Hart Crane's Divided Vision
An Analysis of *The Bridge*

BY
HELGE NORMANN NILSEN

UNIVERSITETSFORLAGET

© UNIVERSITETSFORLAGET 1980
ISBN 82-00-01938-1

Printed in Norway by
Haugesund Bok & Offset A/S
1980

Cover illustration:
Joseph Stella — The Bridge, 1922

Distribution offices:
NORWAY
Universitetsforlaget
P.O.Box 2977, Tøyen
Oslo 6

UNITED KINGDOM
Global Book Resources Ltd.
109, Great Russell Street
London WC1B 3ND

UNITED STATES and CANADA
Columbia University Press
136 South Broadway
Irvington-on-Hudson
New York 10533

PREFACE

We are today in a position to look back on the growth and development of the experimental school in American poetry that flourished during the second and third decades of our century. The period was one of unparallelled innovation and renewal on all literary fronts, and poetry was dominated by such towering figures as T. S. Eliot, Ezra Pound, Wallace Stevens, William Carlos Williams, and Hart Crane. The last two have been slowest in gaining recognition as major artists, but at the present their shares seem to be rising and their work is being reexamined with considerable energy by leading critics. The increased interest in the poetry of Crane, particularly *The Bridge,* may be caused by a general critical trend away from the European traditionalism of T. S. Eliot, and perhaps also by a growing realization of the limitations of the agnostic poetry of Wallace Stevens.

If we ask what Crane's main source of attraction may be, the answer that suggests itself is: his Americanism. Whatever faults he may have, no matter how much the real merits of his work have been misapprehended because of excessive concern with the sensational events of his life and early death, there was never any doubt that this was a distinctly national poet, a true culture child, to borrow one of Waldo Frank's expressions. With the exception of a brief stay in Europe in 1929, Crane spent all his life in the United States, and he strove consciously to continue the Whitmanian tradition in American literature. Though he had little formal education, he was by no means lacking in knowledge; his letters reveal him as a voracious and keen reader and astute critic. His evaluation of a book like *Moby Dick*, for example, was penetrating and anticipated the high praise that was later to be heaped on it. But though he read the Elizabethans avidly, Crane never sought to identify himself with the great literary and philosophic traditions of Europe. He was caught up in a different movement, one concerned with redefining and invigorating American social and literary ideals. This was the aim of writers and artists like Waldo Frank, Van Wyck Brooks, Sherwood Anderson, Carl Sandburg, Alfred Stieglitz and many others and was furthered in magazines like *The New Republic* and *The Seven Arts,* which opened their pages to the advocates of a new American renaissance and the reawakening of the national consciousness.

The following study aims at giving an interpretation of *The Bridge* as a work inspired by a mystic American nationalism. But a doctrine can never fully account for the whole content and value of a poem, which possesses its own unique beauty, and an effort has been made to analyze the poetic organization and the texture of *The Bridge* and approach it as a work of art.

This book is a revised and shortened version of my doctoral dissertation: *Hart Crane's The Bridge: A Study in Sources and Interpretation,* which was originally presented to the University of Bergen, Norway. Parts of dissertation have appeared as printed articles, in somwhat altered form. See «Hart Crane's, Indian Poen» *Neuphilologische Mitteilungen, 72* (1971), and «Hart Crane's 'Atlantis': An Analysis,» *Dutch Quarterly Review of Anglo-American Letters,* 3 (1973/74). Some of the material of the dissertation has appeared in «Hart Crane's *The Bridge* and the Poetics of Faith,» *Edda,* 77 (1977), and in «Crane and Frank: Images of America,» *Hart Crane Newsletter,* Vol. 1, no. 1 (1977).

I wish to express my gratitude to the United States Educational Foundation in Norway and the American Council of Learned Societies for the grants I received from these institutions. I want to thank R. W. B. Lewis for his interest and encouragement, and I thank R. W. Butterfield for his willingness to discuss with me his views on Crane. Other people have also contributed to my work on *The Bridge,* and I am grateful to them. They are Bernard Duffey, Erik Frykman, Sigmund Skard, Georg Roppen, Orm Øverland, Warren Herendeen and Donald Parker. I also want to thank Crane's friend, Emil Opffer, for relating to me his memories of the poet. Finally, thanks are due to Kenneth Lohf of the Special Collections of the Butler Library, Columbia University, for giving me access to Crane's manuscripts.

A note on the text: With the exception of unprinted material, all quotations from Hart Crane's poems, letters and prose are from *The Complete Poems of Hart Crane*, ed. Waldo Frank (Garden City, 1958), *The Letters of Hart Crane,* ed. Brom Weber (Berkeley, 1965), Brom Weber, *Hart Crane* (New York, 1948), and Philip Horton, *Hart Crane: The Life of an American Poet* (New York, 1937). Quotations from Crane's unprinted worksheets of *The Bridge* are from the Hart Crane Collection of the Butler Library, Columbia University, New York.

Trondheim, January 1980

Table of Contents

Our faith comes in moments;
our vice is habitual.
Ralph Waldo Emerson

I. Introduction
A note on the criticism of The Bridge

«What I am really handling, you see, is the Myth of America,» wrote Hart Crane in one of his letters to Otto Kahn, his patron. Ever since the publication of the poem, critics have used the word «myth» in connection with it, often in an imprecise way that tends to deprive the concept of any definable meaning, and sometimes in a too narrow and limited sense which spoils the usefulness of the term. Some critics have hailed Crane as a myth-maker, others have denounced him for failing to create a «myth» or attempting to do so. Historically, the critics of *The Bridge* fall into two categories, one which relates the «myth of America» to the genre of the epic poem and tends to place the poet in a stage of a carefully defined and universally accepted historical development, and another which regards the «myth» simply as a mode of orientation or reaction which can function outside of any historical, or even particular religious, context.

The definition of myth first applied to *The Bridge* by Allen Tate and Yvor Winters is based on a story with a hero, embodying significant aspects and periods of American history in a clear and intelligible manner, so that a profounder, overall force or scheme is applied to this history. The events and the characters of the narrative must be typical of the whole of the American cultural evolution. The «myth of America,» taken in the sense of an ahistorical revelation of a metaphysical principle or poetic vision, is more frequent in the newer criticism of *The Bridge*. The critics who use the term in this way regard «myth» neither as imaginative history, nor as a primitive science, but as a constant mode of discovering the spiritual and esthetic dimensions of reality.

The definition of myth as a religious narrative, or sacred tale, is the most common one, and Richard Chase states that «the word 'myth' means story; a myth is a tale, a narrative, or a poem.»[1] In its original form, a myth nearly always has some kind of narrative element, and the great stories of the Christian, Germanic and classical mythologies are concerned with the historical fate of individual peoples as well as the whole of mankind. Once the notion had arisen that Crane's *The Bridge* was a poem that projected a myth, it is quite natural that the critics should have approached it with certain preconceived ideas derived from their reading of the great epics of Western literature.

Allen Tate critically discusses most of the important issues raised by the poem. In his review of *The Bridge* he is influenced by the classical epic: «It is a sound impulse on Crane's part to look for an American myth, some simple version of our past that lies near the center of the American consciousness, an heroic tale with just enough symbolic morality to give his mind freedom and play.»[2] Tate applauds what he believes is the intention of the poet: to create a sacred tale, originating in a mythical past and giving coherence and purpose to the course of historical events. But he questions the very possibility of doing such a thing. According to Tate, American history is «vast and disordered,» and «there was no settled version for the poet to draw upon and intensify.»[3] Tate goes on to compare *The Bridge*, unfavorably, with *The Divine Comedy,* thus launching a critical tradition of putting Crane and Dante side by side.

In his review of *The Bridge*, Yvor Winters also looks for a historical pattern of the «myth» in the poem, and his reactions resemble those of Tate. Winters asserts: «The book cannot be called an epic, in spite of its endeavor to create and embody a national myth, because it has no narrative framework and so lacks the formal unity of an epic.»[4] Further on in his review Winters makes it clear what kind of definition of myth he has in mind by comparing Crane to Virgil, praising *The Aeneid* for its clear system of values and fine historical structure.[5]

Elisabeth Drew makes another attempt to define Crane's efforts in *The Bridge*. This is her concept of myth: «When the principle of fully coordinated structure, of organic life and power, is expanded from the creation of an individual experience into a vision of the world at large, it results in the myths and stories in which most of the greatest poetry of the word lives.»[6] These references show that Drew holds *The Bridge* up against the epic model and the Western mythologies. Amos Wilder asserts unequivocally that Crane «conceives of his greatest poem as an attempt to give America a religious epic.»[7] This critic is obviously approaching *The Bridge* with Dante or Milton in mind and accordingly makes the observation that the poem is unorthodox and incoherent because of Crane's subjectivism and lack of knowledge. It is the association of myth with epic history that influences Wilder's attitude to *The Bridge*.

In a brief commentary on Crane and *The Bridge,* F. O. Matthiessen takes a historical view and states that Crane's intention is to create a national myth, beginning with the earliest history of the land. Matthiessen is a representative of the critical tradition originated by Allen Tate; his notion of myth implies a historical and cosmological frame of reference within which the poet would be able to create and which would give scope and purpose to his efforts. This dream of an American epic cannot be fulfilled by Crane because his «awareness of American history was hardly more than of a romantic spectacle.»[8] Myth, as Matthiessen sees it, cannot be separated from history; like certain other critics, he wants to find an American Homer or Virgil who in a great epic poem would dramatize the sacred history of the origin, development and fulfillment of America and its people. Similarly, Brom Weber maintains that *The Bridge* fails because «Crane made no effort to grasp the meaning of American history.»[9] Weber also invokes Dante and Virgil, asserting that *The Bridge* fails as a mythical epic.

According to Malcolm Friar, modern poets are confronted with a gap between the Christian myth and metaphysical experience. His idea is that the Christian religion is still present, but the transcendental confirmation of it does not seem to be accessible any more. Consequently the poets may, like Eliot, rely on dogma and not expect very much in the way of divine revelation; or they may, like Crane, attempt to discern a divine design by means of a non-dogmatic experience within the materials of contemporary reality: «Deeply religious yet lacking a religion, Crane sought to span the duality between man and nature by putting 'positive and glowing spiritual content into Machinery'.»[10] Friar comes close to defining Crane's «myth of America» as a revelation of a spiritual coherence between man and his modern environment, but he regards such a spanning of the duality between man and reality as an insufficient and limited effort to create a proper myth. As Friar sees it, *The Bridge* is deficient because it lacks «a series of personifications which embody the ego-ideals of a culture.»[11] These reservations show that Friar has a traditional concept of myth. His call for personifications and ego-ideals is inspired by Greek mythology as represented by Homer, whose culture culminated in the creation of a community of heroes and gods.

Babette Deutsch sees *The Bridge* as an attempt to give a mythic dimension to American history, starting with a vision of Columbus, who assumes a mythical stature. She also mentions the possibility of judging *The Bridge* as an American mythic poem incorporating native folk heroes like, for example, David Crockett. To see the poem in the light of American folk tradition implies a search for characters and events in the work which are mythic in the sense that they loom larger than life and take on a supernatural dimension. The act of mythologizing historical characters is prevalent in American folk tradition, and Deutsch's concept of the «myth» in *The Bridge* is generally that of a folk tale or legend embodied in a popular epic. Summarizing the content of «Powhatan's Daughter,» she points out the parallel between the «hobotrekkers» of «The River» and «the pioneers who wandered, in the childhood of the American dream, across the Great Valley.»[12] However, Deutsch does not develop these views any further, but turns to the same comparison between Crane and Dante that we know from other critics and pronounces *The Bridge* a failure because of Crane's lack of a traditional cosmology.

Vincent Quinn also tends to define the «myth of America» in terms of the epic tradition, and blames the poet himself for the dilemma of classifying his poem: «By far the most unfortunate remark made by Crane was that he was writing an epic. Related to this claim, and only slightly less damaging, was the announcement that *The Bridge* was the expression of a cultural myth.»[13] Quinn left out the rest of the sentence in the letter to Kahn of September 12, 1927, in which Crane calls *The Bridge* an epic of the *consciousness*, implying that no conventional epic is intended. Quinn further points out that *The Bridge* is not a narrative poem, and like the other critics influenced by the epic model he concludes by calling the poem an epic failure because of Crane's lack of knowledge of American history.

In the letter to Kahn, Crane did compare himself with Virgil: «*The Aeneid* was not written in two years — nor in four, and in more than one sense I feel justified in comparing the historic and cultural scope of *The Bridge* to this great work. It is at least a symphony with an epic theme, and a work of considerable profundity and inspiration.» It should be noted, however, that the poet spoke of «a symphony with an epic theme,» not an epic poem in the traditional sense. The comparison with Virgil was mainly motivated by Crane's realization of the scope and the potential importance of *The Bridge* as a national literary document.

But this does not exclude the fact that *The Bridge* has certain epic and historic elements and that some resemblance exists between *The Bridge* and *The Aeneid*. Philip Young has pointed out that the story of Pocahontas and Captain Smith, referred to in *The Bridge*, is related to the story of *The Aeneid* and other epic-mythic tales of the founding of a society.[14] If Crane had built his poem around the narrative of Captain Smith and Pocahontas and given it the dimension of a mythic and national American tale, *The Bridge* might have become a historical and epic poem. But this was not the poet's method; in *The Bridge* he placed himself apart from any conventionally ordered historical context and gathered together several elements, historical as well as contemporary, in a highly personal, poetic synthesis of the American experience.

The critical concept of myth as an heroic narrative embodying the history of a people and presenting a complete cosmology and mythology results in a view of *The Bridge* as an abortive attempt to create an American *Aeneid* or *Divine Comedy*. According to the critics of this school, the poem fails as a mythic epic, has no unity and is at best a collection of occasionally brilliant lyrics. The more recent criticism of Crane and *The Bridge* maintains that the epic-historic definitions of the poem are of limited value, and a number of critics have employed various approaches in which «myth» is regarded as a term denoting an ahistoric, synoptic ordering of experience by means of which a spiritual reality or esthetic dimension is revealed through images and symbols. Within this general perspective most of the individually different ideas of Crane's «myth of America» advocated by these critics can be included.

Hyatt H. Waggoner was one of the first critics who tried to come to terms with *The Bridge* in this new and different manner. His aim is to show how Crane has developed, in poetry, a scientific and cosmic consciousness based on Einsteinian physics and P. D. Ouspensky's mysticism. Waggoner maintains that Crane, by incorporating this new consciousness into his poetry, has performed for our time the task that Whitman, with his «hurrah for positive science,» performed for his. *The Bridge*, then, becomes the great hymn to science of our time, and Waggoner defines its message in this way: «the first step in its creation

13

must be the 'affirmation' of the sum total of the American past and present, the second a 'transcending' of these facts; or that man's increasing technological mastery over nature is a good symbol of his increasing spiritual health and closeness to God.»[15] This is a new and more inclusive concept of Crane's «myth of America.» This critic does not demand an epic or a sacred tale; «myth» to him means a belief in God's presence even in modern reality, or more specifically, in the American culture. Crane's poem, according to Waggoner, is an attempt to achieve a vision of divine order by an assimiliation of the latest scientific theories of the nature of reality so as to bring about a new metaphysical experience.

In Sister M. Bernetta Quinn's analysis of *The Bridge*, the reading is consistently Christian, and it is almost dogmatic in its exegesis of Crane's imagery. The critic demonstrates that the bridge symbol is an archetypal one in the Catholic consciousness and states that the thirteenth-century saint Catherina of Siena used it as a Christ-symbol. Similarly, Crane «presents his Bridge as a concretization of God considered in terms of the Incarnation.»[16] Quinn also sees «To Brooklyn Bridge» as a piece of mystic prayer and analyzes its images of threshold, path and *logos* as expressions of a Christian insight. The main significance of the bridge as symbol then becomes its function as communication; like Christ it is the way to God.

In his essay on Crane, first published in 1956, Clauco Cambon begins by asserting that *The Bridge* offers insights of universal value. Being aware that the epic form could not be resurrected, Crane used his technique of dynamic metaphor and associational structure to incorporate historic and religious themes in his poem. Cambon approaches the various historical and geographical elements in *The Bridge* in a new manner, different from that of the early critics who blame Crane for not giving an orderly presentation of history. The critic defines the structure of the poem as an alogical, montage-like succession of images which reflects the poet's consciousness, and claims that within this structure, the various parts of American history that attracted Crane are organically incorporated. Cambon interprets the bridge as a symbol of the poetic consciousness spanning time and space, a metaphor of the very act of poetic cognition. However, the bridge is not only a symbol, it is also very much a concrete object of contemplation, and Cambon points out that it is nearly like an idol that is being worshipped for its own sake. This critic also regards the insights presented in the climactic sections of *The Bridge* as revelations of a Christian God.[17]

Lawrence S. Dembo has made an extensive and vigorous attempt at a total explanation of *The Bridge*. His main thesis is that Crane was deeply influenced by Nietzsche's views of the poet as he knew them from *The Birth of Tragedy*. Nietzsche's tragic poet combined Apollonian dream-inspiration with Dionysian ecstasy in his creative activity. There was a strongly Dionysian element in Crane's personality, and Dembo interprets his struggles and conflicts as an acceptance of his own personal tragedy and disintegration as a means to achieve a poetic vision.

The concept of myth has no historical connotations for Dembo: «Crane did not lose faith in his myth — that is, in the manifestation of the Absolute in the modern world.»[18] The term «Absolute» suggests a Platonic ideal, and Dembo defines what he saw as Crane's primarily Platonic myth in several places throughout his essay. Regarding the poem as a series of Platonic parables, he maintains that the poet embarks on a quest for the ideal through some of its manifestations: the bridge, the goddess Pocahontas, and the poetic «Word.» This emphasis on Platonic idealism distinguishes this critic's approach both from Sister M. Bernetta Quinn's Catholic-mystic view and Bernice Slote's stress on the connections with American romantic mysticism.

Robert Andreach approaches *The Bridge* on the basis of certain concepts of the stages of spiritual experience which are commonly applied to the teachings of mystics in the Christian tradition. He applies the terminology of Evelyn Underhill in her book *Mysticism* to *The Bridge* because the poem, in his opinion, fits the five-stage division of the spiritual life of the mystics established by Miss Underhill's studies. Crane's poem consists of various forms of spiritual illuminations throughout *The Bridge*; in «Ave Maria,» for example, Columbus has an epiphany, vision of God, but this is no longer possible in the modern world: «The Bridge . . . is a delineation of the decline of Christianity in the twentieth century. Images and symbols are dissociated from their traditionally religious meanings. The experience of Columbus is not possible in a world which lacks the structure and unifying principle of Columbus' world.»[19]As Andreach sees it, Crane's problem throughout *The Bridge* is to recapture the theophany of Columbus in the modern industrial world, but this is no longer possible because the modern universe is not unified and intelligible like the medieval one.

Like Dembo, Alan Trachtenberg interprets *The Bridge* as an expression of Platonic idealism, a search for an abstract ideal of society. He also explores the influence of Whitman, Poe and P. D. Ouspensky on *The Bridge*, but maintains that the Platonic concept of a world of ideas behind appearance is the dominant motive of the poet's quest.[20]

In his extensive analysis of *The Bridge*, R. W. B. Lewis places the poem in a tradition of apocalyptic literature that mainly derives from English romantic poetry, particularly the visionary themes of Shelley's *Prometheus Unbound*. According to Lewis, *The Bridge* describes the gain and loss of a vision that transfigures the world by means of the poetic imagination. Crane's poem, however, is not related to America as such or the potential that the poet saw in it. The subject of *The Bridge* «was not the actual or even the latent greatness of an actual and contemporary America. Its subject was hope, and its content a journey toward hope: a hope reconstituted on the ground of the imagination in action; while the thing hoped for was the creation in *poetry* of a new world.»[21]

In his comprehensive reading of *The Bridge*, R. W. Butterfield maintains that Crane, in trying to create a personal, spiritual synthesis of the American experience, was attempting the impossible. Since, for Butterfield, such a synthesis is an illusion, the optimistic or visionary passages in *The Bridge* constitute an evasion of reality, a form of wish fulfillment. Crane «struggled desperately to build on this imagined synthesis. But in fact, instead of synthesizing America . . . he was merely evading it — or to put it more kindly, transcending it.»[22]

In another large-scale interpretation of *The Bridge,* Sherman Paul draws on the poet's biography and the manifold literary and intellectual sources and influences that played a part in the shaping of the poem. Concerning Crane's «myth of America,» Paul defines it as the poet's combination of certain significant episodes from American history and his search for a more mythic, or Adamic relation to the land. Thus, the «myth» in *The Bridge* «meant both the recurrent pattern — the impulsion — of our 'history' and the mythic, or aboriginal, world beneath it.»[23] Another important feature of Paul's analysis is his emphasis on *The Bridge* as an expression of what he regards as Hart Crane's oedipal neurosis. Hence, Pocahontas, the Virgin Mary, and the other female personae in the poem are seen as images of the mother whom the poet seeks a forbidden union with.[24]

The criticism of *The Bridge* and its «myth of America» is no longer concerned with measuring the poem against the models of the classical epic poem. The discussion now centers around the problem of defining the nature of Crane's approach to the American experience and trying to grasp the unique quality of this approach. *The Bridge* presents an image or view of America that gives rise to interpretations that go beyond the purely literary or esthetic dimension. Philosophical and religious issues are also involved.

In the view of the present writer, the aim of Crane in *The Bridge* was to present a revelation of spiritual unity in America, a sense of «the Whole,» as Waldo Frank puts it. In Frank's preface to *The Complete Poems of Hart Crane*, he maintains that the symbol of the bridge expresses the workings of God in America: «The majority of his fellow citizens prefer to conceive of the Brooklyn Bridge as a passage made of iron from one borough to another rather than as the mythic symbol of how man *in his works* shall immanentize and realize revelation.» The key words here are «*man in his works*». *The Bridge* contains a «myth of America» in the sense that it reveals the divine spirit in the works of America, past and present. Such a radical vision transcends the boundaries of the Christian faith as it has been traditionally understood, so that the Christian readings of *The Bridge* by critics like Sister Bernetta M. Quinn and Cambon do not adequately account for the experience rendered in the poem. Andreach maintains that *The Bridge* is a record of the decline of Columbus' Christian mysticism in our century. However, Crane's use of Biblical references in «Ave Maria» do not betoken any attempt on his part to write a Christian poem. As this study hopes to show, *The Bridge* expresses a mystic American nationalism that derives from the work of Waldo Frank and Walt Whitman, and the Christian imagery of «Ave Maria» is only one of several vehicles for the expression of this theme or ideology.[25]

To read *The Bridge* in terms of Platonic idealism, as Dembo and Trachtenberg do, tends to evoke the impression that the poem is an attempt to express an abstract, otherworldly ideal. Rather, it tries to present a vision of the spiritual within the real, or to render «the Whole» in terms of its parts, as Frank says. Crane knew the work of Plato and used parts of it in *The Bridge*, but it was mainly the «architecture of his logic» and the «grace» of his language that appealed to Crane. (Letter to Gorham Munson, March 17, 1926).

The analysis of *The Bridge* that is the main part of this study owes much to the thorough, often brilliant, interpretations of Lewis, Butterfield and Paul, and there are many similarities between their work and that of the present writer. At the same time, there are certain distinctions and differences that must be pointed out.

R. W. B. Lewis' assertion that *The Bridge* does not deal with the actual or latent greatness of America goes against Crane's own statement that he was handling the «Myth of America» and many similar explanations of the poem that he furnished in his letters. The poem itself illustrates these expressed intentions of his. Lewis also suggests that Crane's hopes for a new world were finally esthetic, or literary, a view which is more categorically stated by Sherman Paul: «The poem is concerned with myth but is itself not necessarily mythic. Nor is it religious.»[26] The Bridge can more justifiably be interpreted as an act of religious faith, and a critic like R. W. Butterfield, who claims that Crane's spiritual convictions were illusions, thereby at least reveals his awareness of the importance of the religious impulse in the poem.

The present study relates *The Bridge* to the work of Frank and Whitman, who both assert that the religious element is the most important one in America. The aim, or method, is thus to explore the influence of a set of ideas on Crane's most ambitious poem. The relevance of the ideas of Waldo Frank, in particular, has not yet been adequately ascertained by students of *The Bridge*. In the analysis of the poem, the poet's letters have been of considerable value, as well as Crane's manuscripts of *The Bridge*. A certain number of the sources of the poem, as well as some undocumented references, have been explored in the hope that they may shed light on the text. An effort has also been made to take into account the many analyses of the text of *The Bridge* that various critics have performed, but to give a full account of all the variations and disagreements, as well as the confluences, between these readings and the present study, would exceed the scope and purpose of this volume. An attempt has been made to analyse *The Bridge* as whole in terms of its leading ideas, and there the method is that of close reading of the text, including the analysis of imagery and symbolism.

II. Walt Whitman and Waldo Frank Parallels and influences

The main theme of Hart Crane's *The Bridge* is the presentation of a lofty image of America that appears in certain passages of the poem. Here, a vision is suggested of a land of beauty and power, with shining cities, strong yet graceful works of technology, and fertile, verdant landscapes. The bond which unites these elements with each other and with the people of the land is a divine, all-pervading presence which the poet relates himself to in his moments of ecstatic inspiration, and the bridge is his chief symbol of this revelation.

A grandly conceived poem like *The Bridge* thus occupies a natural space in the tradition of American national aspirations which is as old as the country itself. More than most countries, America was founded on the basis of an idea, or rather ideal, of perfectibility, of exceptionalism. It was to be a new Jerusalem, a departure from the oppressive conditions of the old world, a second chance for mankind. Of equal importance with the political dimension was the religious aspect of the utopian notion – America would actually become God's own country, a place where the divine will would operate and flourish within each man as well as in his surroundings.

The Bridge has had many critics who have objected to what they regarded as its impossible romanticism and provincial naîveté, but the poem is a logical continuation of a central tradition in American thought, going back most immediately to the native romantic tenets of Emerson, Thoreau and Whitman, to those writers and thinkers of mid-nineteenth century America who constituted «the party of hope,» as F. O. Matthiessen calls it in his *The American Renaissance*. Crane's poetics of faith is linked with the Adamic sensibility and esthetic views of Emerson in his essay on «The Poet» and of Whitman in his Preface to the 1855 edition of *Leaves of Grass* and his *Democratic Vistas*. They both regarded the poet, the creative spirit, as the figure who would

19

more or less replace the priest and assume the function of revealing the spiritual truths about America to its people.

The Bridge, however, does not only contain a hopeful vision, it is also the record of the poet's doubts and misgivings. Though he struggled more desperately with his doubts than Whitman and Waldo Frank, the works of these two spiritual teachers are not blindly optimistic by any means. Both *Democratic Vistas* and *The Re-Discovery of America* are critical as well as hopeful in their views of the American nation.

In his 1855 «Preface» Whitman outlined the task of the American bard in glowing and triumphant terms as that of embracing the whole of the American reality, including society, nature and «exact science.» In his work there would emerge an image of the strong and healthy American states, described in such a way that the beauty and purpose of it all might shine through. Also, this bard would relate his American world to eternity, to the experience of the timeless moments where all ages, places and forms are seen to be related and existing simultaneously. Thus would he penetrate to that mystic vision in which resides the ultimate order of things, and he would replace the churches and priests of the past with his new message of liberty and divine love: «There will soon be no more priests. Their work is done. A new order shall arise, and they shall be the priests of man, and every man shall be his own priest. They shall find their inspiration in real objects to-day, symptoms of the past and future. They shall not deign to defend immortality or God, or the perfection of things, or liberty or the exquisite beauty and reality of the soul. They shall arise in America and be responded to from the remainder of the earth.»[1]

In its most fully realised form, the image of America is a vision of perfect integration, and to experience it requires a certain state of consciousness. At the end of *Democratic Vistas,* Whitman asserted that America is basically a concept, a notion which transcends both the written law and material interest and arises, purified, out of the past: «— so, out of the series of the preceding social and political universes, now arise these States. We see that while many were supposing things established and completed, really the grandest things always remain; and discover that the work of the New World is not ended, but only fairly begun. We see our land, America, her literature, esthetics, etc., as, substantially, the getting in form, or effusement and statement, of deepest basic elements and loftiest final meanings, of history and man.»[2]

In the 1920s, the artistic and philosophic nationalism of American romanticism was carried on by a group of writers and artists whom Crane came in close contact with. More than any other, however, it was Waldo Frank, the journalist, novelist and social philosopher, who strove consciously to reaffirm the vitality of the mystic nationalism of Whitman and tried to convince both his fellow artists and the general public of its continued relevance. In the introduction to *Our America* (1919) Frank asserted that America is a mute giant who cannot articulate his soul. The task is to «lift America into self-knowledge.» This the author set out to do by marshalling the dominant religious and social influences of the past that he thought had shaped America. Then he introduced his central idea, or image, of the America that he envisaged and wanted the people to cultivate in themselves, that of a country infused with spiritual unity: «America is a complex of myriad lights playing upon myriad planes. As a *Unit* it exists only in the eyes of the beholder.»[3] Frank was trying to articulate a vision of a relation to reality which included a sense of a spiritual unity in the materials of modern society. He maintained that this vision would in time grow strong in the people and thereby gradually conform reality to itself: «In this infancy of our adventure, America is a mystic Word. We go forth all to seek America. And in the seeking we create her. In the quality of our search shall be the nature of the America that we create.»[4]

America is a high aspiration, a «mystic Word» that the artist must seek. Similarly, for Crane the revelation of such an America resided in what he in numerous linguistic metaphors referred to as the «word,» «idiom» or «song.» Frank held that American culture was chaotic and fragmented, and that the American people must learn to conceive of reality as an organic whole of which each individual feels himself a part. He discussed the factors in American history that have created this situation and seized on the fact that the American first of all was a pioneer, a man beset by external hardships and driven by a conquering energy which all but obliterated every spiritual and artistic trait in him. The life-denying virtues of the early Puritan settlers mixed with the pioneer spirit; their asceticism became a natural asset to the fighting frontiersman, and the result was a people who were «materialistic» and «unaesthetic.»

According to Frank, Puritanism was the truly anti-religious force in America. The Puritan became pioneer, became externalized and utilitarian, and religion as a «revealed, mystical consciousness» was all but destroyed. It was revived in Whitman, whom Frank applauded for his acceptance of the total American reality as evidence of some ultimate and purposive spiritual design and hailed as the main American prophet of «the Great Tradition» of mystic consciousness of «the Whole.» Frank called his attitude «naturalistic monism,» but only when he acknowledged his indebtedness to Spinoza's philosophy did he emerge with a comprehensive definition: «God is infinite, and man is lost in Him, yet God must be contained within the consciousness of man . . . God is nonanthropomorphic. Yet he is in man's power, since man's mind proves him. He is universal, yet finite mind encompasses His being. All substance, including man, is a part of God . . . And if man, who is finite, knows an infinite world, he is infinite as well. He loses his identity, disappears from the smug center of the universe he had for so long occupied. But he reappears in a far more powerful modification: as an inclusive attribute to the universal.»[5] If we substitute «the Whole» for «God,» we have an explanation of Frank's own theory of the true relation between man and reality, the relation that he sought evidence of in American art and cultural activity both of the past and of his own time.

Our America presented an outline of American culture in which the author found occasional sparks and glimpses of the knowledge of reality as a «Whole:» in the ideas of Roger Williams and Jonathan Edwards and certain of the Founding Fathers, and in some of the poets and writers of the nineteenth century: Whitman, Thoreau and Emerson. However, the period after the Civil War Frank regarded as one of greed, search for power, and cultural disintegration. But in this very chaos there was also evidence of a new, emerging esthetic sense in America which was a sign of the possibility of a new awareness of the land. Frank used a metaphor of this awakening as a morning, an American dawn of which a poet like Carl Sandburg was an important spokesman. His poetry is the birth-cry of a new attitude; coming from the «ravening ugly world» of Chicago he has a rapture in his song: «You cannot mistake it. That is the new god: that is the tomorrow he is so full of. Nothing but this amazing revelation — all in that — that he is alive . . . That cry is not very strong, but it is very wise. Behind it, the deep silences of death and of denial.»[6]

Another American prophet, as Frank saw it in 1919, was Sherwood Anderson, a new and original, almost primitive, personality with a pristine and religious veneration for human life itself. Totally without pretences, like a child and with the true insight of genuine innocence, Anderson saw the real condition of the land: «She has come to the climax of material wealth. She must discover that she is empty, that she is hungry and unclean. She must learn, to the last bitter lesson, the sterility and falsehood of her Puritan, possessive world. She must go forth, and she must go within, to create her own salvation.»[7]

A paramount influence on Frank's thought was *The Education of Henry Adams,* whose theme and terminology parallel those of Frank's own. What the latter called «chaos» or «naked power,» the former named the modern «multiverse,» and Frank's «organic, mystic whole» had its counterpart in the «universe» of medieval French Catholicism as Adams saw it. *The Education* concluded with resignation in the face of cultural decomposition, and Frank compared the book to a tragedy of Sophocles or Ibsen. For Adams the Virgin of faith was dead and could not be resurrected, whereas Frank envisaged a new faith built on the ruins of all old myths. He might use a Spinozistic or Catholic model, but the spiritual content was to be new and wholly American.

Our America ended with a discussion of Whitman, and Frank was moved to panegyrics when describing Whitman's effort, calling him a «great mystic.» Whitman had reached the highest level of consciousness, relating the life of man in America to the universal movements of life and to the infinite, higher being that everything is part of. Whitman's doctrine of «the generic I» was well suited to Frank's philosophy. In «Song of Myself» he wrote «I am large, I contain multitudes,» meaning that he embodied within the self the whole of life and at the same time felt that he was part of this whole. His task, as he saw it, was to transform the minds of his people and make them creative and conscious like himself. His outline of the shortcomings and possibilities of America in *Democratic Vistas* was, according to Frank, the greatest social criticism written by an American.

Frank's book contained a prophetic and revolutionary note in which the after-effects of the great war are felt. The war was the evidence of total failure of all old values, and the soldier, the common man, was becoming aware that society is rotten and the state a criminal. The soldier is the archetype of the new man emerging in America; he stands on the ruins of old worlds as the bringer of a new religion. The great crisis and challenge confronting America is the development of the human self toward the right kind of love of life for its own sake, toward love of *being*. The restless, pioneering energy of America had created an inner void in the individual, and Frank called for a mental revolution: «We must break our impotent habit of constant issuance into petty deed. We must begin to generate within ourselves the energy which is love of life. For that energy, to whatever form the mind consign it, is religious. Its act is creation. And in a dying world, creation is revolution.»[8] *Our America* was a germinal work in Frank's large body of work in social criticism. It contained most of his principal ideas and themes, and they were expressed in a vigorous, youthfully enthusiastic and sometimes flamboyant style. In subsequent books he added more observations and more detailed analyses of America and its possibilities.

In 1929 Frank issued his second major volume of critical observations on the state of American society and culture and called it *The Re-Discovery of America.* It was dedicated to Herbert Croly, editor of *The New Republic,* in which much of the book was printed in instalments throughout 1928. *The Re-Discovery* resumed all the principal themes of *Our America*: the analysis of the roots of American culture, the historical development of the forces shaping American civilization, the nature of the modern American «jungle», and suggestions for a more constructive future course. The book is divided into three parts, the first one called «Causes and Conditions,» the second «Facts,» and the third «The Creating of a People.» This very division suggests the scope of Frank's personality. He was both historian, contemporary observer and prophet of a new social orientation that would develop as the minds of the people changed and became more mature. As in *Virgin Spain* (1926), his general, informing image was that America is the grave of Europe and that the new America would arise, Phoenix-like, out of the ruins of European-instigated chaos and industrial-technical will to power.

The Re-Discovery was weightier and more profound in many ways than *Our America*, and it had a great wealth of thought-provoking and penetrating observations on nearly all aspects of American life and its historical background, ranging from speculations on the philosophy of the Egyptians, the Israelites, the Greeks and the Romans, the «Mediterranean womb of Europe,» to the state of the modern American woman. In the book the grand historical survey dominates the argument; Frank saw America as the final product of an ancient Middle European culture that has manifested itself throughout the history of the western world in various forms, creating a mighty religious structure in medieval times and an upsurge of artistic and scientific achievements during the European Renaissance. After the Renaissance the forces of chaos and disintegration in Europe have grown stronger and have been transplanted to America, the new world in which chaos will spend itself out and a spiritual reorientation will take place.

The idea of a «Whole,» so often mentioned by Frank, signifies the concept of a unified universe which has been breaking up in Europe and is being shattered in America. Since the Renaissance the old, concentrated, spiritual energy of European culture has broken loose and flown across the Atlantic to dissipate itself. Frank described the situation of division and disintegration in America and focussed on the separation of religion and science. Religion, he maintained, is just as important as science, and he regarded their inability to become reconciled as one of the greatest calamities of recent history. Religion creates a sense of order, of wholeness, and so does science in its own way. But the order of science is lifeless and unrelated to man. Science has no body, since the body of man does not enter into a complete relationship with it. A work of art, on the other hand, has such an organic bodily order because it expresses the whole person of the artist. With the artistic object, as with a religious ritual, it is possible for the individual to experience a satisfactory wholeness.

The reason why man seeks this sense of «the Whole» is that his own self is, or should be, such a whole. But there are few men who are fully aware of «the unity of the Whole of Being» in themselves and in the rest of reality. Those who have this awareness, Frank called «mystics:» «Their sense of wholeness, without abandoning the personal which is its core, reaches beyond it. Since they are called mystics, it is well to call their sense of the Whole the mystic sense.»[9] Included among these were figures like Moses, Spinoza, William Blake, Whitman and Hart Crane.

What Frank called «mysticism» is a quality that *can* be expressed in words and images, it is *there* in the works of his great masters. This is in opposition to the more familiar notion that the mystic experience is ineffable and incommunicable. According to Frank, the mystic expresses the «cosmic self» in his work and makes it possible for his audience to gain an insight equivalent to his own. Thus the individual may become a participant in the creation of this consciousness of «the Whole:» «The true mystic meditation is the deed. Prayer and art are one. The Whole exists through its enactments, and its enactments are we creatures of sense . . . it is not for you and me, save as our lives create it; not for America save as America creates it. It is not 'up there' like a heaven or god; not an object like a golden apple to be seen or, unseen, believed in . . . The organic Order which makes the Whole is a matter of *ordering* — is the experience of ordering by you and me. Our knowledge is our participation.»[10]

The main reason for the spiritual chaos of the modern world, the author maintained, is the prevalence of the personal will. Each individual pursues his own ends without feeling part of any larger unity. Such an attitude is not consistent with a sense of «the Whole,» since this transcends the personal will. The man whose world is a mere tool of personal desire has no «universe» at all; he is excluded both from the order of religion and of science and will never feel himself part of any larger, meaningful entity. The «mystic sense of the Whole» is the supremely important thing for modern man, and it is severely underdeveloped. For a new and sound religion to arise in America, man must learn to reconcile science with religion. In the past the constant new discoveries of science have always made religious dogmas invalid. Therefore, a completely new attitude toward both phenomena is needed; science must become spiritual and religion scientific: «the thinkers in psychological, political and social orders build from the debris of worlds a new foundation for the future culminant Whole — our true religion.»[11]

As for industrial civilization, «the machine,» Frank realized that it was here to stay, and he sought a way of incorporating it into his world-view. But in his discussion of man's relation to the machine in *The Re-Discovery*, he was very much aware of the problems it had created for man. He called it a monster, an «anarchic mindless master» which has taken the place of God and is threatening to enslave mankind. The machine has made for a «multiverse» of insulated wills and objects, for example, the automobile. But this is no fault of the machine itself, but of man's attitude toward it. Frank made it clear that he was no nostalgic romantic harking back to a pastoral nature and remarked: «The idyllic Nature of modern man is his tomorrow, not his past: it will contain his machine as surely as it will his body. The machine is an anarchic principle, only so long as man is an anarchic atom.»[12]

This argument resembles that of *The Education of Henry Adams* and its author's speculations on the electric dynamo, symbol of ruthless technical energy without purposeful directions within a larger world-view. But Frank held out a hope: if man himself can become whole, submit to the principle of Wholeness, then the machine may become a means of combining his control of nature with his control of and development of the self.

Frank's discussion of the American art of his time was particularly exacting and dominated by a definite critical program. In the face of the cleavage and disintegration of the human spirit that he observed, Frank turned with passionate hope toward the current arts, in which he discerned a certain promise, a vision which he called «the apocalyptic method.» In a dying culture with nothing but empty forms, this method was the only hope of creating a genuine spiritual relation between man and his environment. By this term was meant an effort on the part of the artists to seek a direct, non-doctrinal and ahistorical vision of beauty, and, on a higher level, of divine presence of revelation, in their materials: «They must literally make the plastic form of their vision from the plasmic substance of their experience — without obedience to conceptual heritage or aesthetic tradition.»[13] The archetypal American artist of this type was Whitman; of those of the twentieth century Frank singled out, among others, Isadora Duncan, William Carlos Williams, Alfred Stieglitz, Eugene O'Neill and Hart Crane.

The photographer Stieglitz was the man whom Frank admired most of all and in whom he found «the essence of leadership.» He argued that Stieglitz demonstrated this quality to those who came into contact with him, and maintained that in a situation such as that of America, with its spiritual vacuum and lack of a religious conceptual idiom with real meaning, the «true word» could only be a non-verbal expression, a «life.» The photographs and the personality of Stieglitz reflected a kind of «proto-citizen» of the new world: «His everyday responses to the American scene have a light from that unspoken dawn; they are linked intimately with our chaos and yet some force moves them obliquely from it, as if a previsioned Order were alive within them.»[14] Frank showed a continuous interest in Stieglitz, regarding him as a leading representative of the emerging new consciousness in America. In 1934 he edited a collection of essays called *America and Alfred Stieglitz* and was himself a contributor.

Toward the end of *The Re-Discovery* the author described the «mystic America» that was a part of his «Great Tradition» of true mystics: the Upanishads, Moses, Pythagoras, Spinoza, Goethe, Blake and

27

Whitman. These all share one all-important quality, their world-view is monistic, they conceive of all reality as One. America must develop into a «symphonic nation» in which the various forces and institutions of the country will work in consort and harmony.

The final chapter of the book was characteristically called «Beginning,» and in it Frank called for the formation of one or more groups of people, artists, intellectuals and so on, who would understand the importance of the new mission, to cultivate the sense of the whole in themselves and others. With a typical American call for action he outlined «Notes on Method;» how to achieve the sense of the self as a whole related to larger wholes. The method is simple enough. First one must become fully aware of one's body as an organic whole and «prehend» it. The author here used the terminology of Whitehead in his *Science and the Modern World* (1926), and adopted Whitehead's concept of «prehension,» the ability to see reality as mysterious entities that are related and whose exact nature no single faculty, such as the scientific intellect, for example, can fully explain.

When one has acquired an image of wholeness by contemplating the body, one will go on to relate it to some larger context, to begin with perhaps simply the room in which one happens to be and later on to larger and more significant wholes. The process will culminate in an awareness of the body as part of, yet encompassing, the whole of life and cosmos. This is the Spinozistic paradox of the self as being part of yet containing an infinite being. When a person has reached this stage he will have given up the idea of an «I» that is an absolute entity: «When he feels, does, thinks, it will be no longer in sufferance to an «I» that images itself as separate, impervious, alone: it will be the Whole — the universe — God (choose your own word) that feels, does, thinks in terms of his own person.»[15]

Frank concluded *The Re-Discovery* with an exhortation to those of his contemporaries who had gone through this process and whose work accordingly pointed the way. These, he was confident, would not stop from «the labour of beauty,» having found wholeness in themselves and having thus lived in «the image of God.»

Frank and Crane met for the first time in New York in 1923, and they remained friends for the rest of the poet's life. Crane read and commented on Frank's works as they came off the presses, and these comments are preserved in his letters.[16] As his plans for *The Bridge* grew, Crane began to feel that he was entering into the «great tradition» of

American mysticism as Frank had outlined it, and especially into the tradition of Whitman: «The more I think about my *Bridge* poem the more thrilling its symbolical possibilities become, and since my reading of you and Frank . . . I begin to feel myself in currents that are positively awesome in their extent and possibilities.» (Letter to Gorham Munson, March 2, 1923).

Frank's influence on Crane can also be detected in some glowing letters that the poet wrote to Alfred Stieglitz at this time. He called the photographer a «great and good man» and started to write an essay on his art. In it he compared Stieglitz' art to Blake's visionary imagination, and spoke of the «clairvoyance» of his photographs and their «invisible dimensions whose vibrance has been denied the human eye at all times save in the intuition of ecstasy.» (Letter to Stieglitz of April 15, 1923).

On July 4, 1923, Crane again wrote to the photographer and explained how close he felt to him and how he had come to regard his life and experience as parts of his own. Their personalities were alike in spiritual orientation because they shared in «common devotions, in a kind of timeless vision.» Crane's own version of this vision was to be expressed in *The Bridge*. He went on to explain to Stieglitz the «new order of consciousness» that he believed was emerging in the art of the photograper, and enclosed in his letter an early draft of «Atlantis.»

In 1924 Frank published a collection of essays called *Salvos,* and Crane read and recommended it. It contained «A Letter to the Annual Whitman Celebration» in which Frank praised Whitman as «the deepest and most creative spirit of the entire Nineteenth Century.» He went on to lament the fact that «Whitman is as much a solitary in the America of 1923 as he was in the America of 1860! His great work has been in no essential way assimilated into American thought, into American literature, into the American intellectual life.»[17] The feeling of the isolation of the saving vision was shared by both Frank and Crane, and yet they felt compelled to go their respective ways trying to create their new vision and communicating it to others.

In the summer of 1926 Crane sailed to the Isle of Pines in the company of Frank, and after they had separated he wrote letters to his friend that revealed both the exaltation that he felt at the remarkable creativity experienced at this time and the equally devastating doubts he had about the validity of a project such as *The Bridge*. Crane was deeply troubled by the fact of the isolation of the «new consciousness» in the society in which he lived, and this feeling of isolation was recorded in a letter to Frank of June 20, 1926, in which he made it clear that his writing of *The Bridge* was motivated by the expectation that his vision would be assimilated into the cultural consciousness as an active principle of faith and action: «The validity of a work of art is situated in contemporary reality to the extent that the artist must honestly anticipate the realization of his vision in 'action' (as an actively operating principle of communal works and faith), and I don't mean by this that his procedure requires any bona fide evidences directly and personally signalled, nor even any physical sign or portents . . . It has always been taken for granted, however, that his intuitions were salutary and that his vision either sowed or epitomized 'experience' . . .»

Further on in this letter, Crane made a comment which showed his growing realization of the isolation of his vision: «Emotionally I should like to write *The Bridge*, intellectually judged the whole theme and project seems more and more absurd.» In spite of moods like these Crane went on to complete the poem, possibly because his sense of having an important mission to fulfill was even stronger than his pessimism. Another reason he had for persisting was Frank's unfailing support, and when he sent a version of «Ave Maria» to him on July 26, 1926, he addressed him as «Dear repository of my faith.» A month later, looking back on moments they had shared together, the poet wrote: «I'm glad to know that *The Bridge* is fulfilling your utmost intuitions; for an intuition it undoubtedly was.» This letter, from August 19, mentioned an evening which the two friends had spent together and during which they had shared in a profoundly emotional and intellectual experience of the essence of their «myth of America:» «You didn't need to tell me that you had 'seen' something that memorable evening, although I was never so sure just what it was you saw, until now. But I have always carried that peculiar look that was in your eyes for a moment there in your room, it has often recurred in my thoughts . . . It is a harmony always with the absolute direction I always seek, often miss, but sometimes gain.»

In 1928 Crane wrote Frank from California and sent him some shorter poems. He received a reply and responded with an enthusiastic letter of March 4 of the same year in which he extolled the then current installments in *The New Republic* of *The Re-Discovery of America*. He spoke about the «glamour and precision» of the book and about how he had grasped its «luminous and essential direction.» He went on to speculate on the necessity for a synthesized knowledge which was of such great importance for a poet with his own ambitions: «some kind of logos, or system, of contact between the insulated departments of highly specialized knowledge and enquiry which characterize the times — God knows, some kind of substantiated synthesis of opinion is needed before I can feel confident in writing about anything but my shoestrings . . . These Godless days! I wonder if you suffer as much as I do. At least you have the education and training to hold the scalpel.»

Like Frank, Eliot and Henry Adams, Crane found himself living in an age which had created an ever widening split between man's various faculties and means of orientation and knowledge. But unlike Eliot and Adams, who mainly diagnosed the situation, Frank and Crane were working toward a new synthesis. Frank was able to formulate his solution in intellectual and scholarly terms, whereas the poet confronted the double challenge of grasping a new religious or philosophical program and articulating it in a poetry whose style is as experimental as anything else written in the twenties.

In February 1929, when Crane was in Paris and was being patronized by the wealthy Harry Crosby, he wrote to Frank and asked him to send a copy of *The Re-Discovery* since he needed it as a balance against the cultural seductions of Europe. At this time he also received an offer from Crosby, owner of the Black Sun Press, to finance the publication of *The Bridge* in a private edition that same fall, and having agreed to this, the poet felt himself under pressure to finish the remaining sections. «Cape Hatteras,» «Quaker Hill» and «Indiana» were still in the process of composition, and it is clear from Crane's correspondence at this time that these poems were finished in something of a rush. After 1930 and the publication of *The Bridge* the correspondence between Crane and Frank subsided, and the letters that were exchanged are all more or less personal and have little of the intellectual and emotional intensity that periodically had existed between the two writers.[18]

Waldo Frank hailed Crane from the very beginning as an American prophet of our time and discussed his work in several contexts. The first item was an article called «The Poetry of Hart Crane» in *The New Republic*, 50 (1927). Frank always emphasized the religious aspect of Crane's work, and in his preface to the 1958 edition of the *Complete Poems,* he summed up the poet's achievement and pronounced him a prophet of the American dream: «There is a tradition in our land old as Roger Williams and the pilgrims. It takes the term *New World* with literal seriousness. America, it declares, shall be the New Jerusalem, the kingdom of Heaven brought from within each man to earth, and expressed in the forms of our American society.» Frank regarded *The Bridge* as a poetic version of the consciousness of America as a mystic whole that he himself was trying to spread in his novels and books of social philosophy.

The Bridge can be interpreted as Crane's attempt to uphold the tradition of mystic utopianism in America and respond to Frank's call for a new consciousness of «the Whole.» In its own, personal way, the work presents a total vision of America, beginning with a poem about Columbus' discovery, then launching into a westward journey across the continent and returning to the poet's New York and the final, mystic apotheosis of the Brooklyn Bridge. Crane's own outline of the poem, included in a letter to Gorham Munson of February 8, 1923, speaks for itself: «Very roughly, it concerns a mystical synthesis of America. History and fact, locations, etc., all have to be transfigured into abstract form that would almost function independently of its subject-matter. The initial impulses of 'our people' will have to be gathered up toward the climax of the bridge, symbol of our unique identity in which is included also our scientific hopes and achievements of the future.» The «mystical synthesis» that Crane speaks of here is another version of Whitman's concept of ideal nationhood and Frank's «mystic America.» In another context, Crane used the word «Cathay» to denote this synthesis of national values: «The theme of 'Cathay' (its riches, etc.) ultimately is transmuted into a symbol of consciousness, knowledge, spiritual unity. A rather religious motivation, albeit not Presbyterian.» (Letter to Otto Kahn, March 18, 1926).

The «initial impulses» of the American people are related to Frank's sense of the high destiny of America, the dream of possessing and inhabiting a terrestrial paradise that Crane attributes to Columbus in «Ave Maria» and that Frank let his Columbus envision in *Virgin Spain*. Like Frank, Crane also included in these «impulses» something of the heritage of the Indian and developed his symbol of the legendary maiden Pocahontas in «Powhatan's Daugher.» It appears that the poet, from the very outset, wanted to establish in *The Bridge* a sense of fusion of several different elements, of unity in a wide range of experience, a «Whole,» in short, and the idea of a bridge occurred to him as a natural symbol of this.

However, Crane's poetic mysticism does not express any devotion to the hereafter. His poetics of faith aimed at a state of illumination of the quotidian, and his religiosity was undogmatic and catholic in the true sense of the word.[19] But he refused to share the view of a poet like Wallace Stevens, who in «Sunday Morning» proclaimed that all gods are dead and that we live in an «old chaos of the sun.» This stance of Crane's had certain consequences for the development of his concept of nature and his attitude toward modern civilization, or «the Machine,» as the phrase went in the twenties. Both Waldo Frank and Gorham Munson speculated on the possible significance and function of the machine in the arts and poetry, and Munson spoke enthusiastically about «the vast struggle to put positive and glowing spiritual content into Machinery.»[20]

Crane discussed the function of poetry in a «Machine Age» in his essay «Modern Poetry,» and here he asserted that this function is the same as always, to present a «synthesis of human values.» He was against any poetic worship of the machine and made it clear that it must be incorporated into a larger, modern concept of nature: «For unless poetry can absorb the machine, i.e., *acclimatize* it as naturally and casually as trees, cattle, galleons, castles and all other human associations of the past, then poetry has failed of its full contemporary function.» Crane did not want to celebrate the machine exclusively as the symbol of man's victory over nature: the most meaningful aspect of the machine would be its function within a larger reality consisting both of «nature» in a conventional, pastoral sense and the impact of technology. Thus the machine might contribute to the creation of an environment in which man would feel at home, or part of a larger «Whole,» as Frank would put it.

On the actual level of literary technique and theory, the poetics of Crane finds expression in what he variously refers to in his essays and letters as «the logic of metaphor» and «dynamic metaphor,» a use of language which led to the creation of incredibly packed and dense sequences of images, words and metaphors which give the appearance of containing nearly infinite associations. But however complex or even sometimes impenetrable this diction of Crane seems to be, the purpose of it is always the same, to capture a vision of integration and harmony. This redemptive vision is pursued throughout *The Bridge* in various epochs and aspects of American history and is suggested by a group of recurring, or structural images that have become familiar to students of Crane's texture. They are the figures of the curve, the circle, the globe, rose and spiral, the imagery of birds, wings, eyes, ships, stars and female goddesses, and the color symbolism of white, gold, silver, blue and green. All these images are gathered up and presented in a combination in «Atlantis,» which Crane, in a letter to Otto Kahn of March 18, 1926, referred to as «the mystic consummation toward which all the other sections of the poem converge.» In other words, the poetic method of fusing disparate elements by means of «dynamic metaphor» has its counterpart within the larger structure of *The Bridge* as a whole, where the sections are linked by these recurring images and references.

III. The text of *The Bridge*
A vision pursued

1. *Proem: To Brooklyn Bridge*

This eleven stanza lyric, which serves as an introduction to *The Bridge*, is one of the most widely read and appreciated of Crane's poems. On July 24, 1926, he wrote to Waldo Frank about it in one of his moods of exhilaration: «That little prelude, by the way, I think to be almost the best thing I've ever written, something steady and uncompromising about it.» The first three stanzas form a dramatic introduction to the central image of the Brooklyn Bridge itself, to which all other details of the lyric are related and whose meaning they define. The famous opening lines evoke the flight of a seagull at dawn over the harbor waters of the city:

How many dawns, chill from his rippling rest
The seagull's wings shall dip and pivot him,
Shedding white rings of tumult, building high
Over the chained bay waters Liberty —

The falling and rising curve of the bird's flight parallels that of the horizontal cables of the suspension bridge and is a symbol of the human spirit's urge for freedom and release. The theme is reinforced by the reference to the actual Statue of Liberty in the capitalization of the word. Moreover, the bay waters are «chained» in contrast to the freedom of the bird and the open sea. The idea of free flight foreshadows the image of the free span of the bridge in stanza four: «Implicitly thy freedom staying thee!» The bridge is a static representation of the soaring flight, it symbolizes latent power. The spinning, pivoting seagull over the bridge creates an illusory picture as of white rings in the air, and the symbolic meaning of its flight is the return of vision, the heightened awareness that occurs with the same organic rhythm as that of the new dawn that succeeds each night. The transitory nature of this experience is accentuated by the swooping fall and rise of the bird as it disappears from the sight of the people in the tall office buildings who are working over pages of figures:

Then, with inviolate curve, forsake our eyes
As apparitional as sails that cross
Some page of figures to be filed away;
— Till elevators drop us from our day . . .

The perfect curve of the seagull's flight and the great cables of the bridge can also be discerned in sails, to which the sight of the gull is compared. These sails are «apparitional,» from the past, and as such they point to «Cutty Sark,» the section in which the poet creates an imaginative vision of clipper ships sailing up the East River. Like the white sails of the imaginary clippers the seagull vanishes from sight, suggesting that the vision is fleeting and impermanent. The sails «cross» the «page of figures» in the sense that the vision passes by the office workers and their filing cabinets. These images indicate the tension between the ideal and the real: the routine, everyday experience associated with the «figures» that have to be filed away, and the moments of elevated consciousness that bring a realization of beauty and freedom and in which events and objects are lifted out of their quotidian spheres and given a splendor and magic power of suggestion.[1]

The poet then turns his attention to another situation which suggests the fact that man is forever in search of a moment's revelation. In the cinemas, the crowd stares at some «flashing scene» which is «never disclosed.» The pictures on the movie canvas are mere shadowy representations of reality, and this parable suggests that human multitudes cannot achieve the experience of the poet. They may hasten toward it as they stare at the screen, but they do not fully grasp it. But it is «foretold» or revealed to the «other eyes» of the poet, or seer.[2] Crane's use of the eye as a symbol is of central importance, and the meaning he attributes to it can be illuminated further by referring at this point to the meaning of this symbol in «Cape Hatteras.» Here, Crane hails the memory of Whitman and sees his eyes in the streets of the city: «Confronting the Excange,/Surviving in a world of stocks . . .» Even in the modern city Whitman's vision survives, and across the expanse of twentieth century America he looks with «Sea eyes and tidal, undenying, bright with myth!» The word «myth» refers to Whitman's belief in an all-unifying principle in nature and human history.

The image of the bridge is then introduced in the incantantory language of a poet-prophet:

And Thee, across the harbor, silver-paced
As though the sun took step of thee, yet left
Some motion ever unspent in thy stride, —
Implicitly thy freedom staying thee!

The language is mythopoetic, the bridge is personified and the intimate relationship between the self and reality which is essential to any religious experience is established. The bridge is the symbol of power in repose, of the magic instrument which the poet wields in his work and by means of which he realizes his sense of «the Whole.» This power is latent in the object of the bridge, it is the «unspent» motion in its «stride» and the voluntary static freedom of its span. In the suggestion that the sun has taken its course from the curve of the bridge lies the key to one of the poet's main intentions, namely to fuse mechanical and natural objects in a larger «nature» which can give the modern poet the kind of inspiration that the poets of the Romantic period derived from an unspoilt nature. The underlying idea of Crane's image is that both the bridge and the sun write the universal figure of the curve and are thus parallel manifestations of a larger geometric order of things.

The bridge of the poetic experience links man with the spiritual by means of the revelation of a dimension in external reality in which a coherence is established between man and a corresponding, universal spirit. The «bedlamite» who presumably throws himself from the bridge into the river is a caricature of the spiritual action suggested by the seagull's flight and the curve of the bridge. His «shrill shirt balooning» is a mockery of the beating of the bird's wing, and his suicidal fall is toward death.[3] The introduction of this figure draws our attention to the tensions in Crane's poetry, the oscillations between an ecstatic faith in his vision and a powerful awareness of the forces of chaos and darkness that were also present in modern American civilization.

The bridge is a symbol of connection between nature and technology, and between man and reality, and this symbolic meaning is expressed in striking and original metaphors. Thus, Crane hoped to create a poetry that would reflect a consciousness of a spiritual whole imbuing both nature and modern, industrial reality. His poetic method was one of drawing together in imagery both natural and man-made objects in a poetic world which is suffused by one creative spirit or principle:

> Down Wall, from girder into street noon leaks,
> A rip-tooth of the sky's acetylene;
> All afternoon the cloud-flown derricks turn . . .
> Thy cables breathe the North Atlantic still.

The metaphor of the rays of the sun sifting down into the streets as a flame of acetylene fuses nature and the machine in an active, forceful image in which a new, living force linking both tenor and vehicle is perceived. Imagery such as this obliterates the conventional barriers between technology and «nature;» a sun-like quality is first attributed to the bridge, and after that the sun's rays are conceived as acetylene flames. These suggest the actual wielding of materials in the building of the bridge, and within that process a universal creative force is envisaged. Such a force connects instead of disrupting, and later in the poem Crane celebrates this power as a «fury» which fuses the bridge into a «harp» and an «altar;» and with defiant rhetoric he poses the question; «How could mere toil align thy choiring strings!»

The seventh stanza deals with the kind of promise, or ultimate redemption, held out by the bridge:

> And obscure as that heaven of the Jews
> Thy guerdon . . . Accolade thou dost bestow
> Of anonymity time cannot raise:
> Vibrant reprieve and pardon thou dost show.

The poet here makes it clear that he has no fixed idea about the exact nature of the reward offered by the bridge symbol to its worshippers. All he asserts is that the bridge, as a divine king who bestows an accolade, emanates or wields magic powers of absolution and redemption. It is, however, also evident that the acquisition of the spiritual power of the bridge to all intents and purposes depends on the individual human being and his own receptivity. The «guerdon» is «obscure» because the poet is aware that he is worshipping a religious symbol of a new kind.

The proem is an incantatory hymn chanted by the enraptured poet-magician, who invokes the sacred powers and approaches his object of veneration. In the climactic eighth stanza he is standing on the threshold of the sacred realm and is addressing the bridge in religious language:

O harp and altar, of the fury fused,
(How could mere toil align thy choiring strings!)
Terrific threshold of the prophet's pledge,
Prayer of pariah, and the lover's cry, —

An altar is a sacred place where human and divine meet, it is a spiritual bridge. Though externally the product of the «mere toil» of human hands, the bridge is ultimately the work of a divine, creative fury working with man as its instrument. There is a purpose behind the construction of the bridge which is parallel to the inspiration of the architects of the Christian cathedrals of the middle ages. In his selection of the Brooklyn Bridge as the symbol of power working in a universal design, Crane was in his own way trying to solve the problem posed by Henry Adams in his speculations on the «multiverse» of uncoordinated knowledge and power of our era as contrasted with the «universe» of faith and order of medieval France.[4] Adams saw an essential difference between his two symbols, the dynamo, representing material energy without spiritual purpose, and the virgin, representing a combination of faith and energy which has died out in modern times.

Crane saw in the bridge what Adams could not see in the dynamo. By stressing that the bridge could not have been built by «mere toil,» the poet declared his faith in a conscious, purposive direction of divine power as it manifests itself in the works of modern technology. This power has been channelled into the construction of the bridge, which thus becomes the meeting-point between these and the poet. On this threshold he holds the key to prophetic insight into both past, present and future manifestations of the creative power that he has envisaged. The feeling he has on the threshold is one of terror and awe and suggests the fear of god which seized the prophets of the Old Testament. Unlike them, however, Crane was never trying to be an instrument of moral castigation, nor did he hold out any promise of personal salva-

39

tion. He only pledges to offer his vision of a spiritual whole which unites nature and the machine and in turn connects man with this reality. The bridge embodies and articulates the diffuse spiritual aspirations of the common man of our time, the «pariah» who is a parallel to the multitudes in the cinema. It is also a symbol of love in the sense of a consummate union between two different elements or principles, and as such it fulfills what the «lover» cries out for.[5]

The proem progresses from dawn to night, and the coming of darkness provides a series of new, luminous metaphors with which to describe the bridge:

Again the traffic lights that skim thy swift
Unfractioned idiom, immaculate sight of stars,
Beading thy path — condense eternity:
And we have seen night lifted in thine arms.

Margaret Schlauch's interpretation of the first three of these lines is so imaginative and accurate that it deserves quotation: «Once more, at night, we can see lights of moving traffic speeding across the bridge like bright moving beads. The arc of the bridge is like a long unbroken idiomatic phrase of language or music; the lights focus a concept of eternity, the uncorrupted music of the spheres: the everlasting and absolute in the concrete and physical.»[6] On the biographical level, it may be useful to refer to Crane's prose description of the bridge at night in a letter to his mother of May 11, 1924: «Look far to your left toward Staten Island and there is the Statue of Liberty, with that remarkable lamp of hers that makes her seen for miles. And up at the right Brooklyn Bridge, the most superb piece of construction in the modern world, I'm sure, with strings of light crossing it like glowing worms as the L's and surface cars pass each other going and coming.»

The traffic lights that become stars and symbols of eternity have numerous parallels throughout *The Bridge*, whose sections abound in sidereal imagery. The expression «lifted in thine arms» connotes a metaphor of the bridge as a woman, and the invocation in the proem of what is presumably the Virgin Mary is in keeping with the general function of the bridge as a symbol of connection between human and divine.

In the second last stanza we have a transition from the previous inspirational flights to an intensely personal experience of the bridge:

40

Under thy shadow by the piers I waited;
Only in darkness is thy shadow clear.
The City's fiery parcels all undone
Already snow submerges an iron year . . .

Standing on the piers beneath the bridge at night, the poet finds himself thrown back into the world of everyday reality after having articulated his symbolic vision of the bridge. This return to the world of fact represents the nether part of the cyclic movement of Crane's imagination. From the apex of the heightened consciousness of a spiritual universe he descends to the «darkness» of the «shadow» of the bridge and stands waiting for a new moment of revelation. As prophet, he feels alienated from society and places himself apart from the city, whose «fiery parcels,» illuminated quarters, darken toward night. The year has come to its end in winter: snow begins to fall, figuratively drawing a veil over the past «iron year» of the poet's life. The word «iron» suggests the modern world of cold, metallic structures and also Crane's personal hardships.

The proem concludes on an affirmative note in the sense that the poet prays to the image of the bridge that his quest through the American experience will yield «a myth to God:»

O Sleepless as the river under thee,
Vaulting the sea, the prairies' dreaming sod
Unto us lowliest sometime sweep, descend
And of the curveship lend a myth to God.

In contrast to the curved flight of the seagull the «curveship» of the bridge is permanent, a tangible symbol of the divine order that the poet seeks. Like the rainbow, whose curve has been traditionally seen as God's finger in the sky, the connective, unifying span of the bridge is the symbol of America's divine destiny, its role as a new cultural synthesis infused with God's presence.

2. Ave Maria

«To Brooklyn Bridge» ends with an exhortation to the bridge to «vault» the sea. «Ave Maria,» the poem about the discovery of America, presents such an act of spanning the ocean and the two worlds of

Europe and America. The bridge of the imagination spans the gap between present and past and stretches across the spaces of oceans and continents, and the sea-poem «Ave Maria» precedes «Powhatan's Daughter,» which deals with the American continent.

Crane read and assimilated a considerable amount of material, historical and other, when he wrote *The Bridge,* searching for characters and events that could inflame his imagination and lend themselves to poetic treatment as parts of his poem. He plunged into a number of books, and in a letter to Gorham Munson of March 5, 1926, he listed the following: William H. Prescott's *History of the Reign of Ferdinand and Isabella, The Journal of Columbus,* Melville's *White Jacket,* Whitehead's *Science and the Modern World,* Waldo Frank's *Virgin Spain* and D. H. Lawrence's *The Plumed Serpent.* It may be assumed that Crane got the general outline as well as certain details for his «Ave Maria» section concerning the life and voyages of Columbus from Prescott's *History* and Columbus' *Journal.*[7]

In «Ave Maria» Columbus is depicted not merely as a voyager, but as a religious visionary who carried out his exploits in answer to the call of a higher purpose. Crane saw the discoverer as a man possessed by a thirst for new discoveries, new knowledge, and his Columbus may be said to belong to a certain type of literary figure, the dreamer-voyager, or *homo viator.* Columbus was eminently suited to become an American *homo viator.* He embodies the original, supreme aspirations of the white man in America, the quest for a new, perfect world. Frank regarded Columbus in the same way: «Even before the Purians, the mystic tradition was planted on our shore. The man who first discovered the Atlantic moved, if confusedly, within it. He thought that he was sailing for the Indies; he dreamed to absorb the scattered East into the Organ of the West. He spoke to Isabel, mystic queen of Spain, and to her monks, of making One the two halves of the world. It was Columbus, first historic man to touch America, who grounded our mystic tradition.»[8] The theme of quest for a new world is launched in the Senecan epigraph to «Ave Maria:» «The ages shall come in the ripe years wherein the ocean shall relax the chain of things and the vast earth shall lie open and Tiphys (Jason's pilot in *The Medea*) shall detect new worlds, nor shall there be an Ultima Thule upon the earth.»[9]

The poem is a dramatic monologue spoken by Columbus as he stands on his ship, homeward bound from the lands that he has discovered. The opening stanza takes us right into the whole human drama of Columbus' situation as he, reflecting on his feat, addresses two of his benefactors at the Spanish court. He has found Cathay, but he is afraid that his ships will never reach Spain. Therefore he wants his helpers to hear his message and invokes their presence:

Be with me, Luis de San Angel, now —
Witness before the tides can wrest away
The word I bring, O you who reined my suit
Into the Queen's great heart that doubtful day;

Columbus had to overcome several court intrigues before Queen Isabella could be persuaded to support his enterprise. Finally, Louis de St. Angel, a fiscal officer of the crown, used his whole influence in order to let Columbus have what he asked for, and he prevailed.[10] According to Crane, St. Angel «reined,» guided Columbus' suit into the queen's «great heart.» Recalling the torment of the conspiracies against him and the spite and ridicule that his plans were exposed to, Columbus keenly feels his triumph as he gazes towards Spain. Now nobody can «riddle or gainsay» the actual discovery he has made, and he brings back Cathay, the promise of further marvellous discoveries. As he stares out over the ocean and recalls his westward voyage, the poem becomes replete with intricate and beautiful sea imagery:

Here waves climb into dusk on gleaming mail;
Invisible valves of the sea, — locks, tendons
Crested and creeping, troughing corridors
That fall back yawning to another plunge.
Slowly the sun's red caravel drops light
Once more behind us . . . It is morning there —
O where our Indian emperies lie revealed,
Yet lost, all, let this keel one instant yield!

This is a very complex metaphor of the sea as a huge soldier or warrior, dressed in the mail of an armor that moves and gleams as he stirs. The image is in keeping with Columbus' idea of a soldier and is linked with the metaphor of the sun as a caravel. Crane is seeing reality in Columbus' terms. Under the «mail» of the waves a vast body lies, with blood-valves and tendons, and its movements are reflected in the armored surface, the topped crests and long «corridors» of the waves.

In the west, the newly discovered land, the sun is rising again; as Columbus sails into the night, the day breaks in his «Indian emperies.» In «To Brooklyn Bridge» the light of dawn symbolizes the visionary moment, and Columbus associates his Cathay with morning. He dreams of an Indian, Oriental empire, but in *The Bridge* this adjective also has another meaning, it is the land of the American Indian as it is celebrated in «The Dance.» The last line of the stanza suggests that Columbus feels himself in the hands of the universal powers of destiny; he is dramatically aware that his discovery, and its potentialities, are lost if the keel of his ship for a moment yields to the force of the waves and causes the vessel to turn over and sink.

The admiral, as he is called in the *Journal,* then looks back on the fateful night hours when his ships first drew near the islands and when he saw the first light ashore. At that moment he remembered the time when he had wandered the streets of his native Genoa, obsessed by a dream which had made him a stranger, an «exile» in his town:

I thought of Genoa; and this truth, now proved,
That made me exile in her streets, stood me
More absolute than ever — biding the moon
Till dawn should clear that dim frontier, first seen
— The Chan's great continent . . . Then faith, not fear
Nigh surged me witless . . . Hearing the surf near —
I, wonder-breathing, kept the watch — saw
The first palm chevron the first lighted hill.
And lowered. And they came out to us crying,
«The Great White Birds!»

This account of Columbus' first sight of land corresponds closely to the *Journal.* According to the entry for October 11, 1492, the admiral «at ten in the previous night, being on the castle of the poop, saw a light, though it was so uncertain that he could not affirm it was land.»[11] This light was seen several times, and two hours after midnight land was sighted. The ships waited for daylight and in the morning they arrived at the first island. The «first lighted hill» refers to the light seen by Columbus, and Crane also describes his nightly vigil, the waiting for dawn to «clear that dim frontier.» The lines vividly convey the suspense of Columbus during these expectant hours, his powerful faith both in the geographical truth of his theories and the divine mission of his voyage. According to the *Journal,* the natives of the West Indies thought that Columbus and his men came from heaven, and their sailing ships quite naturally came to look like great white birds.[12] Similarly, the Aztecs believed that Cortez and his men were incarnations of the god Quetzalcoatl, who had left their country in a mythic past and who was to come back in the shape of a white man. To the natives of America the coming of the white gods meant the downfall of the existing Indian empires and the beginning of a new era, a new world.

As he looks back on the natives' greeting of his ships, Columbus turns his attention towards his present situation, on board a single ship, surrounded by stormy waves and threatened with shipwreck. He prays to the holy Mary, the mediator between man and the almighty God, for salvation:

>   (O Madre Maria, still
> One ship of these thou grantest safe returning;
> Assure us through thy mantle's ageless blue!)
> And record of more, floating in a casque,
> Was tumbled from us under bare poles scudding;
> And later hurricanes may claim more pawn . . .
> For here between two worlds, another, harsh,
>
> This third, of water, tests the word; lo, here
> Bewilderment and mutiny heap whelming
> Laughter, and shadow cuts sleep from the heart
> Almost as though the Moor's flung scimitar
> Found more than flesh to fathom in its fall.

The last, violent storm that Columbus had to endure before reaching the Azores is described vividly in the *Journal* in a long entry of February 14, 1493. The crew were convinced that they would die, and their captain remonstrated with himself for his own fear and lack of faith in divine providence. He and the crew all made holy vows that if saved, they would immediately say prayers in a church dedicated to «Our Lady.» In this same entry is also recorded the writing of a report of the discoveries which was thrown overboard in a wooden barrel in order that the sovereign of Spain might have information even if the ship went down.

Columbus experiences the stormy ocean as a «third» world of water between Europe and America, and in the tempest he sees the powers of chaos and evil at work, threatening to destroy his mission and his faith in divine providence. He also recalls that these same forces operated in the «bewilderment» and «mutiny» of his crew before they reached land on the westward voyage. He conceived of it all as a test of his faith in his mission.

His problems have deprived Columbus of his sleep, which here also means his repose in faith, their «shadow» has «cut» it from his heart in the same way as the «Moor's flung scimitar» cuts flesh. Here is a reference to the war between the Spaniards and the Moors, which had ended just before Columbus left Spain with victory for the Christians, who had conquered Granada. The Arabs, threatening to destroy the Catholic culture of Spain, were also representatives of chaos, and by destroying the Spanish Church they might also destroy «more than flesh,» namely faith itself. Being entrusted with the *word*, Columbus, like the poet himself, subjects himself to the fall from vision, the daemonic darkness which accompanies the prophet and in whose «shadow» he lives.

These reflections represent the lowest point of despair and lack of faith experienced by Columbus in «Ave Maria,» but at this juncture he is reinspired by a visionary moment in which the sea, the setting sun, and the circular horizon combine into a revelatory image of the beautiful and harmonious round globe itself:

              eyes
Starved wide on blackened tides, accrete — enclose
This turning rondure whole, this crescent ring
Sun-cusped and zoned with modulated fire
Like pearls that whisper through the Doge's hands —

Crane is not primarily concerned here with the dramatic representation of the hurricane, but with Columbus' attitude toward the elements that surround him and have him in their grasp. The raging storm reflects the battle in his mind between faith and doubt; he may either see the «tempest-lash» as chaos getting the upper hand, or he may come to terms with the storm as a meaningful test of his faith. As if in answer to his prayer to the Virgin, who here makes her first full appearance in *The Bridge*, he perceives an «inmost sob» beneath the roar of the sea which momentarily reveals God's presence in nature. At this moment the storm has reached its climax, the movements of the wind and sea begin to appear more controlled and measured. Thus is «dissuaded» the «abyss» of the destructive depths of the ocean as well as of the mind which has lost its orientation.

As he stares at the horizon, Columbus experiences a vision of the whole, turning globe which reveals the divine harmony of the universe to him. His eyes, the poet's familiar symbol of the visionary ability, are «starved» because of the endless gazing for land over «blackened tides,» but suddenly the vision emerges. The ring of the horizon, illuminated by the blaze of the setting sun, expands into an image of the round earth, «zoned» into realms of darkness and realms of «modulated fire,» the light of a sun which is another expression of divine power. We have to bear in mind here that Columbus had proved physically, with his own person, that the earth was round; it was on this assumption that he had undertaken his westward voyage to the Orient, and now the globe reveals itself to him as a huge «turning rondure whole.» The word «rondure» occurs in a letter to Frank, July 24, 1926, in which Crane described a return of his creative powers: «I feel an absolute music in the air again, and some tremendous rondure floating somewhere.»

However, «rondure» is also used by Whitman in «Passage to India,» in a section that deals with the voyages and discoveries of the European renaissance and describes «Lands found and nations born, thou born America,/ Thou rondure of the world at last accomplished.» The parallels between «Ave Maria» and Whitman's poem are even more evident in the paragraph immediately following: «O vast Rondure, swimming in space,/ Cover'd all over with visible power and beauty,/ Alternate light and day and the teeming spiritual darkness.»[13] Whitman here asserts his faith in the meaningful design of the universe; his vision embodies the same kind of belief that Columbus has as he stares at the sea. But Columbus voices fears that the riches of his Cathay may inflame the greed of the Spaniards and lead to strife and destruction: «Yet no delirium of jewels! O Fernando,/ Take of that eastern shore, this western sea,/ Yet yield thy God's, thy Virgin's charity!»

Columbus is afraid that his Cathay will be ruined by King Ferdinand, whose «fear and greed» were referred to in the opening of «Ave Maria.» His apprehension is actually a prophecy of the future ravages of the Spaniards in the new world, their delirious, mad search for gold, and within the context of *The Bridge* it points forward to the grimness and spiritual poverty of modern America as seen in «Quaker Hill» and «The Tunnel.» Columbus exhorts the king to take of the «eastern shore» of Cathay without failing to show the same «charity» towards the land and its people that God has shown towards Spain. His warning implies the double nature of the American dream. Ideally, the jewels and riches of Cathay symbolize a perfect land of beauty and plenty, but there is always the possibility of exploitation, of rapacious materialism getting the upper hand.

Columbus' vision of the «rondure» of the earth is an example of one of the dominant images in Crane's poetry, the circle or ball. The drawing together of external objects into some kind of rounded figure always signifies the revelation of a divine harmony and order of things, both in *The Bridge* and in other poems.[14] The eyes of Columbus absorb the sight of the circular horizon and the round, flaming sun and envisage a great, luminous globe, a precious «pearl» that runs through the «Doge's hands,» and this jewel imagery recurs later in the poem as a vision of the «sapphire wheel» of the planets. In «Cape Hatteras» Crane affirms Whitman's vision of total integration, symbolized by «the aureole round thy head/ Of pasture-shine . . .» and in «Atlantis» the circle image is introduced with the positive meaning it had for Columbus: «the circular, indubitable frieze/ Of heaven's meditation, yoking wave/ To kneeling wave.» The sky and the horizon form a circular frieze, an ornament like the «kindled Crown,» and in this universe, governed by divine design, the waves of the ocean are controlled; they are «kneeling» like the waves whose «inmost sob» Columbus heard.

In the third part of «Ave Maria» Columbus, having conquered all obstacles and overcome all dangers, reaffirms his faith in God and in the divine mission that he has been born to fulfill, and as a parallel to the «angelus» of his crew he addresses God in prayer and thanksgiving. Historically we are here dealing with a Renaissance-Catholic God, but Crane portrays the object of Columbus' veneration in terms entirely his own:

O Thou who sleepest on Thyself, apart
Like ocean athwart lanes of death and birth,
And all the eddying breath between dost search
Cruelly with love thy parable of man, —
Inquisitor! Incognizable Word
Of Eden and the enchained Sepulchre,
Into thy steep savannahs, burning blue,
Utter to loneliness the sail is true.

God's being is conceived as a cosmic, all-spanning oceanic bridge
which embodies both this world and the world beyond and unites life
and death in one totality. The organic process of living and dying is the
«eddying breath» of His being; each breath of His covers the life span
of man, and out of His essence He contacts man, and though He loves
him, He tests his faith «cruelly» as in the storm, for God is also fierce
and demanding. «The divine Wisdom simultaneously tests and guides
His fortunate victims, leading them on a course of self-abnegation toward self-fulfillment in Him.»[15]

The cruel yet loving God is an «inquisitor» of man's faith. Crane is
aware that his portrayal of God in terms of an oceanic bridge is a mere
metaphor of the nature of the divine being. That being itself is the «incognizable» *word* or *logos* that became incarnate in the Garden of
Eden and in the person of Jesus and his «enchained Sepulchre.» Columbus is looking back to the time when God moved among men, and
he seeks another revelation in his own time, the word of a new Eden.
He wants to know that his sail is «true,» his voyage guided by God,
whose ocean is like «savannahs,» a metaphor that echoes the imagery
of *Moby Dick*. Melville often compares the sea to plains, meadows
and prairies. The waves are blue and yet «burning,» presumably with
the rays of the setting sun, referring back to the metaphor of the
«gleaming mail.» The color combination of blue or gray, on the one
hand, and gold, fire or red, on the other, recurs in *The Bridge* as a
symbol of the dream of an ideal America.

The metaphor of God as a sea-bridge is sustained, and He is conceived of as a benevolent but exacting taskmaster who in the shape of
the sea wears down or crushes the oars of the sailors and who «argues»
with or tests the mast in the storm. He even «subscribest,» meaning
sanctions, shipwrecks, «holocausts of ships,» as sacrifice. Columbus is
outlining the personality of his God, and he emphasizes omnipotence

and sternness. But he is also convinced that his voyage to the new world is the fulfillment of a prophecy and that he is acting on a higher impulse. He then praises the beauty and perfection of God's creation, the «primal scan,» meaning range or extent of the oceans in which the earth is enveloped and which include the «seignories,» dominions of Ganges, a reference which is in keeping with Columbus' belief that he had found India, the «Chan's great continent.» He recalls various events which he interprets as divine signs sent by God to guide him on his way, a «corposant» and a volcanic outbreak on the island of Tene-riffe.

Columbus goes on to thank God for the assistance he had received in solving the problems of the expedition, particularly in connection with the compass needles:

Of all that amplitude that time explores,
A needle in the sight, suspended north, —
Yielding by inference and discard, faith
And true appointment from the hidden shoal:
This disposition that thy night relates
From Moon to Saturn in one sapphire wheel:
The orbic wake of thy once whirling feet,
Elohim, still I hear thy sounding heel!

According to the *Journal* entry of September 17, the sailors obser-ved that the compass needles did not confirm to the star which was their north point, and they were alarmed. But Columbus realized that this was due to compass variation and explained to his men that the north star made the movement, not the needles. Accordingly the need-les were true. In the poem the needles that seemed to be wrong were «suspended north.» By explaining the variation, using his knowledge to «infer» the real state of affairs and «discard» the false notions brought about by the variation, Columbus succeeded in «yielding» re-newed faith in their direction, here described as «true appointment.» That they were on the right course was confirmed by the observation of the «hidden shoal» that they knew must be near at this stage of the voyage. According to the *Journal* they saw grass and herbs from rocks in the water and gathered that they were near land.

By realizing the mechanisms of compass variation Columbus gained insight into the order of the universe, his expanding knowledge was a conquest of chaos and a revelation of harmony. This «disposition» of reality, seen in the movements and configurations of the heavenly bodies, is «related» to him in a vision of the planets that circle the sun in gem-like wheels. This passage is replete with references to the visions of the prophets of the Old Testament. The very word «sapphire,» and also the figure of the wheel, occur in numerous visions of God that the prophets had. Columbus was a firm believer in the books of the prophets, and he thought that he, like them, was inspired by God. He might well have thought it possible to be given a revelation, a theophany for himself, and he is rewarded. He sees Elohim, or a manifestation of Him; in the nightly firmament he perceives the wake left by the feet that Moses saw and even the sound of God's tread.[16]

At the end of «Ave Maria» Crane portrays Columbus as the archetypal idealist of American history, the poet-voyager in search of a Cathay yet to be realized in time. He distinguishes between the actual land that he has found, the West Indies, and the Cathay that lies somewhere inland:

White toil of heaven's cordons, mustering
In holy rings all sails charged to the far
Hushed gleaming fields and pendant seething wheat
Of knowledge — round thy brows unhooded now
— The kindled Crown! acceded of the poles
And biassed by full sails, meridians reel
Thy purpose — still one shore beyond desire!
The sea's green crying towers a-sway. Beyond

And kingdoms
                naked in the
                              trembling heart —

Te Deum laudamus
                O Thou Hand of Fire

In a letter to Frank of July 26, 1926, Crane described the last part of «Ave Maria» as «the more absolute and marked intimation of the great *Te Deum* of the court, later held, — here in terms of C's own cosmography.» The scene referred to is the court of Isabella at the time when Columbus presented the news of his discovery and a *Te Deum* was performed in praise of God, who had protected the expedition.[17] The discoverer sees his ships readied for yet other voyages, like Matthew Arnold's Ulysses, and the «holy rings» of their sails are matched by the «cordons» or circles of the heavenly bodies, signifying the belief that the expeditions will proceed in answer to a divine will, directed by a human knowledge which has insight into the laws of the universe and makes navigation possible.

The metaphor of the «sea's green towers» refers to «The Port of Columbus,» a fictional dialogue between Columbus and Cervantes which concludes Waldo Frank's *Virgin Spain*. Directly inspired by this dialogue, Crane, in a letter to Frank of March 26, 1926, characterized it as «something of a prelude to my intentions for *The Bridge*.» Frank had a strong and continuing interest in Spain and the Central American as well as Latin American countries, and in his book he attempted to depict America as a fundamentally coherent unity that would include both continents of the hemisphere. The final dialogue has a prophetic note, presenting a vision of America as a world in the process of realizing itself. Several of the images and terms that Frank used in this lyrical interchange were echoed in the poems of *White Buildings* and *The Bridge,* such as towers, gold and white cities. The stage is Palos, the port in Spain from which Columbus first set sail westward, and he and Cervantes, in their old age, stand on a height overlooking the harbor. Cervantes has visions of what is obviously modern America, and Columbus comments on the pictures that are presented to him, holding out his concept of what America will one day be like. He is the spokesman of Frank's own ideals.

Cervantes sees a city of white towers that presents a «glittering order,» a front which hides the real chaos of races and traditions. The people have lost sight of their gods and yet are full of «God-hunger,» so they turn to their own works and worship these. Columbus urges Cervantes to look beyond the towers, which are obviously those of modern Manhattan, and he observes the continent and «childish peoples» that speak in a variety of tongues. According to Frank's Columbus, modern America, with all its technological wonders, its skyscrapers and machines, is really the magnificent grave of European scientific culture, and the true new world will arise when the American people have acquired a new vision of their environment, have learned to see themselves as parts of a more organic, deeply interwoven whole. Columbus outlines this for Cervantes:

Cervantes — (Incredulous) If that is Death yonder across the sea, it is a death most stable and most splendid.

Columbus — Death is the most sumptuous song. This golden-towered America is but the grave of Europe.

Cervantes — I do not understand.

Columbus — What do you find there?

Cervantes — Mighty stones

Columbus — Are not stones of Europe?

Cervantes — Gold

Columbus — Is not gold a lust of the old world?

Cervantes — Marvellous machines

Columbus — Did you, then, not know England, that you should think them new?

Cervantes — Never with us were gold and stone and iron so high a glory.

Columbus — Does not Europe merit a high Sepulcher?[18]

After this, Cervantes witnesses the falling of the towers, and Columbus is jubilant. The city and the chaos are gone, and he exclaims: «The Dream of the Old World, at last — a New World!» The new America will be rooted in the old Spain, whose conquerors sallied forth to claim the American earth for their church. Columbus describes this in terms which reflect Frank's philosophy of America as a spiritually united body. The spirit of Spain is going to be the main inspiration in the construction of a new social and religious consciousness in America. The model is the will of the Spanish Catholic Church to make of America, North and South, the new body of an old religious vision.

At this point it must be stressed that Frank did not intend his ideal America to be a Catholic theocracy; what he hoped for was a new organization of American life which would preserve the sense of the world as Christ's body, as an organic whole, in other words, only completely severed from any already existing doctrine. The faith of the old Spain is a model which Frank employed as a metaphor to describe the *new* faith that must arise in America. In the same way, Crane incorporated Columbus' Catholic world-view into his own vision of the wholeness of America in *The Bridge*.

In the final scenes of «The Port of Columbus,» as the towers are falling, Columbus thanks God for this event and interprets it as a sign of the birth of a new consciousness. The towers are symbols of a triumphant technology and materialism, and their downfall, not necessarily a material one, indicates a changing attitude, a more spiritual orientation. Frank lets Columbus utter these prophetic words: «The New World is in them, underneath the towers. When they have learned that they cannot succeed; that all the towers and all the machines and all the gold on earth cannot crush down this unborn need in them for a true New World — then it will arise.»[19] When Crane has his sea's towers be «a-sway,» ready to fall, it may be intended to show that he sees the new consciousness of America emerging. Frank's thesis is that industrialized and commercialized America has shut off the people from the deeper contact with the land. They have to recover it both physically and spiritually. This contact or recognition is suggested by Crane's metaphor of the «seething wheat of knowledge» which is «pendant,» a potentiality to be realized.

3. *Powhatan's Daughter*

The five poems of this section deal with Pocahontas, the daughter of the chief Powhatan, and she emerges in the text as a symbol of the American earth, becoming an earth-goddess in «The Dance.» In «Ave Maria» the poet explored the possibilities of Columbus' medieval religiosity in the shaping of his vision, and in «Powhatan's Daughter» he sets himself the task of charting the spiritual possibilities of the American land and its various native traditions. The general theme of the section is the search for a religious consciousness of and contact with the living body of the continent, Pocahontas, and the quest is dramatized in sexual terms. The Indian maiden is the poet's waiting bride, and in «The Dance» he becomes united with her. Pocahontas lies somewhere out west and the poet is in New York, and he embarks on a westward journey in the tradition of the old pioneers. Though the journey is also symbolic, it has a great deal of vivid, factual description both of modern city life and of the American landscape.

The theme of the earth is indicated at the end of «Ave Maria» in the image of the «gleaming fields» that await exploration by the white man, but Crane has not followed the logical temporal order after the Columbus section. Instead of recording the early settlements and expeditions historically, he makes a bold chronological leap from the time of Columbus to his 1920s in «The Harbor Dawn,» and from that point he goes backward again to the mythic past of «The Dance.»

This reversal of ordinary time sequence is a consequence of the method of *The Bridge* as outlined by the poet himself, the effort to create «an epic of the modern *consciousness*.»(My italics.) Crane made his leap in time because he did not want the historical awareness that the textbooks present, but a consciousness of the past in and through the present. The structure of «Powhatan's Daughter» is explained in the long gloss of *The Bridge* that Crane sent to Otto Kahn on September 12, 1927:

Powhatan's daughter, or Pocahontas, is the mythological nature-symbol chosen to represent the physical body of the continent, or the soil. She here takes on much the same role as the traditional Hertha of ancient Teutonic mythology. The five sub-sections of Part II are mainly concerned with a gradual exploration of this body whose first possessor was the Indian. It seemed altogether ineffective from the poetic standpoint to approach this material from the purely chronological angle — beginning with, say, the landing of «The Mayflower,» continuing with a resume of the Revolution through the conquest of the West, etc. One can get that viewpoint in any history primer . . . Consequently I jump from the monologue of Columbus in «Ave Maria» — right across the four intervening centuries — into the harbor of 20th-century Manhattan. And from that point in time and place I begin to work backward through the pioneer period, always in terms of the present — finally to the very core of the nature-world of the Indian.

By exploring the «body» of Pocahontas in «Powhatan's Daughter,» Crane was actively trying to tackle a central problem for American poets, the creation of a sense of a really native contact with the earth of the kind that grows out of a tribal or folk tradition. D. H. Lawrence has made some interesting observations on this matter in his discussion of the relation between American literature and «The Spirit of Place.» In an essay on «Fenimore Cooper's White Novels» he writes on the necessity for the white man to absorb the spirit of the primeval inhabitant of the continent; «A curious thing about the Spirit of Place is the fact that no place exerts its full influence upon a newcomer until the old inhabitant is dead or absorbed. So America . . . At present the demon of the place and the unappeased ghosts of the dead Indians act within the unconscious or under-conscious soul of the white American, causing the great American grouch, the Orestes-like frenzy of

55

restlessness in the Yankee soul, the inner malaise which amounts almost to madness, sometimes.»[20] Lawrence eloquently expresses the challenge that confronted American literature and sensibility from the beginning, and he holds that the true contact with the land has not yet been found in America. His idea that the Indian demons must be appeased or absorbed was shared by Crane, who in his gloss of «The Dance» wrote that he became identified with the Indian because this was the only way of ever «possessing the Indian and his world as a cultural factor.»

Crane's Pocahontas is his means of establishing vital contact with the continent that Columbus had found. Living as he did in an industrialized society, the poet felt that this original contact with the soil had been destroyed by the advancement of a soulless, technological civilization. However, he did not seek to annihilate the influence of civilaztion and the machine; after all, his main symbol, the Brooklyn Bridge, is a technological object, and what he wanted was to attribute a spiritual dimension *both* to the machine *and* to the soil. The exclamation in «The River» that America suffers from «an iron dealt cleavage» refers to the artificial separation of technical and scientific achievements from any coherent world-view. For Columbus the expansion of knowledge was a revelation of divine order, and Crane wanted to see the scientific achievements of his own era in the same way. The epigraph of the section illustrates this intention, although in a somewhat oblique fashion. This is a description of Pocahontas as «a wellfeatured but wanton yong girle . . . of the age of eleven or twelve years» who got «the boyes forth with her into the marketplace, and make them wheele, falling on their hands, turning their heels upwards, whom she would followe, and wheele so herself, naked as she was, all the fort over.»[21] The wheel of Pocahontas is moving around on the ground, dancing as it were, and this same kinetic image recurs in «The River,» with its «Pullman breakfasters» that move like «a dance of wheel on wheel.» The figure of a wheel-like circle or dance also occurs in «Ave Maria» and in the early drafts of «Atlantis» and seems to symbolize a higher order or design. Throughout «Powhatan's Daughter» the image of the earth-goddess recurs in several contexts, and the poet's avowed effort to make her a reality is presented symbolically as a love affair culminating in the union between himself and the earth.[22] Crane explains this in the note to «The Harbor Dawn:» «The love-motif (in italics) carries along a symbolism of the life and ages of man (here the sowing of the seed) which is further developed in each of the subsequent sections of 'Powhatan's Daughter,' though it is never particularly stressed. In 2 ('Van Winkle') it is Childhood; in 3 it is Youth; in 4, Manhood; in 5 it is Age. This motif is interwoven and tends to be implicit in the imagery rather than anywhere stressed.»

The Harbor Dawn

The beginning of this poem presents a state of semi-consciousness in the protagonist. Half asleep in the early morning in the city, he vaguely registers the awakening life of the harbor. This strange condition between sleep and wakefulness provides the poet with his first dreamlike and transient vision of the maiden, but first the harbor life itself is vaguely realized:

Insistently through sleep — a tide of voices —
They meet you listening midway in your dream,
The long, tired sounds, fog-insulated noises:
Gongs in white surplices, beshrouded wails,
Far strum of fog horns . . signals dispersed in veils.

The poet's sleep, like that of Rip Van Winkle, who appears in the next poem, is a vehicle for the transport to the past and the body of Pocahontas. «The Harbor Dawn» is a factual, realistic description of a certain place at a certain time, but the poem also contains references to other sections. The «tide» of the voices points back to the «blackened tides» of «Ave Maria,» and the signals that are heard as if through «veils» are linked to the veil that lies upon the bride Pocahontas in «The Dance.» The «beshrouded wails» that are heard link with the passage in «The River» in which the poet listens to the trains going west and hears them «wail into distances I knew were hers.» It is indicated that Pocahontas lies somewhere out west awaiting her lover, and «Powhatan's Daughter» presents a journey westward across the continent and backwards in time, though usually «in terms of the present.»

The poem goes on to evoke more of the activities of the harbor and city in carefully modulated lines and highly selective images. There is an air of realism in these lines, but at the same time a dominant mood of dreamy expectancy prepares for the ensuing love scene: «And if they take your sleep away sometimes/ They give it back again. Soft sleeves of sound/ Attend the darkling harbor, the pillowed bay . . .»

There is a gradual transition from sleep to wakefulness here, as the muffled sounds become more distinct and prominent. On the level of description, mood and atmosphere this must be said to be an excellent impressionistic sketch of the first hours of a wintry dawn in New York city harbor. As a whole «The Harbor Dawn» recalls certain descriptive passages in Crane's letters that deal with the harbor and the Manhattan skyline as he was able to see them from his room in Columbia Heights in Brooklyn. On November 16, 1924, he wrote to his mother about a night and a dawn near the harbor: «All night long there were distant tinklings, buoy bells and siren warnings from river craft. It was like wakening into a dreamland in the early dawn — one wondered where one was with only a milky light in the window and that vague music from a hidden world.»

The impression created in the opening of «The Harbor Dawn,» with its «lumbering truck» and «throbbing» winch engines, is one of potential power waiting to be unleashed. But the power of the machine is not fully dramatized until «Cape Hatteras,» with its «nasal whine of power» that «whips a new universe.» In «The Harbor Dawn» the emphasis is on «power in repose,» which was the intention of the whole section. In the letter of August 3, 1926, to Frank, Crane wrote: «'Powhatan's Daughter' must be that basic center and antecedent of all motion — 'power in repose'.»

The increasing noise of engines is subdued again as the poet returns to the condition of dream and sleep and lets the sounds of the harbor lull instead of awaken him. He imagines that some steam out there between the ships and the derricks is drifting along in the air, «eddied among distant chiming buoys.» The «wavering slumber» suggests that the poet is still in a transitional state between sleep and waking, a condition of meditative quiet that creates a sense of timelessness.[23] It is during such an «immemorial» moment that he begins to perceive the existence of Pocahontas:

And you beside me, blessèd now while sirens
Sing to us, stealthily weave us into day —
Serenely now, before day claims our eyes
Your cool arms murmurously about me lay.

While myriad snowy hands are clustering at the panes —

your hands within my hands are deeds;
my tongue upon your throat — singing
arms close; eyes wide, undoubtful
                    dark
                              drink the dawn —
a forest shudders in your hair!

The dream-image of the woman lying next to the poet is his «bridge» to the American soil, and she is thus linked with the metaphor of the bridge as a woman in the proem. The «cool arms» of Pocahontas provide the poet with the anthropomorphic image which his imagination needs in order to embrace and encompass the continent by means of poetic creation. The description of falling snow seen through the window is very *imagiste* and worthy of Ezra Pound or Marianne Moore, or even e. e. cummings. It has a pictorial value wholly its own.

The climactic passage is italicized and presents the meeting with Pocahontas in erotic images. The poet starts to caress the body of the goddess; his eyes have become «Wide, undoubtful» at this moment of heightened awareness of the true nature and shape of the land. The forests of America become the «hair» of Pocahontas, and there are several such anthropomorphic suggestions throughout the section. In the thunderstorm of «The Dance,» for example, the strokes of lightning down toward the earth and its trees are seen as «twangs/Of lightning deltaed down your saber hair,» and the grass becomes «her hair's warm sibilance.»

The reality of Pocahontas in «The Harbor Dawn» is on the level of dreams, she is not fully known or realized, but appears as a vague promise of an identity that is revealed later. This is indicated by the question which Crane put in the margin: «Who is the woman with us in the dawn? . . . whose is the flesh our feet have moved upon?» Until he has reached into the country, the poet cannot really know Pocahontas, and the main structural principle of «Powhatan's Daughter» is the westward journeying for signs or manifestations of the earth-goddess.

In the two beautiful and evocative last stanzas of «The Harbor Dawn» the poet finally leaves the world of sleep and dreams behind and turns his attention to the outside scene of the sunrise over the harbor:

The window goes blond slowly. Frostily clears.
From Cyclopean towers across Manhattan waters
— Two — three bright window-eyes aglitter, disk
The sun, released — aloft with cold gulls hither.

The fog leans one last moment on the sill.
Under the mistletoe of dreams a star —
As though to join us at some distant hill —
Turns in the waking west and goes to sleep.

After this transient dream-vision of the goddess, the poet turns toward the external world, and the things that he observes condense into images that discreetly reflect and echo the promise of a divine America. Pocahontas has faded now temporarily, but in the harbor setting the poet rediscovers the signs of revelation. His dream of Pocahontas has served as his link with the mythic past, and strengthened by this experience, he has a hopeful vision, embodied in bright images, of contemporary American reality. The windows of the Manhattan skyscrapers become, by a natural metamorphosis, «bright window-eyes aglitter,» and we are reminded of the poet looking through office windows in the proem at the seagull. The window that is filled with daylight and «frostily clears» is linked with the «cold gulls» that refer back to the proem and the white birds of «Ave Maria.» There is also a foreshadowing of the «seagulls stung with rime» in «Atlantis.» The coldness, the snow, the gulls and the glitter of the sun in the windows are all bound together by a common quality, the color white, symbol of the final vision.[24] The circular «disk» of the sun is «released» and rises above the horizon accompanied by ascending seagulls that, as we remember from the proem, fly with «inviolate curve,» describing the spanning, curving movement of the sun across the sky. The star in «The Harbor Dawn» goes to sleep in the western sky; it is the morning star that represents the spirit of the Indian that Crane sets out to revive. In «The Dance,» this star is revealed as the apotheosis of another Indian god, a male counterpart to Pocahontas. Above the «distant hill» the star beckons the poet on toward his merging with the Indian world.

Van Winkle

Having decided to bridge the land to reach the star in the west, the poet starts to celebrate the modern, technical means of spanning the earth.

Beginning with a marginal note, he states: «Streets speed past store and factory — sped by sunlight and her smile . . .» The smile of Pocahontas indicates a promise of union between man and nature. It reappears as the smile of the poet's mother, and in «The Dance» it is perceived in the mountain scenery of the Adirondacks.

The opening stanza of «Van Winkle» is a *tour de force* of kinetic imagery that conveys a sense of breathtaking speed and vast, continental spaces:

Macadam, gun-grey as the tunny's belt,
Leaps from Far Rockaway to Golden Gate:
Listen! the miles a hurdy-gurdy grinds —
Down gold arpeggios mile on mile unwinds.

The first two lines invoke in one bold stroke how modern highways stretch from coast to coast, indicated by the two well-known place names in New York and California. Crane's note explains the last two lines: «The protagonist has left the room with its harbor sounds, and is walking to the subway. The rhythm is quickened; it is a transition between sleep and the imminent tasks of the day. Space is filled with the music of a hand organ and fresh sunlight, and one has the impression of the whole continent — from Atlantic to Pacific — freshly arisen and moving.» The speed of modern higway travelling is rendered in terms of the music that is ground on the handorgan. The speeding traveller that covers miles on miles is suggested by the sound of the grinding of the «hurdy-gurdy.» Another figure connoting speed is the «arpeggios,» rapid succession of tones, that are produced by the organ. Synesthetically, the arpeggios are like gold, a metal that is closely associated with the Cathay-image and plays an important role in «Indiana.»

The figure of Rip Van Winkle has become an important character in American folklore as a voice or message from the past, a living remnant of bygone days. The poet who wakes up in twentieth-century New York is a modern Van Winkle who feels himself connected with the adventurous beginnings of the country's history, its early promise: «The walk to the subway arouses reminiscences of childhood, also the 'childhood' of the continental conquest, viz., the conquistadores, Priscilla, Capt. John Smith, etc. These parallellisms unite in the figure of Rip Van Winkle, who finally becomes identified with the protagonist, as you will notice, and who really boards the subway train with the reader. He becomes the 'guardian angel' of the journey into the past.» In this note the poet identifies himself and the opening of «Powhatan's Daughter» with the early American history that we expect will be drawn into *The Bridge* after the poem about Columbus. The conquistadores invoke the beginnings of the white man's conquest of America, but their savage search for gold is an inversion of Columbus' esthetic and religious vision of the golden new world and echoes his warnings against greed. Captain Smith is associated with the historical legend of Pochahontas, the maiden who bridges the gap between the races.

Sleeping on in his «tenement», the poet as Van Winkle forgets both «office hours» and «pay» and lets time and its affairs pass while he lets his mind remain in the past. Pocahontas, like memory itself, is timeless, or as the poet puts it in a marginal note, «she is time's truant,» who is going to lead him by the hand into the past. He recalls certain incidents from his childhood, the making of paper planes and the hunt for garter snakes:

The grind-organ says . . . Remember, remember
The cinder pile at the end of the backyard
Where we stoned the family of young
Garter snakes under . . . And the monoplanes
We launched — with paper wings and twisted
Rubber bands . . . Recall — recall
                      the rapid tongues
That flittered from under the ash heap day
After day whenever your stick discovered
Some sunning inch of unsuspecting fibre —
It flashed back at your thrust, as clean as fire.

The snakes and the paper planes are the first examples in *The Bridge* of the recurrent symbols of serpents on the one hand and birds or airplanes on the other. The fact that both «The Dance» and «Atlantis» conclude with an image of a serpent joined with an eagle indicates the central importance of this symbolism. In the childhood of the poet, as well as that of his country, the white man tried to destroy the serpent which is a symbol of time as well as the indigenous qualities and beliefs of the Indians. The eagle or airplane symbolizes, in some contexts, the technological conquest of space of the white man. The paper planes of the children thus point forward to Crane's celebration of the Wright Brothers' invention of the airplane in «Cape Hatteras».

However, the children never quite destroy the garter snakes. Under the ash heap of modern civilization they still lie, and when attacked they flash back «as clean as fire.» Serpents are also associated with fire imagery in «The Dance,» where the flames of a sacrificial pyre become the «red fangs» and «splay tongues» of snakes. Crane is articulating the general conflict that he sees between the spirit and accomplishments of the Indian and those of the white man. Like Waldo Frank, the poet regards it as an imperative for the complete presentation of the vision of America that these contrasting influences be reconciled, and that the white man assimilates the Indian world view. «The Dance,» «Indiana,» and parts of «The River» are devoted to the theme of reconciliation between the races.

The poet-Van Winkle, having entered into the double childhood of his own life and that of the land, loses his orientation in time. He does not know what time he lives in and applies the images of the past to the present scene. Under the influence of the past he sees the modern Broadway as a «Catskill daisy chain in May,» a reference to the natural, untouched beauty of America. Later in the poem, the subtle connections between memory and associations are indicated:

So memory, that strikes a rhyme out of a box
Or splits a random smell of flowers through glass —
Is it the whip stripped from the lilac tree
One day in spring my father took to me,
Or is it the Sabbatical, unconscious smile
My mother almost brought me once from church
And once only, as I recall —?

By looking at the «box» of what is presumably the handorgan referred to in the opening of the poem, the poet can remember an old «rhyme.» Seeing some flowers through a window, he recalls a «random smell» associated with them and wonders whether this smell has

anything to to with the «whip» his father once brought him or with the
smile his mother once gave him. The smile of the mother is a glimpse
of what is later to become the smile of nature in the shape of the earth-
mother Pocahontas. There is little emphasis on *individual* women in
The Bridge; the poet is in search of a female principle or element
whose highest manifestation is the Virgin Mary, the heavenly goddess
who supplements Pocahontas.

As the westward journey starts, the reader is abruptly made aware
of it by the repetition of the violent opening lines:

Macadam, gun-grey as the tunny's belt,
Leaps from Far Rockaway to Golden Gate . . .
Keep hold of that nickel for car-change, Rip, —
Have you got your «Times» - ?
And hurry along, Van Winkle — it's getting late!

The poet-Van Winkle boards the subway train and is asked if he has
his «Times,» not only the newspaper, but his poetic time orientation of
the past in the present. It is getting late in the day and in history for his
effort to find the past and connect it with the present. As R. W. Butterfield says, «the poem ends with the indolent, but spiritually harmonious Rip set in ironic contrast against a New York rush hour.»[25]

The River

The westward journey in search of Pocahontas repeats the pattern of
the treks of the American pioneers and is described with gusto and vi-
gor in «The River,» one of the most powerful poems in *The Bridge*. In
American cultural history, the wanderings of the early frontiersmen
have become established as one of the central emotional and imaginative patterns of the American experience and national character.

In this poem, Crane has managed to give one a sense of the ever-pre-
sent actuality and possibility of the westward journey of exploration
and discovery, if only in the imagination, as a journey of the soul.
However, the first part of the poem contains passages of burlesque
that parody many of the absurdities of modern America and its inventions. In the opening lines, this confusion is evoked by the recording of
assorted impressions as seen from the window of a speeding train: bill-
boards with «Tintex-Japalac-Overalls ads,» loose comments from one

tramp to another, and a reference to «Bert Williams,» a contemporary vaudeville artist. The world of advertising, industrial patents and brand names is invoked here. The continent is being overwhelmed by all this humdrum, materialistic activity, during which playbills are «ripped» and chickens stolen. In this context, Horace Greeley's famous advice, suggested in the phrase «going west,» achieves an ironic ring.[26]

Having been transported by the railroad train into the Midwest, the reader joins some tramps near the tracks as they watch the express train of the 20th Century Limited pass by in a rush. The poet employs the image of the speeding train as a metaphor of the cultural disintegration effected by the rapid movement of the life of the modern individual amidst a welter of objects, pursuits and influences that have no coherence. The soulless pursuit of purely materialistic or techonological aims has created a gap between man and nature and thrown all sorts of elements together in one meaningless flood of impressions, and this is the contemporary situation:

- and the telegraphic night coming on Thomas

a Ediford — and whistling down the tracks
a headlight rushing with the sound — can you
imagine — while an express makes time like
SCIENCE — COMMERCE and the HOLYGHOST
RADIO ROARS IN EVERY HOME WE HAVE THE
   NORTHPOLE
WALLSTREET AND VIRGINBIRTH WITHOUT STONES OR
WIRES OR EVEN RUNNING brooks connecting ears
and no more sermons windows flashing roar
Breathtaking — as you like it . . . eh?

The «telegraphic night» implies a criticism of the purely utilitarian conquest of space that Crane saw as the main danger of technology. The telegraph, like the express, «makes time» in the vulgar sense of saving time. The amusing mixing of the names of Edison and Ford, the wonder-boys of American industry, suggests the breathless confusion with which all new inventions are hurriedly introduced and registered by the modern consciousness. Thomas à Becket is also suggested here, to indicate that technology and business have replaced religion and that inventors are the modern saints. Similarly, science, commerce and the Holy Ghost are juxtaposed. With subtle irony, Crane here reminds us of his own purpose of investing both the Machine and the urban scene with spiritual dimensions instead of merely worshipping their efficiency and financial importance.

In modern America everything exists side by side, science and religion, financial exploitation and the dogma of virgin birth, and all sorts of disparate and traditionally irreconcilable influences are promoted relentlessly by individual groups. The radio broadcasts the news of Admiral Byrd's North Pole expedition and the radio contact between him and civilization, and in this medium Wall Street and virgin birth are given equal weight. The total effect is one of a strange equality and levelling of value, everything is just as significant as everything else. The final result, of course, is a total lack of meaning and quality in general. American civilization, adhering to the doctrine of free competition in every field, announcing total spiritual freedom, has produced a culture without standards and without meaning. Its outstanding characteristics are «breathtaking» quantity and speed, and these are contrasted with the poem's reference to Shakespeare's *As You Like It,* a play with a pastoral setting. In the idyllic forest of the play there are «books in the running brooks» and «sermons in stones» (II, i, 16-17).

Thus, the name of the speeding train suggests the severe shortcomings or limitations of the age.[27] However, the train continues on its journey, and the poet turns his attention to the hoboes and the continent itself. The poet has joined the vagrants, and as the 20th Century Limited leaves them behind, they watch the «tail lights» slipping out of sight. These lights «converge,» suggesting the creation of arched lines of light, and thus they point forward to the vision of the apotheosized bridge in «Atlantis,» in which its cables or wires are seen as «sidereal phalanxes» that «leap and converge.» These hopeful images, suggesting another view of the twentieth century, disappear out of sight, but later in the poem the train is decribed more positively again.

Though it is written in a lighter vein, «The River» demonstrates the recurring pessimism that finds fuller expression in «Quaker Hill,» «Southern Cross,» and «The Tunnel,» poems that present what may be called a dark burlesque of the ideal themes of *The Bridge*. In the proem, «Ave Maria» and «Atlantis» the general impression is that an integrating power is at work. Columbus reconciles faith and science, and a divine spirit sings in the cables of the Brooklyn bridge. The burlesque of the opening of «The River» is less demonic and more ironic that that of «The Tunnel,» but it does indicate Crane's continual awareness of the isolated position of his vision of spiritual integration in modern reality.

Crane explained his intention in «The River» to Mrs. T. W. Simpson in a letter of July 4, 1927: «I'm trying in this part of the poem to chart the pioneer experience of our forefathers — and to tell the story backwards, as it were, on the 'backs' of hobos. These hobos are simply 'psychological ponies' to carry the reader across the country and back to the Mississippi, which you will notice is described as a great River of Time.»

Crane's hoboes, who are the main protagonists of «The River,» have something in common with the Indian, in that they have not really been touched by the industrial revolution and have preserved certain elements of a more primitive conception of the land. This entails a different approach to time than that which is prevalent in civilized society, and the poet contrasts two ways of apprehending time:

The last bear, shot drinking in the Dakotas
Loped under wires that span the mountain stream.
Keen instruments, strung to a vast precision
Bind town to town and dream to ticking dream.
But some men take their liquor slow — and count
— Though they'll confess no rosary nor clue —
The river's minute by the far brook's year.

These men have an organic sense of time which contrasts with the mechanical concept of both time and space that the telegraph wires are evidence of. And yet these wires perform the vital function of bridging; they span the «mountain stream» just like the Brooklyn Bridge spans the East River. The tramps relate themselves to time by looking at the river and imagining the time span of its development from a brook. They have a slower, more organic sense of time than those who measure it by the clock. Existing on a more primitive level, they escape the influence of the modern world of «whistles, wires and steam» that has created an «iron dealt cleavage» between the earth and the civilization that thrives on its surface. However, Crane is also sceptical, at this point, with regard to his hoboes. Their primitiveness is devoid of any tribal culture of the kind that the Indians possessed, they have no will or purpose in their lives and roam across the country like a «caboose.» They are the «blind baggage» that is found on any passing train.

In «The River,» Crane has attempted to give a description of a certain segment of the American people, workers and drifters, their mentality and attitude to life, and he brings in several more or less folkloristic elements, popular ballads and local folk heroes. The «people» has always been Carl Sandburg's main subject matter, and at the time when Crane was writing «Powhatan's Daughter» he was also reading Sandburg. In a letter to Frank of August 12, 1926, he wrote: «I'm reading *The Prairie Years* now.» The very scenes with railroad hoboes and work-gangs that we find in «The River» are strongly reminiscent of the Sandburg of such volumes as *Smoke and Steel, Chicago Poems* and *Cornhuskers*. Like Crane, Sandburg uses place names from the Midwest to evoke a certain mood, and Crane's reference to «Kalamazoo» may refer to Sandburg's poem on «The Sins of Kalamazoo» with its lines: «Oh yes, there is a town named Kalamazoo,/ A spot on the map where the trains hesitate.»[28]

Crane's tramps are dreamily poetic in their musings and reminiscences:

> I heard a road-gang chanting so.
> And afterwards, who had a colt's eyes — one said
> «Jesus! Oh I remember watermelon days!» And sped
> High in a cloud of merriment, recalled
> «— And when my Aunt Sally Simpson smiled,» he drawled —
> «It was almost Louisiana, long ago.»
> «There's no place like Booneville though, Buddy,»
> One said, excising a last burr from his vest,
> «— For early trouting.» Then peering in the can,
> «— But I kept on the tracks.» Possessed, resigned,
> He trod the fire down pensively and grinned,
> Spreading dry shingles of a beard . . .

This recording of casual remarks is well done and has a convincing realism about it. A quality of longing for some intangible past or some scene of peace or beauty is attributed to the hoboes throughout «The River,» and this brings them closer to nature and Pocahontas. The smile of «Aunt Sally Simpson» also recalls the smile of the mother in «Van Winkle» and of Pocahontas in «The Dance.» The poet had personal reasons for selecting the name Simpson. Mrs. T. W. Simpson was his housekeeper on the Isle of Pines, where much of *The Bridge* was composed. Crane sent her a version of «The River» along with a letter of July 4, 1927, and wrote: «You'll find your name in it. I kind of wanted you in this section of the book, and if you don't have any objections, you'll stay in the book. For you are my idea of the salt of all pioneers, and our little talks about New Orleans, etc., led me to think of you with the smile of Louisiana.»

Again, Crane makes it clear that his protagonists are mere tramps; they have no high vision and are of the same category as the «multitudes» of the proem. They are «possessed» by the land and are «resigned.» They have no influence on their surroundings. Their lack of insight into a spiritual reality of the kind that Columbus, the poet or Whitman has is suggested by the threading down and extinguishing of the camp fire, fire being an emblem of the divine essence. Crane's reasons for putting the hoboes into «The River» are mostly structural ones, and this is indicated by his note: «My tramps are psychological vehicles, also. Their wanderings as you will notice, carry the reader into interior after interior, finally to the great River. They are the leftovers of the pioneers in at least this respect — that their wanderings carry the reader through an experience parallel to that of Boone and others.» The poet's recollection of the tramps he had seen when a child expresses his pessimism with regard to their human potential with full force:

                                        Behind

My father's cannery works I used to see
Rail-squatters ranged in nomad raillery,
The ancient men — wifeless or runaway
Hobo-trekkers that forever search
An empire wilderness of freight and rails.
Each seemed a child, like me, on a loose perch,
Holding to childhood like some termless play.
John, Jake or Charley, hopping the slow freight
— Memphis to Tallahassee — riding the rods,
Blind fists of nothing, humpty-dumpty clods.

The poet expresses a certain ambivalence in his attitude toward the hoboes. He has compassion for them as outcasts in society, wanderers who cannot find rest and are unable to accept social responsibilities.

These men are like children and have preserved the child's original relation to the universe. Moreover, the poet was able to identify himself and his own fate with that of the tramps, like them he was «wifeless» and «runaway», forever driven and tormented by conflicting desires and needs.

But his sceptical view of the men is revealed in his description of them as «blind fists of nothing, humpty-dumpty clods.» They are mere pieces, chunks of matter, human mechanisms whose whole fate and existence are determined by chance external events and forces. This idea is carried over into the final hymn to the river of time. However, in a highly important shift in the next paragraph, he concentrates on the redeeming trait of the hoboes, their instincitive knowledge of the earth. Again, the poet's divided vision exerts its influence:

Yet they touch something like a key perhaps.
From pole to pole across the hills, the states
— They know a body under the wide rain;
Youngsters with eyes like fjords, old reprobates
With racetrack jargon, — dotting immensity
They lurk across her, knowing her yonder breast
Snow-silvered, sumac-stained or smoky blue —
Is past the valley-sleepers, south or west.
— As I have trod the rumorous midnights, too,
And past the circuit of the lamp's thin flame
(O Nights that brought me to her body bare!)
Have dreamed beyond the print that bound her name.
Trains sounding the long blizzards out — I heard
Wail into distances I knew were hers.
Papooses crying on the wind's long mane
Screamed redskin dynasties that fled the brain,
— Dead echoes! But I knew her body there,
Time like a serpent down her shoulder, dark,
And space, an eaglet's wing, laid on her hair.

The body of Pocahontas, vaguely realized in «The Harbor Dawn,» reappears and is described with significant imagery. The hills and mountains are her «yonder breast,» a metaphor which recurs in «The Dance.» The hoboes have a knowledge of Pocahontas, but it is partial and incomplete. As the margin note suggests, their knowledge is inarticulate; her «name» is known to the poet, who masters language, but the tramps have «touched her, knowing her without name.» In the proem, the «multitudes» have no vision or contact with the divine, but in «The River» the hoboes have at least a limited knowledge of this dimension. Crane's view of the people, or masses, is two-sided. The hoboes' relation to Pocahontas is also indicated in a manuscript version of «The River,» dated December 31, 1929, in which we find this line: «A woman-*mirage* sometimes sleeks their hope.» (My italics). Like Crane himself, the hoboes are in search of a woman-image in nature. The poet then recalls the nightly vigils and reveries that first gave him a vision of the earth-goddess. The «circuit» of the lamplight is linked with the imagery of luminous circles in other sections, and the fact that Pocahontas is seen in dreams and fantasies connects this passage with «The Harbor Dawn.» In both cases we have a dream-vision of the goddess which foreshadows the complete poetic realization of her in «The Dance.» It is implied that Pocahontas as the personification of the earth has Indian roots, and in his dreams, the poet recalls his memory of wailing trains bearing Indian names.[29] Thus, the whistle of the train could suggest papooses screaming the names of native dynasties now dead and gone. But the intention of the poet is to revive these echoes of the spirit of the Indian, and he presents the intriguing, heraldic emblem of Pocahontas as a woman surrounded by the serpent of time and the eagle of space.

It is possible to get a certain visual impression of this symbolism if we consider a remark by Crane in a letter to Samuel Loveman from Chagrin Falls, Ohio, of January 16, 1931. The poet here mentions a stone carving made by Mr. John Church, a local blacksmith, which was rendered on local postcards. Crane enclosed one of these cards and wrote: «What struck me in the first place was the obvious coincidence of a parallel use of symbols, the serpent and the eagle, with my lines on Pocahontas in *The Bridge*. 'Time, like a serpent, down her shoulder, dark,/ And space, and eaglet's wing laid on her hair.' The serpent isn't hard to locate, and you'll see the rather dim outlines of the fore part of an eagle just below where I have indicated in the margin.[30]

The serpent that runs down the shoulder of Pocahontas is the Mississippi, the river of time which runs down the body of the land and symbolizes its history. The eagle is a symbol of its spatial dimensions. Thus, the emblem represents the Indian's sense of inhabiting a living universe. Later, in «Cape Hatteras» and «Atlantis,» the eagle also

71

symbolizes the white man's technology, thus indicating that the emblem of the serpent and the eagle represents a combination of the two cultures.

From the dreams about Pocahontas and the Indians, the poet returns to reality and his westward journey. Having reached the Ozark mountains, he again meditates on the legends of the Indians which are awaiting revival under the surface of civilization:

Under the Ozarks, domed by Iron Mountain,
The old gods of the rain lie wrapped in pools . . .
Where eyeless fish curvet a sunken fountain
And re-descend with corn from querulous crows.
Such pilferings make up their timeless eatage,
Propitiate them for their timber torn
By iron, iron — always the iron dealt cleavage!
They doze now, below axe and powder horn.

These old gods are dramatically alive again in «The Dance,» but in «The River» the emphasis is on the fact that the native contact with the earth has been overwhelmed, submerged, by the crushing impact of the white man's technical civilization, the «iron dealt cleavage.» The references to «axe and powder horn» evoke scenes of early settlers making clearings in the wilderness, ready to defend themselves with rifles. In one manuscript version the line about the gods went like this: «They would sleep now, remembering their morn,» and in «The Dance» the medicine-man is exhorted to «dance us back the tribal morn!»

The central image is that of the fish that «curvet,» leap up from the «sunken fountain» to grab some corn that is dropped by the crows. Their movement describes the curve of the bridge, and the crows overhead recall the seagull's flight in the earlier sections. But the fish in the fountain suggest an absence of vision resulting from the white man's conquest of the land. They are «eyeless» and they «redescend» into their pools. The loss of eye and the downward, sinking movement suggest a lack of spiritual power. But the curves and circles described by the leaping and swimming fish indicate a potentiality which is unleashed in the violently spiralling movements of the gods of the elements in «The Dance.» There are several different worksheet versions of the lines about the fish and the fountain, and instead of the verb «curvet» that was finally chosen, Crane's drafts have variously «spiral,» «swirl,» «entwine» and «ascend.» This shows what an importance he attached to the figures of rotation or spiralling and the need for variation in vocabulary that arose because the figure is repeated over and over again throughout *The Bridge*. The upward and downward moving spiral may be said to symbolize a rise to vision and a fall into death and darkness.

The «iron dealt cleavage» indicates the gap between the white man and the earth which has been created by the «iron» of modern civilization. There is an interesting manuscript variant of these lines that may throw light on the poet's meaning. The worksheet from December 31, 1929, has these lines: «Iron, iron — all this rings vainly, and apart/ Unless her name, a connotation of the Spring,/ Unlatch a sheaf of rainbows in your heart.» Iron is the symbol of the threat of separation between modern industrial reality and the vision of America as a land in which a divine being reveals itself. In the proem this is suggested by the phrase «iron year,» and in the above quoted fragment the danger of a soulless, utterly mechanistic concept of modern technology is suggested by the assertion that the sound of iron «rings vainly» and is something «apart,» isolated from any larger, meaningful pattern as long as there is no connection between the iron and the soil as manifestations of one creative principle. The gap will be there unless one obtains a knowledge of Pocahontas that may effect a higher, all-embracing vision, suggested by the image of a rainbow in the heart.

The ideal of American civilization, the Cathay-Pocahontas image, is always threatened by the nightmarish vision of technological power that works blindly, without direction, and creates chaos. But this threat is counterbalanced by the revelation of spiritual forces at work in the machine, the praise of the structure of the bridge in the proem and «Atlantis.» This same vision now asserts itself in the image of the Pullman trains that speed across the country: «And Pullman breakfasters glide glistening steel/ From tunnel into field — iron strides the dew —/ Straddles the hill, a dance of wheel on wheel.» This is a positive view of the «iron». The train that «strides the dew» and «straddles the hill» invokes the figure of the spanning bridge «vaulting» the prairie, and the steel is «glistening,» suggesting a connection with the sparkle of precious metals. The wheel image appears again, now as a dance of wheels, suggesting that the train-wheels can be the basis of a vision of power working in harmonious design, like a dance.

Crane's Pullman train carries the reader ever closer to the goal of the journey: the river Mississippi, and the atmosphere and lore of the big river are evoked by introducing the names of some of its legendary boatmen and heroes. The poet enjoins the passengers of the train to lean from the window and listen to the voices of the tramps who sing *Deep River.* From the point of view of the hoboes, the poet then addresses the ruling classes of human society, here represented by such figures as «Sheriff, Brakeman and Authority,» and claims that they too «feed the River timelessly,» and thus is prepared the ensuing hymn to the Mississippi as the sovereign symbol of the relentless current of time that carries everybody and everything with it in one grand flow. This hymn is set apart from the rest of the poem by a metric change, and its tone is indicated by the word «largo» which the poet put in the margin of one of his drafts. The verse is divided into regularly rhymed quatrains, and the somewhat loose rhythm of the preceeding passages is tightened and more firmly controlled as the poet invokes the flow of the river of time in his characteristically subtle yet powerful imagery:

> Down, down — born pioneers in time's despite,
> Grimed tributaries to an ancient flow —
> They win no frontier by their wayward plight,
> But drift in stillness, as from Jordan's brow.

> You will not hear it as the sea; even stone
> Is not more hushed by gravity . . . But slow,
> As loth to take more tribute — sliding prone
> Like one whose eyes were buried long ago

> The River, spreading, flows — and spends your dream.
> Who are you, lost within this tideless spell?
> You are your father's father, and the stream —
> A liquid theme that floating niggers swell.

The hoboes were defined as beings without a will or purpose of their own, as pieces of matter passively driven across the country by obscure impulses. This theme is now taken up again and leads naturally into the image of the river of time as an implacable, forward-moving flow in which everything is immersed and in which the individual is destroyed and only the species remains.

Though the period of the settlements is over, the impulse to go west is not, as demonstrated by the hoboes, who are «pioneers in time's despite.» The westward journey and the progress of history is imaginatively fused into one «ancient flow» that the hoboes simply surrender, or contribute to, with their lives. The word «tributary» is a pun here, meaning both someone who pays tribute and a smaller stream that flows into a large river.

The drifting hoboes find no frontiers, neither in reality nor symbolically. They are late in time and they lack vision. The wanderings of the tramps are connected both with the flow of time and the river, they «drift in stillness» as if they were floating downstream. The running stream of water becomes the metaphor of the passing of time, and thus an abstraction becomes concrete. The actual progress of time cannot be heard; it is something even more inaudible and intangible than the pull of the forces of gravity that keep a stone in place.

We are all submerged as mere «tributes» to the flow of the time-river, whose eyes are «buried.» This means that time obliterates individual visions or dreams along with everything else, it «spends» the dream of the individual. With rhetoric of rising power Crane poses the old question: what is the ultimate significance of the individual? The answer is: none, in the river of time all men become alike and there is no difference between one man and his «father's father,» only the species has any identity. The image of floating niggers suggests the ceaseless destruction caused by the flux of time and recurs, strikingly similar, in T. S. Eliot's «The Dry Salvages:» «Time the destroyer is time the preserver,/ Like the river with its cargo of dead negroes, cows and chicken coops.»[31]

The Mississippi is seen as an agent of constant geological change, its march is «alluvial,» carrying soil with it from one place to deposit it in another. The river is a great vein in the body of the land; it is «vascular» with the «silted shale» of substance that is torn loose and carried away. The theme of geological change and evolution is taken up again in the opening of «Cape Hatteras,» where the formation of the landscape throughout time is described. The flux of the time-river is like a «quarrying passion,» it has a will or motivating force indicated by its «undertowed sunlight.» With the «jungle grace» of a lynx it stretches out and prepares for the final leap into the sea, the «biding place.» The poet sustains and brings to a climax the rhapsodic tone of his hymn to the river in this concluding section:

Over De Soto's bones the freighted floors
Throb past the City storied of three thrones.
Down two more turns the Mississippi pours
(Anon tall ironsides up from salt lagoons)

And flows within itself, heaps itself free.
All fades but one thin skyline round . . . Ahead
No embrace opens but the stinging sea;
The River lifts itself from its long bed,

Poised wholly on its dream, a mustard glow
Tortured with history, its one will — flow!
— The Passion spreads in wide tongues, choked and slow.
Meeting the Gulf, hosannas silently below.

De Soto was a hero and discoverer of Columbus' type, but Crane
does not try to recreate his vision or spirit in any way. The river of time
has flowed over his bones and there is nothing left of his greatness. As
Crane sees it, the southward flow of the river recapitulates centuries of
American history, from   sixteenth-century De Soto to nineteenth-
century «ironsides.» This is a reference to De Soto's burial in the Mississippi after his death in the wilderness. On its way to the gulf the river
passes a city of «three thrones,» which is probably a reference to New
Orleans, which was under the rules of the thrones of both Spain, England and France. The final lines of «The River» discreetly introduce
the metaphor of the river as a serpent that «heaps itself free» from its
inland imprisonment and leaps into the gulf. Crane often associates rivers or bays with bonds or trammels and the open sea with freedom, as
in the «chained bay waters» of the proem and the «laughing chains» of
the river in «The Dance.»

Up to this point the meaning of the hymn to the river seems to have
been an admission of resignation and defeat. Time and history progress and destroy all ideals and individuals. However, the river is «poised wholly on its dream,» and though its will is to flow, it preserves a
«dream,» the utopian consciousness of America that has inspired the
poet and that will live after him. The imagery of the last two stanzas
suggests renewal of hope and vision. The river moves towards its freedom and lifts itself, describing a glowing arc or curve that finally merges with the ocean. Both the river and the ocean here finally become

symbols of divine revelation, as indicated by words like «Passion» and «hosannas.» As R. W. B. Lewis states, the river's passage is «a movement out of time — not from earth to paradise, but from the actual to the mythic.»[32]

The Dance

This poem represents a climactic effort to revitalize the native past, and in his gloss on it Crane wrote that he was working backward in his spiritual progress to «the very core of the nature world of the Indian.» In the recreation of the primitive world of the Indian lies an important element of the «synthesis of America.» Similar views were held by Frank, who in *Our America* had written that America is a land of «buried cultures,» the civilizations of Indian tribes and empires. The Indian «knew not iron,» wrote Frank, but «he lived in a spiritual world so true and so profound, that the heel of the pioneer has even now not wholly stamped it out.»[33]

According to his own synopsis of the poem in the letter to Kahn, Crane saw the main idea of «The Dance» as a fusion of himself and the Indian by means of which he would take possession of the latter's spirit:

Here one is on the pure mythical and smoky soil at last! Not only do I describe the conflict between the two races in this dance — I also become identified with the Indian and his world before it is over, which is the only method possible of ever really possessing the Indian and his world as a cultural factor. I think I really succeed in getting under the skin of this glorious and dying animal, in terms of expression, in symbols, which he himself would comprehend. Pocahontas (the continent) is the common basis of our meeting, she survives the extinction of the Indian, who finally, after being assumed into the elements of nature (as he understood them), persists only as a kind of «eye» in the sky, or as a star that hangs between day and night — «the twilight's dim perpetual throne.»

By means of his identification with the Indian in «The Dance,» the poet tries to bridge the gap that has arisen between the white man and the Indian. Drawing on various primitive beliefs, Crane presents the maiden Pocahontas as a native goddess, and as a supplement to this figure he creates a male persona who is variously an Indian chieftain, the poet himself, and the Aztec god Quetzalcoatl, who manifested himself in the shapes of a serpent with feathers and the morning star. By identifying himself with the Indian in his beliefs, the poet takes part in a ritual burning of the chieftain which is accompanied by the latter's apotheosis as a star.

Recreating the world view of the Indian, Crane begins with the beginning, the genesis of the earth, which is often accounted for as the fall of a goddess from the sky at the beginning of time. This goddess becomes the universal mother, and from her body grows the earth itself. An ancient Iroquois legend relates how the woman Ataensic fell through a rift in the sky which separated heaven and earth and plunged into the primeval waters beneath. After giving birth to two sons she died, but she was resurrected again in the organic life of the soil.[34] The opening stanza of «The Dance» offers a dramatic portrait of Pocahontas which seems influenced by a legend of this kind:

> The swift red flesh, a winter king —
> Who squired the glacier woman down the sky?
> She ran the neighing canyons all the spring;
> She spouted arms; she rose with maize — to die.

As earth mother, Pocahontas is also a fertility goddess and is made the object of the death and rebirth ritual commonly associated with such deities. In the spring she rises to life in the growing maize and in the autumn she dies again, only to be ressurrected next spring. As the creator of all life on earth, it is she who sent the horses running through the canyons in spring.[35] The opening line presents the sexual opposites that run through the poem: the «red flesh» of the maiden which denotes the soil itself, and her lover the «winter king», who later occupies the «throne» of the «twilight» as a star. As Sherman Paul states, «the masculine and feminine elements of the cosmos figure immediately in the question with which the poet begins the poem.»[36]

From this venture into the past, a transition is made to the poet's present environment, the American earth as it is after the destruction of the Indian and the departure of his gods. The spiritual barrenness created by the white man's invasion is symbolized by an autumn drouth:

And in the autumn drouth, whose burnished hands
With mineral wariness found out the stone
Where prayers, forgotten, streamed the mesa sands?
He holds the twilight's dim, perpetual throne.

The protagonist here is the poet, who in his search for the native past holds the key to a new cultural fusion of the two races. He can recover the spirit of the Indian and inhabit «the twilight's dim, perpetual throne,» the abode of the Indian gods of the dawn. The reference to the sands of the «mesa» mountains shows that the poet is exploring the southwestern part of the continent, in which these particular mountains are found. Here he goes in search of the old rain gods of the Aztecs. According to one of their beliefs, a big stone once fell from heaven and broke into many pieces, each of which became a god. They also believed that a stone was shot from the sky with each thunderclap. Thunder was followed by rain, and the stones became rain gods.[37] The poet finds such a stone, or totem, and invokes the «forgotten prayers» associated with it. In this way, he hopes to recover and adopt the faith of the Indian.

The first two stanzas summarize the whole spiritual action of the poem: the absorption of the consciousness of the Indian. They form the first division of «The Dance» and foreshadow the more detailed fictional expedition of the poet into the Indian past. But first he identifies himself with the white explorers in general as they first broke into the American wilderness:

Mythical brows we saw retiring — loth,
Disturbed and destined, into denser green.
Greeting they sped us, on the arrow's oath:
Now lie incorrigibly what years between . . .

The «brows» belong to Pocahontas, the personification of nature, and she recedes before the white invasion, «disturbed» by the conquerors and «destined» to become subdued.[38] For Crane, the brows of Pocahontas suggest the Indian's consciousness of a living universe, and in «Ave Maria» God is revealed in the stellar universe as «brows unhooded now.» The poet regards Columbus' Old Testament Christian outlook and the religion of the Indian as elements to be bridged by his poem so that a common American spiritual synthesis could be found in the context of the past. Though the years of the white man's history in America «lie incorrigibly» between past and present, a phrase which records his profound doubts about his project, the poet nevertheless embarks on his Indian pilgrimage in order to bridge the gap between the two cultures.

Pocahontas is seen as a bride awaiting her mate on «a bed of leaves,» wearing a veil, and she is wooed by the Indian chieftain with which Crane identifies himself. She is the embodiment of an anthropomorphic conception of nature, and throughout «The Dance» the landscape is described in terms of the female body with a «brown lap» and «bridal flanks and eyes.» Thus the poet tries to restore the «broken play» of the tribal rituals by means of which the Indian maintained his harmonious rapport with nature, and he sets out in pursuit of the earthgoddess in a journey through time and space:

I left the village for dogwood. By the canoe
Tugging below the mill-race, I could see
Your hair's keen crescent running, and the blue
First moth of evening take wing stealthily.

What laughing chains the water wove and threw!
I learned to catch the trout's moon whisper; I
Drifted how many hours I never knew,
But, watching, saw that fleet young crescent die, —

And one star, swinging, take its place, alone,
Cupped in the larches of the mountain pass —
Until, immortally, it bled into the dawn.

The whole magic of the Indian world, the pristine beauty of his natural environment, is superbly evoked here. The journey up the Hudson river in a canoe suggests the first, legendary expeditions of the white man into Indian territory, and it thus brings in the theme of the American frontier, which is important in *The Bridge* and particularly in «The River.» In that poem, the reader was transported across the country from New York to the Mississippi, and thereafter, wrote Crane, «I also unlatch the door to the pure Indian world which opens out in 'The Dance' section, so the reader is gradually led back in time to the pure savage world, while existing at the same time in the present.» (Letter to Mrs. T. W. Simpson, July 4, 1927.)

Having left his village, the poet-protagonist is lured on by certain partial appearances of Pocahontas, and he first perceives her hair in the moon's «keen crescent running.» The moth which rises from the «laughing chains» of the river waters surrounding the canoe symbolizes the upward flight toward the freedom which the Indian possesses after his metamorphosis: «Thy freedom is her largesse, Prince.» The flight of the moth is parallelled in the opening stanza of the proem, where the seagull's wings dip and hurl it, «building high/ Over the chained bay waters Liberty.» In both instances we have a closely corresponding sequence of imagery, a winged flight over waters that are chained, imprisoned by land. The star appears after the moonlight has faded, and then, «immortally,» it disappears at sunrise. Both the Aztec god Quetzalcoatl and his Iroquois counterpart Ioskeha, son of Ataensic the earth-mother, are gods of the dawn and manifest themselves as the morning star. Its appearance is foreshadowed in «The Harbor Dawn,» where it shines in «the waking west.» Like Pocahontas, the star is asleep, expecting the poet to resurrect its power and spiritual significance.

After leaving his boat by the river and climbing a «portage» and a «further valley-shed,» the protagonist is beckoned on by more glimpses of Pocahontas. He sees her feet in the «wat'ry webs» of mountain falls, and the leap of the stream over the edge of the rock becomes her «white veil.» The whiteness of the veil relates it to the symbolic function of white in *The Bridge;* from the «white rings» of the seagull in the proem and the «White Birds» of «Ave Maria» whiteness recurs as a symbol of purity and beauty. At the ledge of the mountain range the journeying poet gains a panoramic view of nature, and Pocahontas offers him her «steep, inaccessible smile.» Thus, the poet suggests the possibility of union with nature by means of his use of mythopoeic imagery. However, the smile of the goddess is inaccessible, and thus the poet, even here, in the «pure savage world,» voices his doubts about the feasibility of this undertaking.

In his imagination, the poet approaches an Indian village, and a romantic forest scene is evoked with tepees «tufting the blue knolls» and smoke swirling up between the trees of a «yellow chestnut glade.» Here, in a «boding shade,» he anticipates the drama of the ensuing rituals. First there is a description of a growing thunderstorm in which the powers of nature second the ritual drama of the extinction and metamorphosis of the chieftain Maquokeeta. His dance and the storm itself are fused in a coherent chain of imagery. The growing «thunder-bud» that moves across the sky refers to the gathering clouds, and then the poet hears the «rhythm» of a «padded foot within» in the sounds of the thunder. There is a suggestion here that the native gods of the thunder are at work in their cosmic dance.[39]

By identifying himself with the Indian and conceiving of nature in his primitive mythic manner, the poet becomes renewed and reborn into a primeval state of being. This experience drains the «black pool» of the influence of modern civilization from his «heart's hot root.» The heart's desire has been frustrated by the black pool of evil and dis-belief, but in the imaginative experience of Indian rituals this pool is drained, and the poet's heart is cleansed and made receptive. In «The River» the native gods were «wrapped in pools,» oppressed by the «iron» of white civilization, but in «The Dance» they are released and become active forces in Crane's new synthesis of past and present. The Indian's response to reality will even be carried over into our modern world of machinery, as in the description of the train in «The River» as a giant who «straddles the hill» and whose feet, in this case the wheels, perform a dance. At the same time, as part of his desire to synthesize, the poet takes pains to see nature in terms of the white man, using machine imagery: «A cyclone threshes in the turbine crest.»

Maquokeeta's dance and subsequent burning at the stake are dramatized as universal events, and further allusions to Indian religion enter into the poetic texture. Maquokeeta's is a dance of death, and it reflects and blends with the violent winds of the storm. The «eagle feathers» of his costume point to the serpent and eagle symbolism at the end of the poem, and it also connects him with nature insofar as the eagle is an Indian god associated with wind, thunder and lightning. The impending death of the chieftain is dramatized as the fall of a «tamarack,» and this reference to a tree points back to the poet's canoe trip and the star that he saw between «the larches» of the mountains. The fall of the «Sachem,» or leader, is seconded by a turbulent dance of the powers of nature in the climax of the thunder-storm. The birches and oaks are being bent by the wind and the leaves are hurled into the air. Crane undoubtedly employs the pathetic fallacy here; Pocahontas «grieves,» she is nature mourning the destruction of her child the Indian.

In Indian religions there is a widespread worship of the snake, and snake-gods abound. According to one belief, the lightning is a great serpent, and the reason for entertaining such an idea is that both snakes and lightning move with rapid, flashing darts and turns. Crane uses serpentine imagery in his picture of the lightning that strikes down to earth along the «saber hair» of Pocahontas, thus recalling the «serpent down her shoulder» that adorns the earth-goddess in «The River.» The fire which is going to consume the chieftain is being lit by the lightning, and the flames are conceived in terms of serpents' «red fangs» and «splay tongues.» The metaphor of fire as a serpent foreshadows the subsequent metamorphosis by fire of Maquokeeta in the shape of Quetzalcoatl, the «plumed serpent.» The metaphor of flames as tongues was also used in «Van Winkle,» where we have «rapid tongues that flittered from under the ash heap.» The fire is the symbol of the death and rebirth of the well-known Indian deity, Quetzalcoatl. It is this divine essence that the poet sets out to discover and identify with by means of primitive myth.

The Indian performs his snake dance, and in his later burning at the stake the poet himself blends with him:

Dance, Maquokeeta! snake that lives before,
That casts his pelt, and lives beyond! Sprout, horn!
Spark, tooth! Medicine-man, relent, restore —
Lie to us, — dance us back the tribal morn!

The snake dance is a ritual practised by many Indian tribes, and anthropologists have interpreted it variously as a fertility and immortality rite. In the present context the dance symbolizes the apotheosis of Maquokeeta. Though physically destroyed, the Indian achieves immortality by being transformed into a star, and the dance is a ritual expression of this. According to primitive belief the snake, with its habit of casting its skin, is an immortal creature. By performing rituals and ceremonies with snake skins the Indians believed that they would gain immortality. The reference to sprouting horns carries the same meaning as the snake dance; the deer casts off its antlers in the process of growth. The poet, however, is not just translating the myth into his own verse, he identifies himself with the burning god: «I could not pick the arrows from my side.» Symbolically, «wrapped in that fire,» the poet atones for the suffering inflicted on the Indian by the white man, and he also sacrifices himself, his own happiness, for the sake of the new poetic and religious vision that he brings. However, the doubts expressed earlier in the poem about the possibility of resurrecting the Indian myths are now stated in very clear terms. The medicine man is asked to «lie to us,» the poet and his audience. Crane feels that, on a rational level, it is impossible to believe in the myth, and yet he continues, in an attempt to «sustain myth against the ravages of fact.»[40] Unable to solve the dilemma, he chooses to express both his faith and his doubt, honestly recording the division within himself. Crane takes a leap into faith, almost as though he had to create his own godhead, and it remains an as-if divinity in «Atlantis,» the final section: «As though a god were issue of the strings.»

In his rendering of the metamorphosis of Maquokeeta, Crane has employed the myth of Quetzalcoatl, the Aztec god who departed from his empire, ascended into heaven and became the morning star.[41] According to his letters, the poet was familiar with more than one version of this myth. Deena P. Metzger, who has studied the influence of the Quetzalcoatl legend on *The Bridge*, claims that «the direct sources of Crane's knowledge of the salient elements of the myths were probably *Orpheus* and William H. Prescott's *History of the Conquest of Mexico*.»[42] All versions of the Quetzalcoatl myth agree on the point that he was to return to Mexico in the shape of a white man with a long beard, and we know that the Aztec ruler Montezuma and his people thought that Cortez and his followers were returning gods who came to institute a new order. However, none of the two versions of the myth that Metzger mentions seems to be the one Crane used when he wrote «The Dance.» In Prescott's *History*, the god sails away from the land in a wizard skiff, and in *Orpheus: Myths of the World*, Padraic Colum repeats this story and gives an additional one according to which the god threw himself into a funeral pyre on the shore and his heart rose and became the morning star. According to D. H. Lawrence's *The Plumed Serpent,* however, a book which Crane mentions in a letter to Gorham Munson of March 5, 1926, Quetzalcoatl throws himself upon a pyre on the top of a volcanic mountain. This version seems to be closest to Crane's poem. Quentzalcoatl was the god of art and culture, and both his departure and return were events of great importance in the religious tradition of the Aztecs. His return was believed to signal the creation of a new civilization and thus had both a tragic and heroic aspect. As Lawrence tells it, Quetzalcoatl «climbed the steep of the mountain, and over the white snow of the volcano . . . So the old god reached the top of the mountain and looked up into the blue house of heaven . . . Then fire rose from the volcano around the old Quetzalcoatl, in wings and glittering feathers. And with the wings of fire and the glitter of sparks Quetzalcoatl flew up, up, like a wafting fire, like a glittering bird, up, into the space, and away to the white steps of heaven . . . Night fell, and Quetzalcoatl was gone, and men in the world saw only a star travelling back into heaven.»[43]

This is how Crane has recreated this story in his poetry:

I heard the hush of lava wrestling your arms,
And stag teeth foam about the raven throat;
Flame cataracts of heaven in seething swarms
Fed down your anklets to the sunset's moat.

O, like the lizard in the furious noon,
That drops his legs and colors in the sun,
— And laughs, pure serpent, Time itself, and moon
Of his own fate, I saw thy change begun!

And saw thee dive to kiss that destiny
Like one white meteor, sacrosanct and blent
At last with all that's consummate and free
There, where the first and last gods keep thy tent.

The first of these stanzas describes the burning of the god on top of the volcano. In the second we have the apotheosis, and the serpentine imagery of the snake dance is reintroduced. According to the old belief, Quetzalcoatl assumed the shapes of both bird and snake; he was the feathered serpent whose image is carved in stone on the walls of the Aztec temples. The etymological meaning of the very name Quetzalcoatl is in fact «serpent with feathers.» By turning himself into a «pure Serpent» the Indian, as Quetzalcoatl, has conquered «Time itself,» obtained immortality. Here we have to bear in mind another meaning of the serpent symbol in primitive thought. The image of a snake biting its own tail, thus forming a circle, is a mythic symbol of eternity. Finally, the chieftain, in the shape of Quetzalcoatl, has reached a paradise which is «consummate and free,» and the aspirations of the moth in its flight are fulfilled.

In the last section of «The Dance,» the past is left behind and the poet, in his own time, addresses the Indian, who now has taken possession of the throne of the twilight as winter king, morning star and bridegroom of Pocahontas. From his timeless abode he gazes into history and the «angered slain,» the Indian victims of the white man's conquest of the continent. The transcendent immortality achieved by the chieftain is accompanied by the organic immortality of the earthgoddess, the «bride immortal in the maize.» The «pyramid» of the Aztecs slumbers, and «other calendars now stack the sky.» This is a reference to the famous calendar of the Aztecs, which they believed had been invented by Quetzalcoatl. In spite of this, says the poet, Pocahontas still retains her power, hidden «on paths thou knewest best to claim her by,» paths that the poet pledges to follow. It is one of the ways in which he can recapture a sense of «the Whole» of nature and reality in America and apply it to the modern world. As Frank wrote, «The Indian's culture is prophetic of what our culture must be. His nature is a guide to the understanding and achievement of our own . . . The Amerind was profoundly, beautifully adjusted to the land.»[44]

Having penetrated to the core of the Indian mysteries, the poet experiences a new rapport with the land in its beauty and fertility, recovering his Pocahontas:

High unto Labrador the sun strikes free
Her speechless dream of snow, and stirred again,
She is the torrent and the singing tree;
And she is virgin to the last of men . . .

The poet has attained the anthropomorphic consciousness of the savage and employs his primitive symbolism to create a panoramic vision of the land. Here as elsewhere in *The Bridge*, Crane goes back to a basic habit, found in all religions, of conceiving the earth in terms of the human body. By making Pocahontas function as an earth-mother, he is able to revitalize nature and once again regard her as an organic entity. His image includes both prairie grass and the snow of Labrador, a reference which harks back to the «glacier woman.»

At the end, the poet again addresses Maquokeeta and recalls the dance:

And when the caribou slant down for salt
Do arrows thirst and leap? Do antlers shine
Alert, star-triggered in the listening vault
Of dusk? — And are her perfect brows to thine?

We danced, O Brave, we danced beyond their farms,
In cobalt desert closures made our vows . . .
Now is the strong prayer folded in thine arms,
The serpent with the eagle in the boughs.

This is a beautiful evocation of a hunting scene with Indians on the watch and alert deer, but the implications are wider than that. The poet asks himself whether he in his poem has succeeded in recreating the Indian world and merging with Pocahontas, and in the last stanza he answers the question in the affirmative and claims that the union of himself and the Indian has been achieved and the harmonious vision of Pocahontas been assimilated. The poet «affirms that 'the strong prayer,' which in the beginning of 'the Dance' brought water to the 'mesa sands,' is no longer 'forgotten' but 'folded in thine arms,' the bride 'immortal' in the organic 'maize' of the Indian's natural world.»[45] The perfection and symmetry of the Indian world-view are symbolized by the emblem of the united serpent and eagle, which suggests his consciousness of the land as a harmonious and comprehensible whole. The meaning of the symbolism was first indicated in «The River,» where the eagle is said to represent space and the serpent time in the emblem in the final line of «The Dance,» and thus the theme of the returning god and the founding of a new world is repeated.

Indiana

Crane's note on this poem, in his 1927 letter to Kahn, refers to an early version of it, but it still gives us some clues to the meaning and function of the poem within *The Bridge:* «It will be the monologue of an Indiana farmer; time, about 1860. He has failed in the gold-rush and is returned to till the soil. His monologue is a farewell to his son, who is leaving for a life on the sea. It is a lyrical summary of the period of conquest, and his wife, the mother who died on the way back from the gold-rush, is alluded to in a way which implies her succession to the nature-symbolism of Pocahontas.» In the final version of «Indiana» it is the wife of the farmer who survives and returns, and she speaks the poem's monologue. Her son Larry is going to sea, and she recalls their earlier life as she says farewell to him. The poet intends to carry over into later periods the Pocahontas symbolism and makes the white pioneer woman the center of the maternal attraction of the earth. The marginal note to «Indiana» reads: «and read her in a mother's farewell gaze.» The Pocahontas theme connects the poem with the rest of «Powhatan's Daughter,» and the description of the gold-rush carries the westward journey of the section to its geographical end.

For the woman and her husband the dream of America means quite concretely the finding of gold, and the gold symbolism in «Indiana» links with the Cathay image. In the beginning of the poem the woman has returned to Indiana and, appropriately, at the break of a new day on the farm she looks back on the search for gold in the west and the long homeward journey. The reference to the «morning-glory» that grows over the lintel of her house is linked with the general symbolism of dawn in *The Bridge*. Just as the poet in «The Harbor Dawn» dreamt of Pocahontas, so the woman of «Indiana» recalls the quest for «Eldorado» in the morning hours. Her son Larry was born on the way back:

And bison thunder rends my dreams no more
  As once my womb was torn, my boy, when you
Yielded your first cry at the prairies' door . . .
    Your father knew

Then, though we'd buried him behind us, far
  Back on the gold trail — then his lost bones stirred . . .
But you who drop the scythe to grasp the oar
    Knew not, nor heard

Three kinds of search are indicated in «Indiana.» The first one is the quest for gold, here represented by Jim, the father who was buried on the «gold trail.» The mother's journey to Indiana is a return to the soil and the life of a farmer. But Larry rejects such a «scythe» and takes the «oar» instead, choosing to voyage on the seas in search of his meaning. Atlantis is the name of his goal in the ocean and is linked with the «Belle Isle» that lies at the end of the sea-quest in another

Crane poem. In the final section of «Voyages» there is an image of «Belle Isle, white echo of the oar,» and Larry of «Indiana» takes the oar, too.

The mother then describes the westward journey prompted by the promise of gold:

How we, too, Prodigal, once rode off, too —
   Waved Seminary Hill a gay good-bye . . .
We found God lavish there in Colorado
   But passing sly.

The pebbles sang, the firecat slunk away
   And glistening through the sluggard freshets came
In golden syllables loosed from the clay
   His gleaming name.

A dream called Eldorado was his town,
   It rose up shambling in the nuggets' wake,
It had no charter but a promised crown
   Of claims to stake.

America is the earthly kingdom of God, and He reveals Himself in the shape of gold, which was «lavish there in Colorado.» The «golden syllables» of His name presented themselves in the grains of gold «loosed from the clay.» The divine appears as a name, a word, the «idiom» of the bridge and Columbus' «word» of Cathay. In «The Dance» the native Indian deities are important, but in «Indiana» the language of «Ave Maria» comes back. Like Columbus, the family from Indiana went in search of gold, and like him, they never found it and acquired it for themselves. As always in *The Bridge,* the golden land of Cathay is never realized; it remains a promise, or hope, a dream of which the boom town «Eldorado» is the evidence. Like Cathay, Eldorado is a name that suggests a realm of fabulous riches, and its «crown» of claims reflects the «kindled Crown» of Elohim that Columbus saw in the sky. The only thing that the people from Indiana got out of their trip was a «gilded promise, yielded to us never».

The second half of «Indiana» tells the story of the return journey of mother and infant son, and the race motif is introduced. The union of the poet and the Indian in «The Dance» was acted out on a highly symbolic and ritualistic level, but the reconciliation between the squaw and the pioneer woman and her son is described in conventional and straightforward verse. The east-bound wagon-train meets a «homeless squaw,» who is

> Perhaps a half-breed. On her slender back
>   She cradled a babe's body, riding without rein.
> Her eyes, strange for an Indian's, were not black
>   But sharp with pain
>
> And like twin stars. They seemed to shun the gaze
>   Of all our silent men — the long team line —
> Until she saw me — when their violet haze
>   Lit with love shine . . .
>
> I held you up — I suddenly the bolder,
>   Knew that mere words could not have brought us nearer.
> She nodded — and that smile across her shoulder
>   Will still endear her.

These lines are probably the ones that are responsible for the criticism of sentimentality so often directed at «Indiana.» The very theme of interracial love is one that can be easily vulgarized, a fact which is evident in the mass of sentimental literature on the subject. But Crane defended himself against these charges in a letter to William Wright, Nov. 21, 1930: «I admit having felt considerably jolted at the charge of sentimentality continually leveled at the 'Indiana' fragment . . . Right now it is more fashionable to speak otherwise, but the subject (or emotion) of 'race' has always had as much of sentiment behind it — as it has had of prejudice, also. Since 'race' is the principal motivation of 'Indiana,' I can't help thinking that, observed in the proper perspective, and judged in relation to the argument or theme of the Pocahontas section as a whole, the pioneer woman's maternalism isn't excessive.»

Pocahontas is the bridge between the white man and the American soil, and it is clear from Crane's explanation that he intended to let the Indiana woman preserve the earth-mother principle first indicated in the Pocahontas image in «The Harbor Dawn» and the mother figure in «Van Winkle.» By returning to the farm, the pioneer woman functions, like Pocahontas, as a basic point of orientation, she is «power in repose,» whereas her son is a voyager-poet who takes to the sea.

The central scene in «Indiana» is this one between mother and son and the Indian squaw. The latter pays no attention to the other people in the wagon-train, but she smiles at the sight of a woman with child like herself. We may take this to mean that the squaw accepts the white race as represented by mother and child and acknowledges the white boy's right to possess the continent. This is also suggested by the fact that the squaw is moving westward, having been dispossessed of the land, whereas the others are moving east to settle for good in former Indian territory. The reconciliation and merging of the two races seems to be further indicated by the suggestion that she may be a half-breed and the fact that her eyes are «strange for an Indian's» and «violet.»

The white boy Larry is blessed or baptized as his mother lifts him up to receive the smile of the Indian woman, the token that the land is granted to him. He is its true heir, the «first-born» of the family, and he has also inherited the dream that drove his father west. Jim and Larry are representatives of the dream of America, but it is a significant fact that neither of them realizes the dream. Jim «won nothing out of fifty-nine,» and Larry is leaving the land for a life at sea. However, the mother sees the dream reflected in his eyes and feels drawn toward it. Eyes are clearly symbolic in this poem. The eyes of the squaw are full of love for the white child and his mother, and Larry has got his father's eyes, with their expression of longing, their dream of gold. The mother imagines the gold in the «engaging blue» of Larry's eyes, and she recalls her own vision of the golden West and sees it preserved in the eyes of her son, «where the stubborn years gleam and atone, -/Where gold is true!» Although the pioneers did not heed Columbus' warning not to exploit the «plenitude» of Cathay, but threw themselves into the gold rush, the spiritual values are not completely gone, but reflected in the symbolism of the blue and gold that is perceived in Larry's eyes. As R. W. Butterfield says, «the gold in the Western hills had been America's fake grail; in the eyes of the voyager, spiritual scion of Columbus, was the true gold which would redeem America.»[46]

The mother, representing the maternal attraction of the earth, beseeches Larry to come back one day:

Come back to Indiana — not too late!
  (Or will you be a ranger to the end?)
Good-bye . . . Good-bye . . . oh, I shall always wait
  You, Larry, traveller—

                stranger,

                   son,

                      — my friend —

Once more Crane's poet-voyager heads for the sea, but it is suggested by the mother's supplications that Larry's true home is ashore. He has a «pledge» (cf. «the prophet's pledge» of the proem) and carries with him a «word,» a poetic image of America. But the question whether he will return or not is left open, he is «traveller» and «stranger» as well as «son» and «friend».

«Indiana» functions as a connecting link between the poems preceding and following it. From the Indian past of «The Dance» and the poet's own present in «Cutty Sark,» the mid-nineteenth-century of «Indiana» forms a transition. The westward journey that is the structure of «Powhatan's Daughter» is completed in «Indiana,» and an eastward movement is begun which leads into the sea again in the figure of Larry and carries over into «Cutty Sark.»

4. Cutty Sark

This section is about the era of the Oriental trade that was carried on by means of American and British clipper ships during the nineteenth century, and the title is the name of both a famous clipper and Crane's favorite whisky. The epigraph from Melville sets the tone in what in many ways is a Melvillean poem, and it is taken from his «The Temeraire,» in which he laments the loss of the old sailing ships that was the result of the emergence of newer, ironclad battleships. For Crane the Yankee clippers become representatives of a glorious and promising past, their magnificent white riggings repeating the symbolism of the «White Birds.» «Cutty Sark» is a return to the sea, to New York harbor and the Brooklyn Bridge. An important clue to the poem is in the note furnished by the poet in his 1927 letter to Otto Kahn. According to the note, «Cutty Sark» is «a phantasy on the period of the whalers and clipper ships. It also starts in the present and 'progresses backwards.' The form of the poem may seem erratic, but it is meant to present the hallucinations incident to rum-drinking in a South Street dive, as well as the lurch of a boat in heavy seas, etc.» The poem is written in what can best be described as an imitative or expressive form:

I met a man in South Street, tall —
a nervous shark tooth swung on his chain.
His eyes pressed through green glass
— green glasses, or bar lights made them
so —
    shine —

                    GREEN —

                                    eyes —

stepped out — forgot to look at you
or left you several blocks away —

in the nickel—in—the—slot piano jogged
«Stamboul Nights» weaving somebody's nickel —
    sang

O Stamboul Rose — dreams weave the rose!
Murmurs of Leviathan he spoke
and rum was Plato in our heads . . .

The arrangement of the lines does indeed suggest a heaving, swaying motion that associates itself both with a state of drunkeness and the rhythms of a moving ship. The shark tooth talisman around the sailor's neck swings like a lantern at sea, and his eyes are green like the ocean itself. Eyes are symbols of vision, but these are the green eyes of one who has become disintegrated by the contact with the sea.[47] In «Cape Hatteras» green is the color of vitality as expressed in Whitman's work, but this is hardly the significance of the color in «Cutty Sark.» Instead it is suggested that the sailor-voyager has lost all coherent understanding and become blinded, in a sense, by the sea. He seems to have utterly succumbed to the disintegrating effect of his experience at sea rather than undergoing any such metamorphosis toward the revelation of eternity as that granted to the protagonists of certain other poems by Crane that seem relevant here. One thinks of the mariners of «At Melville's Tomb» and the lovers of «Voyages,» and in the final poem of this cycle the swimmer-poet sustains a kind of purification by the sea:

My eyes pressed black against the prow,
— Thy derelict and blinded guest

Waiting, afire, what name, unspoke,
I cannot claim: let thy waves rear
More savage than the death of kings,
Some splintered garland for the seer.

His eyes are black and blinded, but he is afire with the waiting for the vision that lies in store for him beyond the waves and the garland that they weave. In «Cutty Sark» the vision, the «imaged Word,» emerges brokenly and in incoherent fragments, in the popular tune «Stamboul Rose» that is being played by the nickel-in-the-slot piano.[48] Its voice alternates with those of the sailor and the poet, and the meaning of this structure is explained in Crane's note: «'Cutty Sark' is built on the plan of a *fugue*. Two 'voices' — that of the world of Time, and that of the world of Eternity — are interwoven in the action. The Atlantis theme (that of Eternity) is the transmuted voice of the nickel-slot pianola, and this voice alternates with that of the derelict sailor and the description of the action.»

The Atlantis theme functions in «Cutty Sark» as an image of a spiritual America in a manner which is complementary to the function of the name «Cathay» in «Ave Maria.» Though these are both sea poems, the former finds its dream in the sea whereas the latter directs itself toward the discovery of some fabulous realm ashore. Atlantis, the sunken continent, reinforces the dominant maritime background of «Cutty Sark,» and it is boldly transformed into a single image of a rose woven by dreams. There is a parallel between the gradual development of the Atlantis theme in the second half of *The Bridge* toward its culmination in the final section and the evolution of the Pocahontas figure throughout the poems of «Powhatan's Daughter.» In both instances the symbols are at first vaguely suggested and then progress toward a heightened realization.

The nickel of the pianola is connected with the nickel for car-change in «Van Winkle» and the one the poet uses to enter the subway in «The Tunnel.» In the former poem it precedes the journey into the past and toward the west, in the latter it signals a descent into darkness. In «Cutty Sark» the nickel introduces the voice of eternity, of the ideal land Atlantis. The atmosphere of the opening paragraph strongly suggests the world of *Moby Dick;* there are references to sharks and Leviathans that foreshadow the succeeding visions of clippers, and the association of Platonic idealism and a state of intoxication or unconsciousness remotely suggests Ishmael's ruminations in chapters like «The Mast-Head» and «Cisterns and Buckets.» The physical and mental disintegration of the sailor in South Street is suggested by his drunken, incoherent talk. The main thing that is expressed in his rambling remarks is a chaotic sense of time. He asks the poet to remember his hour of departure, confesses that he is unable to keep time and that he even keeps «weak-eyed watches» at sea. This weakness contrasts him unfavorably with the keen seafarer Columbus who vigilantly kept his watch as the new world was drawing near.

The hands of the sailor are «bony,» he is like a skeleton or derelict thrown ashore by the sea. He has also been a whaler at one time, and he is thus associated with «the dice of drowned men's bones» that «beat on the dusty shore,» the remnants of the crew of *The Pequod* described in «At Melville's Tomb.» His life at sea, the monotony of the surroundings, and especially the voyages through the sterile whiteness of snow and ice of the Arctic regions have «killed» his ability to orient himself in time. He does not possess the mechanical concept of time as a sequence of well-defined entities, and, on the other hand, the changeless, white Arctic has destroyed in him the ability to relate to time in the manner of the hoboes of «The River,» in terms of the seasonal changes of birth, growth and death. This whiteness of the Arctic, somewhat like the whiteness of the whale in *Moby Dick,* represents an absence of time, a nothingness.

Crane was also preoccupied with the significance of the color white and treats it somewhat ambivalently. It is associated with dawn, revelation or insight in some poems, but the Arctic whiteness in «Cutty Sark» symbolizes not a positive experience of eternity, but a negative loss of time, a nothingness.[49] Similarly, in «North Labrador,» the whiteness of the Arctic regions suggests a sense of timelessness induced by the absence of seasonal change:

Cold-hushed, there is only the shifting of moments
That journey toward no Spring —
No birth, no death, no time nor sun
In answer.

In this world there is no evidence of beginnings or ends, of progress or decline, past or present, merely a meaningless «shifting of moments.»

The piano refrain in «Cutty Sark» is repeated with slight modulations in phrasing throughout the poem. There are actually two different refrains, one dealing with the Atlantis theme, the other with the clipper ships. In the case of the first one the rose of Atlantis is first woven by «dreams,» then by «drums,» and here may be a reference to «The Dance,» in which drums accompany the ritual by which Pocahontas is revived. Like the Indian maiden, Atlantis is a symbol of an elevated state of consciousness, and the realm of Indian myth is reintroduced by means of the sailor's ruminations on his wanderings in Central America, in Panama and Yucatan.

It seems that he gave up the sea for a while to tramp around in these regions, and he even observed the volcano Popocatepetl. Ashes run down the sides of the mountain and its top is like a «birdless mouth.» This is Crane's way of asserting that the time of the great Indian myths is over; the deserted volcano contrasts with the scene in «The Dance» where Quetzalcoatl ascends from the top of the volcano like a flaming, birdlike serpent. However, the sailor returns from his inland excursion to the coast again, and now the Atlantis refrain becomes more insistent and detailed: «*Rose of Stamboul O Coral Queen —/ teased remnants of the skeleton of cities —/ and galleries, galleries of watergutted lava.*» The rose becomes a queen, and the Pocahontas image blends with the Atlantis theme. The lava of the volcano has sunk to the bottom of the sea along with the ancient cities of the lost continent. There is an echo here of Poe's «The City in the Sea,» a poem which is closely linked with «The Tunnel.» Poe describes his sunken city of death in lines like these: «There shrines and palaces and towers/ (Time-eaten towers that tremble not!)/ Resemble nothing that is ours.»[50] The mythic constellations in «The Dance,» the Pocahontas image and the rose have been drowned, literally and figuratively; but even in this picture of the disintegration and drowning is suggested the existence of an Atlantis, of possibilities that are fully articulated in the «Atlantis» section.

The sailor, driven back to the sea, finds that he cannot live on land. He exclaims that life is a «geyser,» an image that refers both to a volcanic outburst and the spiracle of a whale. He is aimlessly and eternally searching without knowing exactly what he is searching for, and he is a far cry from the determined Columbus. He is more like the hoboes of «The River» and has glimpses of beauty and integration in the sea in the same way as they have premonitions of the earth as the goddess Pocahontas.

However, the relations between the sailor and the images that suggest the positive possibilities of America are chiefly grotesque and chaotic:

> Or they may start some white machine that sings.
> Then you may laugh and dance the axletree —
> steel — silver — kick the traces — and know —

> *ATLANTIS ROSE drums wreathe the rose*
> *the star floats burning in a gulf of tears*
> *and sleep another thousand*

> interminably
>
> long since somebody's nickel — stopped —
> playing —

> A wind worried those wicker-neat lapels, the
> swinging summer entrances to cooler hells . . .
> Outside a wharf truck nearly ran him down
> — he lunged up Bowery way while the dawn
> was putting the Statue of Liberty out — that
> torch of hers you know —

> I started walking home across the Bridge

The nickel-in-the-slot piano becomes a white machine; the color white, the references to machinery, steel and song recall the technological symbolism of the proem, of the «dancing» Pullman trains in «The River» and point forward to the «Atlantis» section. The sailor's behavior is a burlesque on this dignified symbolism, his dancing and his kicks comically reflect the circular, dancing movements of powerful machinery such as that of the derricks of the proem and the speeding trair s of «The River.» Similarly the «One Song» of «Atlantis» has been reduced to the blare of a pianola. The sailor is all dissolution, bits and pieces float through his mind: frontiers, steel, silver, the last word ironically pointing to the «silver-paced» bridge of the proem, but he is unable to integrate his impressions into any harmonious whole.

The «Stamboul Rose» of the piano tune becomes the rose of Atlantis, the legendary sunken continent that has haunted man's dreams for nearly two thousand years and which may remain a dream for another millenium, as suggested by the image of the sleeping star. This same star went to sleep in «The Harbor Dawn» and was restored to its full glory in the metamorphosis of Quetzalcoatl in «The Dance.» In «Cutty Sark» the star is drowned, like Atlantis itself, but it «floats» in «tears,» which indicates a possibility of renewed visionary experiences, tears being a symbol of both suffering and insight.[51]

As the music of the piano runs out, the episode of the drunken sailor is over. He leaves the South Street dive and staggers up through the Bowery. The external setting is the same as that of «The Harbor Dawn,» sunrise over New York harbor, and the same images and objects return: a wharf truck, the grayish light of dawn, and the Statue of Liberty, suggested in the proem, emerges clearly here, the fire of its light recalling the pervasive fire imagery of *The Bridge.*

Dawn is the hour of revelation, of the renewal of vision, and it fittingly introduces the second part of «Cutty Sark,» the hallucinatory procession of clippers seen from the Brooklyn Bridge, the «phantom regatta» as Crane called it: «Blithe Yankee vanities, turreted sprites, winged/ British repartees, skil-/ ful savage sea-girls.» The rhythms and movements of the drunken sailor and the pianola refrain are carried over into this impressionistic portrayal of the imaginary ships, ironically named «vanities» and «repartees» to emphasize the unceasing competition between individual ships. A new, comical and shanty-like refrain is substituted for the Atlantis theme, and the poet makes a sharply ironic comment on the old tea trade by juxtaposing opium and tea, recalling the evils of opium smuggling that were also part of the era of the clippers.

The imitative or expressive form of the poem is explained in a letter

from Crane to Edgell Rickword, editor of *The Calendar,* to which
«Cutty Sark» was submitted on January 7, 1927: «I must risk a pre-
sumption on your interest in the poem in order to emphasize the necessity of printing 'Cutty Sark' as closely as possible to the form as ty-
ped herewith, especially in regard to the third page, which is a 'carto-
gram,' if one may so designate a special use of the calligramme. The
'ships' should meet and pass in line and type — as well as in wind and
memory, if you get my rather unique formal intentions in this phantom regatta seen from Brooklyn Bridge.»

In his use of the evocative names of ships and places, Crane is
drawing on the rich lore of the old sailing ships, their perilous passage around Cape Horn, across the Pacific and into Asian waters, the
constant racing between them and their fabulous speed records. In
his note to «Cutty Sark» the poet wrote: «It was a pleasure to use historical names for these lovely ghosts. Music still haunts their names
long after the wind has left their sails.» The final paragraph of the
poem reminds one of a Whitmanian catalogue of names:

> *Thermopylae, Black Prince, Flying Cloud* through
>   Sunda
> - scarfed of foam, their bellies veered green esplanades,
> locked in wind-humors, ran their eastings down;

>   *at Java Head freshened the nip*
>   *(sweet opium and tea!)*
>   and turned and left us on the lee . . .

> Buntlines tusseling (91 days, 20 hours and anchored!)
>   *Rainbow, Leander*
> (last trip a tragedy) — where can you be
> *Nimbus?* and you rivals two —

>   a long tack keeping —

>   *Taeping?*
>   *Ariel?*

Here are references to the races of some of the most famous American and British clippers, and the poet goes out of his way to convey a
sense of the marvellous speed and grace of the ships, which are ador-

ned with «scarfs» of foam as they plunge ahead across the «green esplanades,» the great open spaces of the sea. There may be a pun on the word «scarfed» here; it may also refer to the cutting of a whale, in which case the foam of the waves is compared to the white blubber that is being turned up by the sharp edge of the knife, the ship's prow.

Locked on to the prevailing winds, the clippers run their easterly course through the tropical seas, stopping only at «Java head» for replenishments and then anchoring after making new records. That the clippers are real is testified to by Crane in a letter he wrote to Malcolm Cowley and Peggy Baird, July 29, 1926: «It happens that all the clippers mentioned were real beings had extensive histories in the Tea trade — and the last two mentioned were life-long rivals. Rather touching . . .»[52]

However, there is also a symbolic significance in the use of some of the ship's names. In *The Bridge* the rainbow is one of the symbols of beauty, aspiration and vision, and the clipper *The Rainbow* was one of those which foundered. Like Atlantis itself the rainbow has sunk to the bottom of the ocean; in «Cape Hatteras» it is resurrected. *The Leander,* whose last trip was a «tragedy,» apparently suffered the same fate as *The Rainbow.* Leander is the Greek boy who is the hero of Christopher Marlowe's love poem *Hero and Leander.* Marlowe was one of Crane's favorite poets, and the epigraph to «Three Songs» is from *Hero and Leander,* in which Leander is seen swimming the Hellespont to visit his beloved Hero. Neptune fell in love with him and pulled him down to his kingdom of the ocean depths, but when he discovered that the boy was about to drown, Neptune set him free and he reached Sestos, the abode of the fair maiden. The tale is a perfect illustration of a central, recurring pattern in much of Crane's poetry, the drowning or transformation of the poet-voyager which involves a metamorphosis and a gaining of a new and deeper insight. This is a dominant design within *The Bridge,* in which the drowned images of the ideal and of love in «Cutty Sark» are resurrected in «Cape Hatteras» and «Atlantis.»

«Cutty Sark» is the last poem of the first half of *The Bridge*, and Crane insisted on this division in a letter to Caresse Crosby, December 26, 1929. Three photographs of the Brooklyn Bridge by Walker Evans adorn the Paris edition of *The Bridge,* one is of the span, one of the cables, and the third portrays the river and some barges as seen from the bridge. This is what Crane wrote about the placement of this latter picture: «will you see that the middle photograph (the one of the barges and tug) goes between the 'Cutty Sark' Section and the 'Hatteras' Section. That is the 'center' of the book, both physically and symbolically».

Having arrived at this «center,» the poet's next task is to bring with him, into modern America, the spiritual tools he has forged from the past and employ them in his wider synthesis of American civilization. He begins this venture on a note of sober realism or even scepticism, contrasting the noble Maquokeeta of «The Dance» with the drunken sailor of «Cutty Sark.» The Atlantis motif is introduced in connection with this sailor and is only a broken refrain on a pianola, and in the sections of the second half the poet will have to confront much harsher realities. Nevertheless, he is able to draw on further inspirational elements from the more recent past and from his own era: clipper ships, Walt Whitman, the airplane, Isadora Duncan, Emily Dickinson, his own experience of the Brooklyn Bridge. In this way, he sets out on his quest into the modern world, and at the end of it, in the finale of the poem, he presents his synthesis, his Atlantis.[53] Walking home across his bridge at the end of «Cutty Sark,» the poet is back in twentieth century New York and America again, preparing to span the diverse elements of his own era in the bridge of his poetry, and to bridge the gap between present and past. He is sustained by the apparition of the clipper ships, whose «baronial white» sails have the same function here as they had in the proem: to recall the poet to his vision of the «Whole,» or the «All.»[54] In the next section, Whitman becomes his guide and mentor in this undertaking.

5. Cape Hatteras

Though *The Bridge* as a whole shows the influence of Whitman, «Cape Hatteras» is the only section entirely devoted to the reaffirmation of his vision. Crane conceived of Whitman's message in the same way as Waldo Frank — Whitman is the seer who embraces the whole of American reality in his consciousness. *Our America* ends with a discussion of Whitman, and here Frank calls him «a 'great mystic'» and an American prophet who «talked with God, standing upon America as Moses upon Sinai. He talked with God, speaking our tongue. America therefore is holy land to us . . . in this juncture of his spirit and our land is revelation.»[55]

The epigraph to «Cape Hatteras» is the second of these lines from «Passage to India:»

Reckoning ahead O soul, when thou, the time achiev'd,
The seas all cross'd, weather'd the capes, the voyage done,
As fill'd with friendship, love complete, the Elder
                                        Brother found,
The Younger melts in fondness in his arms.[56]

Crane felt related to Whitman's powerful transcendental optimism, the belief in the power of the soul to maintain its integrity in all vicissitudes and to journey beyond all earthly limits and touch the divine. We recognize here the metaphor of the struggle of the spirit as a sea voyage that both poets employ in a number of contexts. By choosing the above passage, Crane may have thought of himself as the «younger brother» of Whitman. In «Modern Poetry» Crane discusses the future of American poetry and draws the conclusion that Whitman's approach to the native scene remains the most valid one: «The most typical and valid expression of the American *psychosis* seems to me still to be found in Whitman. His faults as a technician and his clumsy and indiscriminate enthusiasm are somewhat beside the point. He, better than any other, was able to coordinate those forces in America which seem most intractable, fusing them into a universal vision which takes on additional significance as time goes on. He was a revolutionist beyond the strict meaning of Coleridge's definition of genius, but his bequest is still to be realized in all its implications.»

It may be maintained that a tradition is only alive when it adjusts itself to changing conditions. American culture and civilization underwent profound changes during the period between Whitman's and Crane's creative efforts. The older poet was able to support himself on the tradition of New England transcendentalism, whereas Crane lived in an era whose catchwords were chaos and disintegration and whose dominant poetic monument was *The Waste Land*. Carl Sandburg is sometimes referred to as the heir of Whitman, but it may be that his affirmation of modern America and its people was made possible only at the cost of profundity and inclusivenes, of a «universal vision.» Crane focussed on Whitman's world-view, his sense of reality as an ultimately spiritual whole that Frank admired in him. In «Cape Hatteras» Crane launches forth in the world seeking proof of Whitman's prophecies and attempting to relive his visionary experience. In this way, he tries to fulfill Whitman's demand for a «poet of the modern.» It is clear, in what he wrote about Whitman in the essays and in the letters to Waldo Frank and others, that Crane wanted to share the older poet's beliefs, which fundamentally were the same as those of Frank. «Cape Hatteras» is a record both of Crane's hopes for the modern world as well as his awareness of its evil, and thus repeats the emotional pattern that we know from the previous sections of *The Bridge*.

The point of view in the opening paragraph is that of an observer on board a ship drawing near the Cape Hatteras coastline. A central theme of the poem is the nature of power, natural or mechanical, and the first lines present a grand view of the long-range geological development of the land itself:

Imponderable the dinosaur
          sinks slow,
               the mammoth saurian
               ghoul, the eastern
                          Cape . . .
While rises in the west the coastwise range,
                 slowly the hushed land —
Combustion at the astral core — the dorsal change
Of energy — convulsive shift of sand . . .

Here is created a sense of the slow, immemorial processes of paleontological evolution by referring back to the age of the giant reptiles and imagining their gradual extinction. The dinosaurs and the cape off the eastern seaboard sink down, and the «hushed land,» the mountainous and varied continent of America itself, gradually rises and acquires its present shape. The opening of the poem describes the rise of America in geological, but also symbolic terms, in contrast with the stagnation of the Mediterranean «capes» of Europe. Moreover, the poet attempts to bridge, in his imagination, the enormous time span of the history of the planet itself.[57] The rendering of the formation of the land echoes the hymn to the Mississippi in «The River,» where the silent flow of the river becomes a natural metaphor for geological change. The moving power behind it all is the «combustion» in the interior core of the earth of which the convulsions in the external crust are the result. Fire is the symbol of power, energy in its purest form as it manifests itself in the sun, in lightning and volcanoes in the earlier sections. On another level, fire is a manifestation of the divine, the fiery hand of God that stretches out toward man.

From a geological past «Cape Hatteras» moves into the present, and the situation is that of modern Americans returning to their native coast after having visited older countries and cultures, presumably those of Europe. The poet himself went to France and England in 1929 and worked intensely on «Cape Hatteras» during that period. He also wrote Frank, February 7, from Paris: «Please don't forget to send me your *Re-Discovery of America* now, as soon as possible. I need it as a balance against the seductions of Europe.» It is the American culture problem that Crane returns to in the opening part of «Cape Hatteras;» the need for a national poetic and religious expression:

> But we, who round the capes, the promontories
> Where strange tongues vary messages of surf
> Below grey citadels, repeating to the stars
> The ancient names — return home to our own
> Hearths, there to eat an apple and recall
> The songs that gypsies dealt us at Marseille
> Or how the priests walked — slowly through Bombay —
> Or to read you, Walt, knowing us in thrall
>
> To that deep wonderment, our native clay
> Whose depth of red, eternal flesh of Pocahontas —
> Those continental folded æons, surcharged
> With sweetness below derricks, chimneys, tunnels —
> Is veined by all that time has really pledged us . . .

The strange languages of the peoples of the foreign countries, with their castles and fortresses, respond to nature with their own «names,» the categories that have sprung from their own cultural environment. Crane's sense of the cultural identity of France and the contrast between that country and his homeland is reflected in a letter of May 1, 1929, to Isidor Schneider, written in southern France: «For even here by the blue inland sea, with ancient citadels and fortifications crowning the heights of a lovely whitewalled, village — I can't help thinking of my room out there in Paterson.»

Crane implies that his returning Americans are innocents, the eating of the apple suggests that they are Adams and Eves. They recall the songs of France and the rituals of Indian priests, but then they turn to their own prophet, Whitman, knowing that only he can express the spirit of their land. Crane here fuses his Pocahontas image with Whitman's celebration of the land. To express his sense of the unity of the land Whitman also employed the female personification, and in «Thou Mother with Thy Equal Brood» he sees America as a great mother. The concept of the motherland, the transcendental union of the American states, is here expressed in more philosophic and abstract terms than Crane uses with his figure of Pocahontas, who is seen as the body of the continent lying beautiful and fertile under the mechanical structures of civilization that cover the surface. However, like Whitman, Crane regards nature as a manifestation of something higher, of the infinite. This is what the land has «pledged» and what man should strive for: to discover the eternal in the temporal, the native clay. A manuscript version of line 22 supports this: «The veins of that eternity that's pledged us.»

From the earth the attention is shifted towards space, the element which has been so dramatically conquered by modern machinery:

> The captured fume of space foams in our ears —
> What whisperings of far watches on the main —
> Relapsing into silence, while time clears
> Our lenses, lifts a focus, resurrects
> A periscope to glimpse what joys or pain
> Our eyes can share or answer — then deflects
> Us, shunting to a labyrinth submersed
> Where each sees only his dim past reversed . . .

Space is no longer free and undisturbed; radio waves and the wireless have «captured» it and made long-range communication possible. This also implies that the age of exploration of unknown continents is over; no Columbus keeps «far watches» in distant seas. The great discoveries have been made, and history has cleared the «lenses» of modern man, made it possible for him to see the land that Columbus discovered. Using a modern invention, the periscope, as his symbol of the poetic vision in our time, the poet suggests that both joy and pain are part of a larger, meaningful whole. However, this elevated perspective does not last, because time also has in store the soul's sinking into the dark «labyrinths» of the completely isolated self.

The poet goes on to explore the relations between modern science and technology and man's search for the infinite: «But that star-glistered salver of infinity,/ The circle, blind crucible of endless space,/ Is sluiced by motion, — subjugated never.» As both Whitman and Crane saw it, spatial conquest has no meaning if it does not point beyond itself to the sphere of the spiritual. Endless space, the universe, is seen as a circle, and it can never be «subjugated,» not even by the newest inventions. However, infinity can be approached imaginative-ly, through the development of the consciousness. To seek re-estab-lishment of contact with the eternal has been a goal ever since the fall of man, which severed «Adam» from the divine sphere here symbolized by «Hesperus,» the evening and morning star.[58] A similar feeling of distance between man and star is suggested at the end of «The Tunnel:» «How far away the star has pooled the sea.»

The airplane, the supreme modern instrument of journeying, is in-troduced, and it is ironically implied that though we are equipped with such an invention, space, by virtue of its endless size, «consumes us.» It drives home to man the fact that he cannot reach infinity by mecha-nical means, and thus its flight produces both laughter at the joy of flying and tears at the realizations of its limitations. The great strides made by physical science and by industry have revolutionized the world and seem to have established a purely materialistic world-view, a new «realm of fact» in which man is reduced to an «atom.» On the ot-her hand, the machine age holds out the greatest possibilities for man, as an «engine in a cloud» he seems closer than ever to the fulfillment of the Icarus dream. Throughout «Cape Hatteras» the poet explores the possibilities and dangers of airflight and tries to see it as a modern poe-tic symbol of the journey of the soul that Whitman celebrated in «Pas-sage to India» and «Song of the Open Road.»

Crane poignantly and beautifully expresses his yearning for Whit-man's vision and his pledge to carry it on:

«— Recorders ages hence» — ah, syllables of faith!
Walt, tell me, Walt Whitman, if infinity
Be still the same as when you walked the beach
Near Paumanok — your lone patrol — and heard the wraith
Through surf, its bird note there a long time falling . . .
For you, the panoramas and this breed of towers,
Of you — the theme that's statured in the cliff.

O Saunterer on free ways still ahead!
Not this our empire yet, but labyrinth
Wherein your eyes, like the Great Navigator's without ship,
Gleam from the great stones of each prison crypt
Of canyoned traffic . . .

                                    they also range
Across the hills where second timber strays
Back over Connecticut farms, abandoned pastures, —

References to poems by Whitman abound in «Cape Hatteras.» In «Recorders ages hence» he admonishes the historians of posterity to regard him not primarily as a writer of poems, but as a great lover who was proud of the «measureless ocean of love within him.» The «syllables of faith» refer not only to Whitman's belief in love, but also to his conviction that his efforts would be remembered and appreciated for ages to come. Crane goes on to create a variation on the theme of «Out of the Cradle Endlessly Rocking,» in which Whitman listens to the song of a bird calling for its mate and renders it in human terms. The bird is a forlorn lover who sees the shape of his bride in nature itself: *«Land! land! O land!/ Whichever way I turn. I think you could give me my mate back/ again if you only would . . .»*[59]

The theme of a lover's longing is developed into the soul's reaching out into the universe for an answer to its deepest needs. The poem reaches the conclusion that it is «the low and delicious word death» which carries the ultimate answer to man's incessant craving and yearning. Death is the passage to infinite peace and to immortality. Whitman was able to obtain rapport with the infinite while walking on an American beach listening to a bird's song and the roar of the sea. For him even modern America would have been «holy land,» both the «panoramas» and the Manhattan towers, in the «theme» of his poetry this world has a transcendental dimension. The open road is Whitman's symbol of the state of mind that conceives of reality as perpetual movement or progress toward a meaningful and sublime end. This end belongs to another dimension that that of mere technical progress, and therefore Crane, in «Cape Hatteras,» sees the «free ways» of Whitman's vision as lying beyond even the realities of the twentieth century, which are more like a labyrinth than an open road.

Here is an echo of Whitman's «Song of the Universal,» a poem which deals with the need of the poet to perceive in the chaos of America the essential quality or force which links all together and which is ultimately benevolent. Some seers have the capacity to see through to this dimension; in the midst of «the mad Babeldin» they see this whole, this universal: «O the blest eyes, the happy hearts,/ That see, that know the guiding thread so fine,/ Along the mighty labyrinth.»[60] They behold the essential America, the culmination of history: «thou America,/ For the scheme's culmination, its thought and its reality,/ For these (not for thyself) thou hast arrived.»[61]

It is probably more than coincidental that Crane also uses the metaphor of the world as a labyrinth through which the seer's eyes guide us; he is incorporating Whitman's poem into his own text to show that the situation has not changed. The struggle is always going on between the forces of blind materialism and those of an integrated consciousness of reality as spiritual whole. Whitman's eyes symbolize this consciousness which is able to encompass all. From the Stock Excange they range over the continent itself, taking the open road of the soul's journey, unhampered by the fact that the Connecticut farms have become «abandoned pastures» and are being used as summer homes for city people.

The eyes are «undenying,» the attitude of total acceptance is the only way of assimilating the American experience and extricating its spiritual meaning. Crane found it harder to maintain a view like this in his own time than Whitman did in his, and the next paragraph of «Cape Hatteras» expresses some of his doubts about the meaning or purpose of the ever growing technical power of the industrialized society that America has become:

The nasal whine of power whips a new universe . . .
Where spouting pillars spoor the evening sky,
Under the looming stacks of the gigantic power house
Stars prick the eyes with sharp ammoniac proverbs,
New verities, new inklings in the velvet hummed
Of dynamos, where hearing's lash is strummed . . .
Power's script, — wound, bobbin-bound, refined —
Is stropped to the slap of belts on booming spools,
     spurred
Into the bulging bouillon, harnessed jelly of the stars.
Towards what? The forked crash of split thunder parts
Our hearing momentwise; but fast in whirling armatures,

As bright as frogs' eyes, giggling in the girth
Of steely gizzards — axle-bound, confined
In coiled precision, bunched in mutual glee
The bearings glint, — O murmurless and shined
In oilrinsed circles of blind ecstasy!

In the proem the poet found it possible to celebrate the power engaged in the construction of the bridge, but the later sections demonstrate his profoundly ambivalent and uncertain attitude towards the machine. In the above passage he begins with a forceful, yet emotionally quite neutral, description of the unleashing of electric currents in a power plant.[62] The currents describe a whipping, churning, spiralling motion, and electricity being an omnipresent phenomenon, its discovery and increasing utilization may be said to have changed our view of reality and created a «new universe.»

The impact of constructions like the power house has made for a new conception of nature, and the observer is impressed with the mighty pillars and «looming stacks» that rise against the sky, though he has none of the religious reverence toward them with which he confronted the bridge in the proem. Seen through the structures of the plant, the stars take on new meanings which are more in keeping with a scientific definition of nature. This definition prompts a search for the essential meaning of this new universe, what «new verities» that may be revealed in the hum of the dynamoes. In the electric installations power has been trapped and made to reveal its design or «script,» the currents race around in the «spools» of the power house and from there are released in cables across space, which thus is conquered like a «harnessed jelly of the stars.»

However, the fundamental question, «Towards what?,» remains unanswered. Whitman was able to feel that everything was evolving according to plan toward a supreme fulfillment, but the only thing Crane is able to perceive at this point is the existence of power itself. The spectacle of electrical machinery is bright and shiny and conveys an impression of power and efficiency, but it is a power that has no purpose and significance beyond itself. Its «whirling» motion is one of «blind ecstasy.» The power house represents the machine at its least integrated level; it is power isolated from any meaningful whole as Henry Adams saw it and as also Waldo Frank feared that it would continue to be. The latter warned against the lure of a superficial worship of the machine, of the tendency of the American to love the machine «autoerotically:» «Its body of surfaces must shine, as if it were the body of the beloved. It must gleam with oil as with ointment, glide silently as in soft raiment.»[63]

After the power house episode, the effects and functions of the airplane, the primary object of both hope and despair, are evaluated. Crane takes a loosely historical approach to the subject, describing first man's old dream of free flight and the first experiments with airplanes made by the Wright Brothers on the famous sand dunes and hills at Cape Hatteras: «Stars scribble on our eyes the frosty sagas,/ The gleaming cantos of unvanquished space . . ./ O sinewy silver biplane, nudging the wind's withers!» The phrase «unvanquished space» invokes the Columbus theme again, the exploration of the unknown. Having more or less finished the conquests of sea and land, modern man turns toward the air and even toward empty space itself, and in these exploits grand adventures beckon the voyager — the word «cantos» suggesting Homeric feats and great poetry suited to them. The first, historic flights at Kitty Hawk are a modern instance of the voyage of discovery of men like Columbus.

The brothers in their craft wrestle with the wind, which has both «withers» and «flanks,» and as they gain control of the new element, the poet asserts that the movements of the plane are «ciphers» that indicate the fulfillment of a prophecy. The airplane has opened up tremendous possibilities for voyages that may embody the double function of the material and the spiritual. However, though beyond the earthly atmosphere the «new latitudes» of the universe beckon, the new instruments have brought the threat of destruction and are «rife of doom.» The planes are dragon's issue, and while they may inspire poetic emotion as «Iliads glimmer through eyes raised in pride,» they also bring a «hell's belt» of bombing and air combat. The fighting planes are like mad dogs in the «fiery kennel» of the sky.

Crane's description of war in the air is a violent burlesque of the positive themes and figures of *The Bridge*. The planes, like the seagull, describe circles in their flight, but they are «marauding,» spreading «rancorous grenades» of destruction in their path. However, in the next paragraph the poet again turns his attention toward the spiritual and aesthetic meaning of this modern conquest of the air and creates a rhapsodic address to the spectacle of formations of planes taking off and soaring through the skies, and now the imagery of wheels, revolving motion, wings and dawn are repeated and glorified:

Wheeled swiftly, wings emerge from larval-silver hangars.
Taut motors surge, space-gnawing, into flight;
Through sparkling visibility, outspread, unsleeping,
Wings clip the last peripheries of light . . .
Tellurian wind-sleuths on dawn patrol,
Each plane a hurtling javelin of winged ordnance,
Bristle the heights above a screeching gale to hover;
Surely no eye that Sunward Escadrille can cover!
There, meaningful, fledged as the Pleiades
With razor sheen they zoom each rapid helix
Up-chartered choristers of their own speeding
They, cavalcade on escapade, shear Cumulus —
Lay siege and hurdle Cirrus down the skies!

The machine has become something meaningful and promising, and the hope is raised that the surging motors will carry man to his ultimate goal as the planes rise through the clear air. The wings are spread and alert, capturing the faint, peripheral glimpses of light. Flying on the tracks of the wind, the planes master it and even hover over the gales, and their movement has a purpose and ordnance, the longing for infinity, suggested by the metaphorical comparison of the planes and spears thrown upward. This spear-arrow symbolism recurs in «Atlantis». At this point the formation has become a part of a larger whole, nature itself, and takes its place among the stellar figurations of the sky. The spiral of their ascension is like a «helix», and unlike earthbound choristers they can power their own spiritual uplift. But the ambiguities persist. Even in its glorious flight the threat of war accompanies the airplane as it lays «siege» around the cloud formations. In spite of the brilliance, the poet does not take us much further than to celebration of the spectacular and adventurous aspects of the speeding craft as they cut through the high cloud masses. The splendor of another modern wonder of the air besides the airplane is indicated by the dirigible which glides along the «pendulous auroral beaches» of the clouds, having «splintered» space.

But then we are more forcefully reminded again that these are machines of war, and an imaginary air fight over Cape Hatteras is being staged. Being armed, the planes are seen as «moving turrets,» and the idea of a dogfight is reintroduced by their being compared to «scouting griffons.» The imagery becomes more scientific, and also more demonic: the air masses are like «gaseous crepe» and the rays of searchlights penetrate the «foaming anthracite» of the sky. The main hero emerges, the pilot himself, the modern heir of Columbus and the potential bearer of the Whitmanian ideal of the open road. This pilot is a «corsair,» which suggests a connection between the flier and the figure of an ocean voyager that occurs elsewhere in *The Bridge*. In «Atlantis,» the passages by sea and air are fused into one and the same journey. Techno-scientific metaphor reappears in the «bicarbonated white» of the pilot's eyes, and he occupies a position supremely fitted for the vision of infinity. His eyes are «white» and he rises at great speed through the air, following a path above even the «levin's lance.» He may be said to have the position ascribed to the gods of «The Dance,» who, «thewed of the levin,» sit at the mainspring of thunder and lightning and gaze through «infinite seasons.»

He must aspire to the vision of the gods, but the doom is with him and the ambiguous significance of his flight is sustained. Its great possibilities are suggested by the «Sanskrit charge» which is invested in him and by means of which he may «conjugate,» verbalize, infinity anew for modern man. Sanskrit suggests India and the Cathay image, and the linguistic metaphor refers to the motif of the *word*. This is a clear echo of the following lines from «Passage to India:» «O soul, voyagest thou indeed on voyages like those?/ Disportest thou on waters such as those?/ Soundest below the Sanscrit and the Vedas?»[64] The Sanskrit terminology also occurs in «Reliquary,» one of Crane's «Uncollected Poems.» Reflecting on his death, the poet asks what is to become of his vision: «Who is now left to vary the Sanscrit/ Pillowed by/ my wrist in the vestibule of Time?» The arm is on the pillow, and so is the vision, seated as it is in the pulsating veins. A vestibule is a place where one waits, and time itself is nothing but waiting before the approach of death. The concern here is with the continuance of the tradition, the «varying» of the message.

However, in «Cape Hatteras» the «Falcon Ace» is shot down, receiving the «benediction of the shell's deep, sure reprieve!» The poet seems to say that though the possibility of achieving the vision through manned flight may be uncertain, death is a sure entrance to eternity, and thus the pilot suffers the fate of the «bedlamite» that fell from the bridge in the proem. The language is highly expressive and imitative in the manner of the opening of «The River» and of «Cutty Sark,» the machine is seen «twisting» and «gyring» down «whizzing Zodiacs» and is finally drawn down into «gravitation's vortex,» ending in «crashed dispersion» and death.

«Cape Hatteras» is divided into two parts, and the first one ends with the downfall and crash of the airplane. The second part of the poem is a more direct apostrophe to Whitman, and here Crane affirms his own personal participation in the older poet's emotion and pledges allegiance to his belief in immortality:

> The stars have grooved our eyes with old persuasions
> Of love and hatred, birth, — surcease of nations . . .
> But who has held the heights more sure than thou,
> O Walt! — Ascensions of thee hover in me now
> As thou at junctions elegiac, there, of speed
> With vast eternity, dost wield the rebound seed!
> The competent loam, the probable grass, — travail
> Of tides awash the pedestal of Everest, fail
> Not less than thou in pure impulse inbred
> To answer deepest soundings! O, upward from the
>   dead
> Thou bringest tally, and a pact, new bound,
> Of living brotherhood!
>   Thou, there beyond —
> Glacial sierras and the flight of ravens,
> Hermetically past condor zones, through zenith havens
> Past where the albatross has offered up
> His last wing-pulse, and downcast as a cup
> That's drained, is shivered back to earth — thy wand
> Has beat a song, O Walt, — there and beyond!

Reading his destiny in the stars, man has been used to believe in a fate that he must succumb to and that he was unable to influence. Whitman erected a faith in the unlimited possibilities of the soul and in eternal life, and from the heights of his vision he was able to survey the whole of existence, the continuous motion and flow of all things toward a spiritual fulfillment. Invoking Whitman in a manner similar to the traditional invocations of the muse, Crane feels the «ascensions» of his genius working in himself. Dwelling in eternity, the older poet now occupies «junctions elegiac,» but through his inspiring example he still wields the seeds of the vision which has rebounded, returned to his disciple.[65] Conforming to the tradition, Crane celebrates the loam and grass of the earth because they still embody answers to the deepest soundings of the visionary imagination. The grass is evidence of a superior design, and so is the evolution of the earth, suggested by a new instance of the geological vision of the opening, the Asian continent (Everest) emerging from the primeval sea. The grass image suggests its function as a symbol of divine design in «Song of Myself.»

Crane proclaims a brotherhood pact between himself and his master and then goes on to develop a variation on the archetypal pattern of Whitman's imagination, the voyage toward infinity. In «Song of Myself» he writes: «I tramp a perpetual journey» and describes, in terms echoed by Crane, the flight of his spirit high above the Earth: «My ties and ballasts leave me, my elbows rest in sea-gaps,/ I skirt *sierras,* my palms cover continents,/ I am afoot with my vision.»[66] (My italics).

Crane paraphrases this journey in terms of birdflight carrying the soul into successively remoter areas. Rising higher than a raven can fly, it passes beyond the realms of the condor. It even goes beyond the last wing-beats of the albatross, a bird always found in the remotest parts of the oceans. This bird has become a literary symbol of strangeness and remoteness, for example, in works like Coleridge's *The Rime of the Ancient Mariner,* Richard Dana's *Two Years before the Mast,* and Melville's *Moby Dick.* It generally suggests the boundaries of earthly existence and the transition to eternity.

Whitman's spiritual journey goes beyond all boundaries; it is the song of the open road and is less concerned with the goal than with the journey itself as such. As long as the voyage continues, one can rest assured that the end will be a good and worthwhile one. As he expresses it in «Passage to India,» it is safe to «steer for the deep waters only,» for they are all «the seas of God.» This emphasis on faith, daring and movement is conveyed by Crane through the repetition of the word «beyond.»

Standing on the Cape, Crane calls it «the ghoul-mound of man's perversity,» referring to the destructive use of the airplane. He addresses Whitman as the great «Mourner» of wars from «Appomattox» to «Somme.» He was the one whose faith was strong enough to survive confrontation with the worst kind of suffering and evil. From the recurring speculations on war and destruction, the poet then shifts to a beautiful, nostalgic praise of the pastoral American nature that he experienced as he for the first time let himself be guided by Whitman's vision: «Cowslip and shad-blow, flaked like tethered foam/ Around bared teeth of stallions, bloomed that spring/ When first I read thy lines.» The closest parallel to this passage is the description of virgin nature in «The Dance.» Crane is recreating man's first, pristine experience of his natural environment, when everything was fresh and alive and he himself felt completely part of it. The Indian quest led to Pocahontas, and Whitman's lines reveal the divine beauty of the «loam of prairies.» The color blue or violet links both with the Virgin and Pocahontas, and the «Pontiac rose» links with the rose of Atlantis in «Cutty Sark» and «Atlantis.» A panoramic sense of the whole of the continent is evoked: the prairies, the mountain ranges, the forests, the rivers and valleys, the great sequoia trees of the west and the snows of Alaska.

Approached in this way the details of the landscape embody a revelation of the spiritual principle that links everything into a harmonious whole, and the poet celebrates his nature in a language worthy of Whitman. Crane envisages the landscape in such a way that nature becomes his temple of the universal spirit. The thunder speaks through the «arcades» of the forest, and «trumpets,» suggesting angelic presences, sound from each small grass tuft. With the «gold» autumn the color of Cathay reappears, and in «crowning» the hill it indicates its divine source, referring back to the crown of Elohim in «Ave Maria.» Whitman's spirit is identical with the power of love, the prime mover and merger of all things into a unity. In «I am he that aches with love» this power is celebrated as the great unifier: «Does the earth gravitate? does not all matter, aching, attract all/ matter?/ So the body of me to all I meet or know.»[67]

From the «lover's cry» under the bridge to the hymn to love in «Atlantis,» the theme of love in various manifestations runs through *The Bridge*. In «Cape Hatteras» Crane focusses on Whitman's steady power, his «eyes tranquil with the blaze/ Of love's own diametric gaze.» However, in the great tradition of love Whitman is neither the «first, nor last» advocate, but his is the native voice that is near to Crane and that convinces him of the existence of a tradition that will last beyond himself. Whitman's vision of wholeness in love is both «familiar» and «evasive» as «dayspring's spreading arc.» The imagination's fluctuating rhythm between vision and darkness is made quite explicit, and the bridge symbol, fused as it is with the light of dawn, is invoked. It suggests the revelation of total fusion and coherence through the universal power of love:

Our Meistersinger, thou set breath in steel;
And it was thou who on the boldest heel
Stood up and flung the span on even wing
Of that great Bridge, our Myth, whereof I sing!

The bridge of love creates the mystic sense of «the Whole,» and it works in the non-human world as well as among men. A universal brotherhood, writes Whitman in *Democratic Vistas,* is «the old dream of earth,» and he goes on to say: «Not that half only, individualism, which isolates. There is another half, which is adhesiveness or love, that fuses, ties and aggregates, making the races comrades, and fraternizing all. Both are to be vitalized by religion, (sole worthiest elevator of man or State,) breathing into the proud, material tissues, the breath of life. For I say at the core of democracy, finally, is the religious element.»[68] The «breath of life» in the material tissues corresponds to Crane's «breath in steel.»

Crane then invokes the poem «Years of the Modern,» a vision of the future America and the world which is to see the fulfillment of democracy and the technical progress and interlinking of all lands under American leadership. Whitman had the ability to appreciate science and technology without subordinating everything else to them and always ranking the life of the soul first. In «Song of the Universal» he writes: «Yet again, lo! the soul, above all science,/ For it has history gather'd like husks around the globe,/ For it the entire star-myriads roll through the sky.»[69] This passage is paraphrased in «Cape Hatteras:»

                                        O, something
    green,
Beyond all sesames of science was thy choice
Wherewith to bind us throbbing with one voice,
New integers of Roman, Viking, Celt —
Thou, Vedic Caesar, to the greensward knelt!

America, the land that fuses all peoples and all creeds, is in itself the supreme bridge that will unite all the different spiritual traditions of the history of mankind into «one voice,» the «One Song» of «Atlantis.» Something green lies beyond all science, the color suggests rebirth, eternal life. Standing on the foundations of mankind's older beliefs, Whitman built new «integers,» syntheses of faith suited to the American reality.

In a final affirmation of the airplane, Crane is able to see it as a Whitmanian symbol of the open road and accept its flight as something ultimately meaningful and benevolent. The lines now reach the desirable mythopoeic intensity: «And now, as launched in abysmal cupolas of space,/ Toward endless terminals, Easters of speeding light —/ Vast engines outward veering with seraphic grace . . .» The flight of Icarus is maintained, as it were, and the final fall does not occur. In this high vision the speeding planes elevate, really and symbolically, man's mind to the level of consciousness suggested by the concept of the open road, this «span» or bridge that fuses all into a whole and directs the soul to its ultimate goal.

At the end of «Cape Hatteras,» the rainbow appears in the sky over the Cape, the «ghoul-mound» that has seen the invention of the supreme instrument of destruction as well as spiritual expansion, the airplane. The rainbow is a natural symbol of the Whitmanian vision, it describes the arching curve of wholeness of the bridge:

And see! the rainbow's arch — how shimmeringly stands
Above the Cape's ghoul-mound, O joyous seer!
. . .

Yes, Walt,
Afoot again, and onward without halt, —
Not soon, nor suddenly, — No, never to let go
    My hand
     in yours,
      Walt Whitman —
       so—

Crane pledges his allegiance by invoking the poem «Whoever you are holding me now in hand,» in which Whitman makes clear that any disciple of his will have to go his own way. He describes his own poetry as a mere hint toward a direction that his followers must find for themselves, and asserts that he cannot even define this direction:

> For it is not for what I have put into it that I have
>   written this book,
> Nor is it by reading it you will acquire it,
>   . . .
> For all is useless without that which you may guess at
>   many times and not hit, that which I hinted at;
> Therefore release me and depart on your way.[70]

Whitman completely liberates his heirs, he states that the trend that he follows cannot be communicated by him, only experienced anew from generation to generation and individual to individual. Only by adhering to this paradox can the true followers of Whitman emerge, and by concluding «Cape Hatteras» with this reference Crane may have wanted to suggest that his profound allegiance was based on independence.

Whitman's vision can be reclaimed, not by passive disciples, but by new creative geniuses, and therefore he is a perpetual challenge, not a static model. This same view was strongly advocated by Frank in his «A Letter to the Annual Whitman Celebration:» «I say that a mere passive love of Whitman is not enough. We must work very hard and very deep upon the message of Whitman and upon its application to ourselves, if he is indeed to become our cultural possession.»[71]

6. Three Songs

The transition from «Cape Hatteras» to «Three Songs» seems somewhat abrupt to begin with, but in the larger context of *The Bridge* the reasons for the inclusion of this section become clear. The journey into the past of part one of *The Bridge* returns to its starting point, the Brooklyn bridge from which the poet sees his phantom clipper regatta. In part two the direction of his quest is into his own reality, and he launches forth, equipped with the visions of the past and pledges his allegiance to Whitman's consciousness of cosmic wholeness and love in «Cape Hatteras.» Like Whitman Crane wants to go beyond individual, romantic love to a realization of love as a universal force. Love of woman becomes love of a feminine principle, a goddess who manifests herself either as the heavenly Virgin Mary or the virgin earth-mother Pocahontas.

The bridge symbol functions everywhere in the text: Mary is the bridge between man and god, Pocahontas bridges the gap between the white man and the Indian, and Whitman, holding the poet's hand, is his bridge to the experience of infinity. Having tested the Whitmanian vision against his contemporary world, the poet seeks to recapture the Mary-Pocahontas of love and mythic unity of being in the modern world of «Three Songs.» The starting-point here is that of sexual love, which is depicted in the whole range of its aspects as indicated by the significant sequence in which Eve, Magdalene and Mary are named in «Southern Cross.» The love theme of the three songs is suggested by the epigraph from Marlowe's *Hero and Leander,* whose main subject is the universal power of love. The beautiful Hero dwelt in Sestos, and across the Hellespont Leander lived and pined for his beloved. His dramatic swimming across the Hellespont to join her is a symbolic bridge of love corresponding to the bridge across the East River. The epigraph is from the first sestiad of the poem:

> On Hellespont, guilty of true love's blood,
> In view and opposite two cities stood,
> Sea borderers, disjoin'd by Neptune's might;
> The one Abydos, the other Sestos hight.[72]

Again it is an image of the past that haunts Crane, and in the poems of «Three Songs» he measures a love such as that of Hero and Leander against his own realization of woman, the modern versions of Eve, Magdalene and Mary. The fallen Eve is the first woman, and the love for her becomes degraded to the pursuit of pure lust in Magdalene, the harlot who appears as a burlesque dancer in «National Winter Garden.» As mother of Jesus, Mary represents love of the pure and universal kind, and a hope for its continued possibility is raised in the last song, «Virginia,» in which a modern Mary emerges.

The three songs describe the curve of the imagination from the middle to the nether world and up again toward the higher regions, and this pattern is repeated on a larger scale in the final three sections of *The Bridge.* «Southern Cross» corresponds to the quotidian, middle level of «Quaker Hill,» «National Winter Garden» foreshadows the descent into the underworld of «The Tunnel,» and the higher aspirations of «Virginia» reach full orchestration in the massive chorus of «Atlantis.»

In this poem we are at sea again; the poet voyages through southern waters towards his home in the north. We may recall that «Three Songs» was written during a sojourn on the Isle of Pines. The poet meditates on a sunset on the ocean, searching for a revelation of the ideal female principle in nature. At this point, the woman images of the preceding sections have disintegrated, only a diffuse search for some female manifestation remains. It is both a principle and a living, physical woman, not a «Wraith,» that is sought after. The sun, a slowly sinking fire, is setting, the stars of the Southern Cross are emerging, and night is released. This is conceived as a process of denudation in which the «girdles» of daylight that keep night in place are removed. The night sky is associated with the Mary of «Ave Maria,» in which it appears as her «mantle's ageless blue.» The denudation of night has faintly sexual overtones here, as the night-woman is relieved of her «girdles.»[73] The fire of the sun leaves «scars» in the sky, and this image of injury and wounds contrasts with the beauty of the sunset that occurs in «Ave Maria» and creates a «modulated fire.»

The poet has lost the grasp he had of Mary in the Columbus section and of Pocahontas in «The Dance,» and he is unable to establish contact with this woman of the south, his modern goddess of beauty and universal love. His call for her remains unanswered:

Whatever call — falls vainly on the wave,
O simian Venus, homeless Eve,
Unwedded, stumbling gardenless to grieve
Windswept guitars on lonely decks forever;
Finally to answer all within one grave!

The figures of Venus and Eve blend into a female persona who is both love goddess and mother of the race, Venus Genitrix. But this Eve cannot be rediscovered in apotheosized form, in the stars, like Mary, and the deprivation of vision calls forth, as always, despair and grief. The homeless and gardenless Eve recalls the fall of man, «Adam's answer in the forest» in «Cape Hatteras.» Since the fall, both Adam and Eve, man and woman, have been condemned to grieve forever, separated from god in nature.[74] The word «simian» suggests the ugliness of a world without spiritual coherence, as in «Recitative,» where «darkness, like an ape's face, falls away./ And gradually white buildings answer day.»

In the barren world of «Southern Cross,» the tread of God's feet is no longer apprehensible, but the pattern of His movement re-emerges in hellish caricature. Columbus saw the «orbic wake» and heard the «sounding heel» of Elohim, but no such revelation appears in the wake of the ship that carried the poet toward the north:

And this long wake of phosphor,
                                    iridescent
Furrow of all our travel — trailed derision!
Eyes crumble at its kiss. Its long-drawn spell
Incites a yell. Slid on that backward vision
The mind is churned to spittle, whispering hell.

The characteristic feature of demonic inversion in *The Bridge* is the pulling down of the ideal figures, images and patterns to a lower level. The wake of heaven becomes that of the sea, the phosphor of the morning star gleams in the water, which is iridescent like a rainbow. Even the basic theme of the voyage toward God emerges as movement without meaning, inviting derision. Focussed on this wake the eyes «crumble» and go blind.

Though it is reversed, it is a vision we are dealing with here too; the nether realms of Crane's poetic world that reside in the shadow of the bridge's span. The self has entered its own infernal regions and swirls or «churns» around within them. The mind is its own hell, an idea which is restated forcefully in «The Tunnel,» in which the poet speaks of «the chasms of the brain» and states that «The phonographs of hades in the brain/ Are tunnels that re-wind themselves.» This inferno-imagery reminds one of that of Dante, in whose «Inferno» the souls of some of the damned are driven around in eternally flying circles or spirals. Such sinister gyrations abound in the second part of *The Bridge,* in which the demonic, godless powers rally themselves more strongly than in the first part, where the burlesque is comparatively light, as in «The River,» or jocose, as in «Cutty Sark.»

It may be helpful at this point to draw on Northrop Frye's categorizations of the archetypal organization of the literary universe. One important distinction which he makes is the one between the apocalyptic and demonic realms. In the former there may be a divine order, represented by One God, a human world, represented by an archetypal man, and a vegetable world, the ideal manifestation of which is the One Tree of Life. In opposition to this stands the demonic world, which is equally real to the imagination but rejected and abhorred by man. The most typical religious and literary instances of these opposites or antinomies are the Biblical Heaven and Hell and Dante's Paradiso and Inferno. What makes the demonic realm particularly repulsive is that it resembles its counterpart as far as formal patterns and arrangements go. Heavenly love becomes perversion or prostitution and the circle of saints is transformed into the spiralling, driven souls of sinners in hell.[75]

«Southern Cross» is the first poem in *The Bridge* whose main emphasis is on division and alienation instead of bridging and unification; its nether world of despair signals the more extensive laments on twentieth-century conditions that are to follow. The search for revelation remains unrewarded, the stars yield no answer, and the poet finds himself set apart from them. He is like the Adam of «Cape Hatteras,» whose Hesperus is perceived in the water, the «lucid pool.» But he remembers his vision of Mary and Elohim, and the Southern Cross evokes the fierce longing for a sense of mythic union that the poet feels even in his isolation. The starry cross glows in the sky, and the response of the protagonist is vaguely and tentatively mythopoeic; the divinity he seeks has no name. And yet, in his «blood» the impulse lurks and the fiery words of vision are still on his lips. The word «stammer» suggests struggle, and this battle to articulate insight is also indicated in the following line from «Atlantis,» in which both sight and speech, image and word, are referred to: «Eyes stammer through the pangs of dust and steel.» The woman image that finally emerges and asserts itself in «Southern Cross» is that of Eve, who is a semi-mythological figure in the Western tradition. In his version of her creation Crane envisages a female figure who carries several associations:

All night the water combed you with black
Insolence. You crept out simmering, accomplished.
Water rattled that singing coil, your
Rehearsed hair — docile, alas, from many arms.
Yes, Eve — wraith of my unloved seed!
The Cross, a phantom, buckled — dropped below the dawn.
Light drowned the lithic trillions of your spawn.

The woman ascends from out of the ocean, and the myth of the birth of Aphrodite is suggested, the «lounged goddess» of «Voyages.» But the situation has a different coloring, the woman of «Southern Cross» reminds us of Medusa rather than Venus, her hair being compared to coiling snakes. The hair-serpent image suggests that she is a low version of Pocahontas, who had time like a serpent down her shoulder. She was virgin to the last of men, whereas Eve is nothing but a female animal, handled by many arms. She has none of the mythic proportions of Pocahontas and cannot inspire any earth-mother vision. The poet has a sensual perception of the «red flesh» of Pocahontas, the earth, but Eve, woman of flesh and blood, remains a ghost, a «wraith» to him. The coming dawn causes the vision of Eve and her progeny, «spawn,» to disappear, and the starry cross also fades. This «spawn» has a double meaning. It refers both to the innumerable stars that disappear in the morning, and to the human race, or man, who is spiritually drowned, inert as a stone.[76] The implication is that the Christian faith, of which the cross is the symbol, is losing its power in our time, which will see the dawn of the new faith, articulated more strongly in the visionary passages of *The Bridge*.[77]

National Winter Garden

This poem continues to explore the possibility of union through woman, and the image of the fallen woman that was suggested by the figures of Eve and Venus in «Southern Cross» is fully developed into the harlot and burlesque dancer who is the protagonist of «National Winter Garden.» The modern «Magdalene» of this poem is a true caricature of Pocahontas, the virgin earth-mother. The lyrically pure, erotic attraction that she had for the poet throughout «Powhatan's Daughter» has vanished; of the individual love that ideally leads to a sense of universal union, only the most elemental phase, animal lust, remains.[78] Like Pocahontas, the dancer invites pursuit, but nothing except lust can be satisfied through her. She is the embodiment of the provocation and frustration that go with the dedication to mere sensual pleasures that do not lead beyond themselves.

The «sweating cinch,» referring to the band around the waist of the woman, is a caricature of the holy circle that symbolizes unity of being. It also points forward to «the final ring,» another demonic image, that appears in the third stanza. The movements of the dancer also suggest the act of intercourse, a basic symbol of fusion, union, and we have a sexual burlesque on the bridge symbol itself. The dancer is primarily a caricature of Pocahontas, and the flying hair, one of her chief attributes, becomes the peroxide attribute of the blonde prostitutes that let themselves be picked up in the smoky room. The smoke invokes the world of «The Dance,» in which it swirls from tepees through the forest, signalling or introducing the ritual dance of Maquokeeta. A dance is also begun in the smoky theatre, but instead of being accompanied by sacred drums, a «tom-tom scrimmage» attends on the vulgar performance. The harlot frustrates the desire she awakens — by its very nature the desire for her is one that cannot be satisfied.

«National Winter Gardern» stages a complete burlesque on the dance and metamorphosis of Maquokeeta, which united the protagonist with Pocahontas. Hers is the image that is half visible behind the gaudiness and lewd spasm of the dancer:

And shall we call her whiter than the snow?
Sprayed first with ruby, then with emerald sheen —
Least tearful and least glad (who knows her smile?)
A caught slide shows her sandstone grey between.

Recalling the whiteness of the «glacier woman,» the poet ironically contrasts her with the tawdry and heavily made-up dancer with her sham jewelry and decorations, cheap echoes of the gem images associated with the Cathay motif. The colors, the red of ruby and the green of emerald, are suggestive of exotic eroticism and also hark back to the «red flesh» of Pocahontas. Throughout «Powhatan's Daughter» the poet was led on by the avatars of her smile, having some concept of her identity, but the harlot-dancer is expressionless, showing neither tears nor laughter. The contrast between faked glory and sordid reality is very insistent throughout the poem. The burlesque queen promises much and gives nothing; in her the emblems of harmonious movement and unity of being have become the bizarre and barren gestures of the mimicry of lust. The dancer, of course, has no vision; her energy, like that of the «armatures» of the powerhouse in «Cape Hatteras,» is purposeless and isolated, represented by pearls swinging around her hips. The upward moving spiral appears in the rings that shake and move around her arms, but real gold and silver has been replaced by «tinsel,» cheap imitations of precious metals. This is indeed a «metallic paradise» of the kind that is described in the second part of «For the Marriage of Faustus and Helen.»

The image of Pocahontas blends here with that of Shakespeare's Cleopatra. Both are associated with snakes, the emblem of Pocahontas includes both serpent and eagle, and the «snake rings» of the harlot reflect both the Pocahontas image and the circle of «the Whole,» of unity of being. Cleopatra is an exotic and lustful female character who fits in quite well as a background figure in this poem. In *Antony and Cleopatra* she is described more than once in terms of a snake and calls herself the «serpent of old Nile.» (I, V, 25).[79]

As the dancer reaches the climax of her performance, the writhing body sinks to the floor in an imitation of the ecstasy of sexual union:

We wait that writhing pool, her pearls collapsed,
— All but her belly buried in the floor;
And the lewd trounce of a final muted beat!
We flee her spasm through a fleshless door . . .

Yet, to the empty trapeze of your flesh,
O Magdalene, each comes back to die alone.
Then you, the burlesque of our lust — and faith,
Lug us back lifeward — bone by infant bone.

The serpent image is sustained implicitly in her writhing movements, and her gestures, not portraying real passion, become lewd as she stretches herself out in a spasm before the final collapse, which is accompanied by a drum beat. The climax of Maquokeeta's dance is the union between himself and Pocahontas, but the burlesque dancer, though she promises union, in effect creates a feeling of utter isolation. The spectators flee her at the crucial moment, instead of bridging and wholeness we get division and separateness.

But man is compelled to copulate, an act which Crane sees as both a death and rebirth. Maquokeeta died when being united with Pocahontas and was reborn into immortality, but to Magdalene «each comes back to die alone.» Lust without faith has no meaning beyond the mere spending of a certain amount of energy. Magdalene's body is an «empty trapeze,» a metaphor of the mechanical act of coition. The swinging trapeze may draw an invisible curve which is like that of the bridge, but its meaning is isolation, not fusion. The figure of Magdalene is a travesty of lust itself because her act is mere imitation of passion, and she also mocks the faith in womanhood as a general principle of the universal order represented by Mary and Pocahontas. The desire for her does not point beyond itself, but it does direct man «lifeward» in the sense that the reproduction of the race is secured.[80] The «bone» refers both to the male organ and the formation of the bones of the foetus. Thus, the last line emphasizes the power of sexuality and fertility and may be said to suggest a renewal of hope that points toward the bright atmosphere of the last of the three songs. As John R. Willingham says: «No matter how degraded the sexual function of woman has become, its vast possibilities for religious knowledge are still present; woman requires only a man who approaches her with his lust purified into love.»[81]

Virginia

This is the shortest and slenderest of all the poems of *The Bridge* and may seem trifling and insignificant when compared to some of the grander sections. And yet its function within the whole is an important one and also one which is in keeping with its fragile and almost hesitant texture and rhythm. Crane has provided the clue to the essential meaning of the poem in a letter to Frank of August 12, 1926, in which he explains the title «Virginia» as «(virgin in process of 'being built').» Having envisaged a medieval Mary in «Ave Maria» and a virgin earth-goddess in «Powhatan's Daughter,» the poet faces the challenge of religious revelation anew by seeking to translate the figure of the heavenly virgin of pure love into modern and American terms. Again, he finds himself in the Whitmanian situation, employing the 'apocalyptic method' of religious revelation that Waldo Frank had defined as the method of American art in *The Re-Discovery of America*.

The uncollected poem «To Liberty» also deals with the theme of «building» a Virgin figure directly from experience, and Brom Weber maintains that this poem may have been the original version of «Virginia.» However that may be, the two poems are obviously closely related in their treatment of the theme of poetic recreation of a religious tradition originating in a non-American culture:

Out of the seagull cries and wind
On this strange shore I build
The virgin. They laugh to hear
How I endow her, standing
Hair mocked by the sea, her lover
A dead sailor that knew
Not even Helen's fame.

Light the last torch in the wall,
The sea wall. Bring her no robes yet.
They have not seen her in this harbor.[82]

In «Virginia» the scene is that of the skyscrapers of lower Manhattan; in «To Liberty» it is the familiar picture of New York harbor which is invoked. The female figure here is suggestive not only of the Virgin Mary, but of the goddess of liberty. In both cases the last line is a satirical comment on people in America, who have no knowledge of either of the two principles represented by these figures. Crane's *alter ego,* the drowned sailor, appears again here. He is the visionary in America, deprived of mythic traditions, here symbolized by Helen of Troy.

The «strange shore» is America, the new world where the poet has to be a prophet as well and bring the image of the goddess to the people, who ridicule him, being unreceptive like the «multitudes» of the proem. As in «Virginia» she is only vaguely and tentatively realized, her «robe,» Mary's mantle, still lacking. However, in «Virginia» she is not a chimera of seagull cries and wind, but a flesh-and-blood secretary in a downtown Manhattan skyscraper, presumably the Woolworth tower, which Crane refers to in one of his lyrical prose descriptions of the New York skyline and harbor in a letter of May 11, 1924, to his mother.

After the disillusioned portrayal of lust in «National Winter Garden,» an attempt is made to rediscover the principle of pure, virginal love in the person of a young woman working in her office. She is addressed by a protagonist who appears to be her young lover, and the whole tone of the verse is light and romantically hopeful:

O rain at seven,
Pay-check at eleven —
Keep smiling the boss away,
Mary (what are you going to do?)
Gone seven — gone eleven,
And I'm still waiting you

O blue-eyed Mary with the claret scarf,
Saturday Mary, mine!

The foremost quality of the blessed Virgin of the Catholic tradition is chastity, and this girl repulses the sexual advances of her employer by «smiling» him away. The smile typifies the mother in «Van Winkle» and Pocahontas throughout the rest of «Powhatan's Daughter;» it signifies the higher universal love that the burlesque dancer denies. Color is another attribute that is employed in the «building» of the Virgin — the blue of her eyes corresponds to the blue of Mary's mantle and is also associated with Pocahontas. The «claret» of her scarf recalls the fire imagery of «Ave Maria» and «The Dance.» The setting is also significant. The office girl stands at the window of a high tower and is observed and addressed from below. It is suggested that the love of this woman is of a higher, more satisfying nature. The office skyscraper is becoming transformed into the bell-tower of a cathedral, «popcorn bells» functioning as «Carillon.» Such a tower and the music of its bells are symbols of poetry as insight into the essence of spiritual love. It is part of Crane's method to seek spiritual beauty in the materials of modern America, including skyscrapers. «Virginia,» then, is not a satire on «the false brightness of the city routine» and «the absurdities of ornamental architecture.»[83]

In his last poem, the powerful «The Broken Tower,» as well as in «Virginia,» Crane suggests a Catholic Christian frame of reference; the tower of the former poem belonging to a certain church in Mexico. Launched before dawn, the sound of its bells, «antiphonal carillon,» spreads across the world, announcing the presence of divine love and harmony, and the poet pledges allegiance to this principle, at the same time revealing the non-dogmatic, profoundly personal basis of his commitment:

The bells, I say, the bells break down their tower;
And swing I know not where . . .

And so it was I entered the broken world
To trace the visionary company of love, its voice
An instant in the wind (I know not whither hurled)
But not for long to hold each desperate choice.

Love is the unifying power that can redeem the «broken world,» an idea that was put forth in «Cape Hatteras,» but the poet remains uncertain about it, realizing perhaps even more clearly here than in *The Bridge* that his belief in love is dependent on momentary inspirations. He goes on to speculate on whether his poetry, his «word,» has its ultimate source or fountainhead in a male god, the «tribunal monarch of the air,» or in the Virgin Mary, «she/ Whose sweet mortality stirs latent power.»

In «The Broken Tower» the tone is more passionate and solemn than in «Virginia,» in which the poetic quest is rendered in singularly lighthearted verse. The poem has none of the climactic intensity of «Ave Maria,» «The Dance» and «Atlantis,» nor is it grotesque or demonic like «National Winter Garden» or «The Tunnel.» Its atmosphere of freshness and anticipation reminds one most strongly of «Van Winkle,» the poem that introduces the journey toward Pocahontas. «Virginia» aspires to portraying a rebirth in the city, the center of the modern world, of the female, virginal element required in a complete synthesis of America. Spring is the season of rebirth, and the pigeons that fill the streets and the air invoke the familiar image of winged flight, emblem of hopefulness and the uplift of the spirit. The upturned gaze and the sense of height which culminate in «Atlantis» are emphasized again in the exhortation to the American Mary to let down her «golden hair» from her high tower.

In «The Harbor Dawn» and «The Dance,» Pocahontas' hair is a symbol of fertility and vegetation. The golden hair of Mary, on the other hand, has somewhat different connotations. Gold is the color of Cathay-Eldorado, cf. «Indiana,» and it symbolizes spirituality, revelation from above on a plane different from the dryadic and earthly figure of Pocahontas. For the modern Mary to let down her golden hair would be like a ray of light from the godhead shining down into the city street; the situation recalls the descent of the bridge in the last stanza of the proem, the outstretched hand of fire in «Ave Maria», and the rainbow's arch over Cape Hatteras in the poem by that name.

In the third section of «Faustus and Helen,» golden hair is attributed to the girl in the streetcar who is the modern avatar of Helen of Troy in much the same way as the office girl of «Virginia» is an embodiment of the Virgin. This Helen is the symbol of the elevated and spiritual beauty that the poet believes in and pledges to seek or «drill» out from the midst of the chaos that surrounds him:

> Laugh out the meager penance of their days
> Who dare not share with us the breath released,
> The substance drilled and spent beyond repair
> For golden, or the shadow of gold hair.

The poet's indifference toward the blind «multitudes» has here become active scorn of the timidity of people at large who are enslaved by a mechanical, routine existence in the city and never come near the poetic vision suggested by the «golden hair.»

The final stanza of «Virginia» repeats the imagery of flowers and verdant spring in the American wilderness that runs through *The Bridge* from the «*Catskill daisy chain*» of «Van Winkle» to the pursuit of Pocahontas as dryad into the savage beauty of the «Appalachian Spring» of «The Dance» and the mountain spring of «Cape Hatteras.» The flowers behind windows and on cornices in Manhattan are not intended as burlesque on the pastoral American nature, but reinforce the bright and hopeful tone of «Virginia» and suggest reconciliation between nature and the city:

> High in the noon of May
> On cornices of daffodils
> The slender violets stray.
> Crap-shooting gangs in Bleecker reign
> Peonies with pony manes —
> Forget-me-nots at windowpanes:

> Out of the way-up nickel-dime tower shine
> > Cathedral Mary,
> > > shine! —

In this arrangement of flowers, the violet stands out because of its symbolic value. Its color blue associates it with Mary's mantle, but also with the Pocahontas figure as it appears in «the violet wedge of Adirondacks» in «The Dance» and the «violet haze» of the eyes of the squaw in «Indiana.» The ramifications of the use of the color blue seem to indicate that Pocahontas and the Virgin Mary are not kept completely apart in *The Bridge* as separate figures; they blend into each other to a certain extent.

In keeping with its light, jocose tone the texture of «Virginia» mixes the lyrical and the quotidian, and the probing for a vision of the goddess does not exclude observations of «crap-shooting gangs» in the streets. In its attitude to the city and its people this poem seems both realistic and hopeful and presents a balanced outlook not encountered very frequently in *The Bridge*. The apotheosis with which the poem concludes is different from the devotional and impassioned incantations at the end of some of the other sections. The call for revelation is a sanguine wish and a modest prayer that the light of a superhuman dimension of love may issue forth from the woman in the tower, now become «cathedral Mary.»

7. Quaker Hill

This poem is not mentioned in the notes to *The Bridge* provided in the letter to Kahn of September 12, 1927, and it appears to have been conceived and written at a later date than any of the other sections. Crane first mentioned it in a letter to Caresse Crosby of September 6, 1929, at the time when *The Bridge* was already going to press. On December 26 the same year he sent the final version to Mrs. Crosby with a letter that plainly shows that he was feeling great outside pressure to finish the poem and that he might have preferred to work more on it if permitted by circumstance: «I am hastily enclosing the final version of 'Quaker Hill,' which ends my writing on *The Bridge*. You can now go ahead and finish it all. I've been slow, Heaven knows, but I know that you will forgive me. I haven't added as many verses to what you took with you as I had expected. I had several more, roughly, in notes, but think that my present condensation is preferable. 'Quaker Hill' is not, after all, one of the major sections of the poem; it is rather by way of an 'accent mark' that it is valuable at all.»

From time to time Crane wrote in the letters that *The Bridge* as a whole was a failure or was out of place in time and environment, but he usually showed a firm belief in the poetic value of each individual section. «Quaker Hill» is the only poem that he was really apologetic about, and the reason probably was that he was prevented from giving it the same amount of prolonged thought and revision that most of the other sections of its scope and length had received. According to Philip Horton, it was «completed in a rage of disappointment.»[84]

Crane's characterization of the poem as an «accent mark» is very apt. «Quaker Hill» is less of an independent and self-contained lyrical incantation than, for example, the proem, «Ave Maria» and «Atlantis;» it is expository, polemic and autobiographical to an extent which makes it clearly exceptional. Its closest parallel is «The River,» particularly that part of it which precedes the final dithyramb to the Mississippi. The two poems also have a common theme insofar as they contain a criticism of the American people, the tramps or lower classes in «The River» and the businessmen and speculators in «Quaker Hill.» The latter come off worse than the former; they lack the knowledge of Pocahontas which is the redeeming trait of the hoboes.

«Quaker Hill» accentuates and develops more fully the satire on contemporary conditions that was begun in «The River» and carried on in «Cutty Sark» and, with more emphasis, in «National Winter Garden.» Owing to its discursive texture «Quaker Hill» is more directly satirical than demonic or burlesque, it juxtaposes the ideal promises of the past and the dissatisfying present in a very overt manner which is untypical of Crane. The worksheets of the various sections of *The Bridge* nearly always show a tendency to condensation and toughening of the verse; what was a simple idea becomes complex poetic language. The few work-sheets that exist of «Quaker Hill» demonstrate that this process was under way with regard to this poem too, and the lack of time must account for the prosaic and lamely argumentative quality of parts of the poem.[85]

The first of the two epigraphs of the section is a statement by Isadora Duncan: «I see only the ideal. But no ideals have ever been fully successful on this earth.» In a letter to Isidor Schneider, March 28, 1928, Crane mentions having read a book by the dancer, in all likelihood her autobiography, *My Life.* The epigraph suits the theme of this poem, which holds the ideal America up against modern New England.

Isadora Duncan was a favorite of both Waldo Frank and Crane, and they saw in her art a genuine and wholehearted commitment to beauty. In *The Re-Discovery of America,* Frank claims that «With the exception of Isadora Duncan, America has yet to produce a woman artist sufficiently free of the inferiorities which American life has put upon her sex, to create a fully liberated plastic work.»[86] Duncan's dance was one of the more decisive experiences of the young Crane, and her total devotion to her art and to beauty was part of the inspiration behind «Faustus and Helen.» After attending one of her performances in Cleveland, Crane wrote about it to Gorham Munson, December 12, 1922: «It was glorious beyond words, and sad beyond words too, from the rude and careless reception she got here. It was like a wave of life, a flaming gale that passed over the heads of the nine thousand in the audience without evoking response other than silence and some maddening cat-calls.» Crane was engaged in the composition of «Faustus and Helen» both during 1922 and 1923, and this poem shows the same worship of beauty and indignation at the stupidity of the masses that is evident in the words about Isadora Duncan. When writing «Quaker Hill» years later, the poet was overtaken by the same mood of disgust at the vulgarity of modern man that he had felt so strongly that night in Cleveland.

Since «Quaker Hill» is comparatively personal and seems to be tied to certain experiences of the poet, it may be useful to keep in mind that in it Crane is referring to people, mostly visitors and property owners from the cities, whom he observed in the New York and Connecticut countryside near Patterson, New York, where he lived, first with his friend Slater Brown during the summer of 1925 and later with Allen Tate in the winter and spring of 1926. The house that he shared with the Tates was located in the hills along the border between New York and Connecticut.

The poem opens with a description of the cows that graze near the home in the countryside:

Perspective never withers from their eyes:
They keep that docile edict of the Spring
That blends March with August Antarctic skies:
These are but cows that see no other thing
Than grass and snow, and their own inner being
Through the rich halo that they do not trouble
Even to cast upon the seasons fleeting
Though they should thin and die on last year's stubble.

And they are awkward, ponderous and uncoy . . .
While we who press the cider mill, regarding them —
We, who with pledges taste the bright annoy
Of friendship's acid wine, retarding phlegm,
Shifting reprisals ('til who shall tell us when
The jest is too sharp to be kindly?) boast
Much of our store of faith in other men
Who would, ourselves, stalk down the merriest ghost.

The animals, of course, have no vision of the ideal, they are docile and see no difference between skies of winter and fall. They do not see beyond the immediate grass or snow and are dependent on the «stubble» that the fields offer them. Later in the poem, in stanzas four, five and six, Crane criticizes the weekend visitors from the city, but in the opening stanza he is referring to cows, not the weekenders, as a number of critics have thought.[87]

Even in comparison with the cows, the poet and his friends, representatives of humanity, do not make the best use of their potential and are unable to preserve their friendship. Crane is here referring to the disharmony and hostility that occurred in spite of the good fellowship he and his friends enjoyed in the house of Slater Brown. The stay with the Tates took a highly unfortunate turn and a quarrel ensued which nearly ruined the friendship between Crane and Allen Tate.[88] The real irony of it is that those who regard the city people with scorn and believe themselves to have faith in man are the very same ones who are ready to «stalk down the merriest ghost,» meaning, one assumes, that they would let jealousy or enmity carry them to any length against their fellow men.

The poet then turns his attention toward the invaders from the city and the hotels and the golf courses that have made their inroads on the landscape. The name of the hotel, «Mizzentop,» also refers to certain topsails of sailing vessels, and forms an ironic contrast to the white sails of the proem, of «Ave Maria» and «Cutty Sark,» which are symbols of promise. The «palatial white» of the hotel may look splendid enough, but it is a sham glory, like the tinselled hands of the burlesque dancer in «National Winter Garden.» The description of the building progresses on an upward course toward the ceilings with their dormers, and the familiar pattern of ascension to a high point of vision is repeated. Height symbolizes the elevation of consciousness that accompanies the achievement of the vision of «the Whole» and that is exemplified in, for example, the gazing star of Quetzalcoatl in «The Dance» and the aeroplane pilot in «Cape Hatteras.» The image of the eye that gazes from above suggests the ideal, total vision; in the proem it belongs to the poet behind the window of a skyscraper, and the window image recurs again in «Quaker Hill,» metaphorically identified with the «dormer portholes» along the ceiling of the hotel.

But the window-eyes stare into a forgotten, ideal past, the «former faces» of a mythic, personified nature such as that of the Indian, and later in the poem the «slain Iroquois» are asked to be the poet's guide to the land. The «faces» invite comparison with the «smile» of mountain and earth as Pocahontas. The gleam of the window panes at sunset «crowns» the hillside on which the hotel stands, and we have another echo of beauty lost, the Adamic landscape of Whitman's America where «gold autumn . . . crowned the trembling hill» that occurs in «Cape Hatteras.» Seeing three states falls far short of the ideal aim of the consciousness, to achieve the vision of the whole continent and of reality as a whole. The golfers have the most limited kind of vision both spatially and figuratively; all they are concerned about is their «turf-won scores.» The game they play is in itself an insignificant preoccupation with a highly restricted kind of space and time, and it concentrates on petty measurements of the soil of Pocahontas. The leading idea, again, is that of isolation and disunity. By playing golf these people devote themselves to a soulless and mechanical activity that very effectively prevents them from feeling themselves to be parts of a larger nature or whole. American sport, wrote Waldo Frank, is «a combination cult of the machine and success.»[89] The golf game represents an imposition of the isolated will on reality and deprives man of the organic relationship with nature. The «death's stare» revealed to the poet suggests the sterility and the decay which accompany the mechanical regulations that man imposes on nature.

Man's perversion of the land takes several forms, and the worst violators are those for whom the earth is nothing but an object of trade. Against these and other speculators the poet directs his attack:

This was the Promised Land, and still it is
To the persuasive suburban land agent
In bootleg roadhouses where the gin fizz
Bubbles in time to Hollywood's new love-nest pageant.
Fresh from the radio in the old Meeting House
(Now the New Avalon Hotel) volcanoes roar
A welcome to highsteppers that no mouse
Who saw the Friends there ever heard before.

What cunning neighbors history has in fine!
The woodlouse mortgages the ancient deal
Table that Powitsky buys for only nine-
Ty-five at Adams' auction, eats the seal,
The spinster polish of antiquity . . .
Who holds the lease on time and on disgrace?
What eats the pattern with ubiquity?
Where are my kinsmen and the patriarch race?

Here Crane is referring to a noble American tradition that comes from a different historic source than Columbus' dream of Cathay; the belief of the colonial New Englanders who regarded America as the New Jerusalem where the true God revealed himself to his chosen people. Though he regarded the Puritan tradition as an anti-religious one, Waldo Frank also maintained that the first Puritans, led by Roger Williams and men like him, established a society that was a true spiritual whole. Speaking of «the mystic tradition,» Frank states that «it was the Puritan who made the tradition organic, by establishing it as the Law in their bleak towns. Prophets like John Cotton, Thomas Hooker, Ann Hutchinson, John Eliot, Roger Williams staked in the wilderness of New England little worlds where humankind might be one. Each in his faltering way worked toward unity of rule and service, of deed and prayer: visioned an America free of the divisions of Europe — an America dawn to bring the day.»[90] Crane was proud of his «Pilgrim Father» ancestry and felt that he could use the spiritual legacy of the early settlers as part of his cultural synthesis in *The Bridge*.[91] This does not mean, as R. W. Butterfield claims, that he suddenly, in «Quaker Hill,» became a «nostalgic, regional reactionary.»[92]

What united the early Puritans was their faith in a godhead who possessed a power of love vastly greater than man, and this is exactly where the modern Americans sin the most. Love, honesty and morality have been replaced by the exploitation of man by man, by the sham facades of a double standard and by the mimicry and perversion of love as performed by Hollywood's moviemakers. Their economic exploitation of man's need for love corresponds to the faked sensuality of the burlesque dancer of «National Winter Garden.» Universal love, as represented by the bridge symbol, by the Virgin Mary and Pocahontas and Whitman's vision, is denied and made a mockery of in«National Winter Garden» and the first half of «Quaker Hill,» but the love vision never leaves the poet completely. At the end of «Quaker Hill» his faith is reaffirmed as he seeks strength in the idealism of women like Emily Dickinson and Isadora Duncan.

Another violation of the past and of a tradition of human love and worship has been inflicted on an old «Meeting House» of the Society of Friends that has been turned into a hotel, ironically named «the New Avalon,» a reference to the island of Arthurian romance to which King Arthur repaired after his last battle to heal his wounds. Avalon belongs to the literary-mythic tradition of the blessed isle or Elysium which is very active in Crane's poetry. One may recall the «Belle Isle» of «Voyages» and the «Atlantis Rose» of «Cutty Sark.» The use of the name Avalon for a country resort suggests that people have lost their sense of noble aims and ideal aspirations and are vulgarizing their heritage. The din of their noisy music and dancing roars over the countryside, and one is reminded of the opening of «The River» with its rendering of the «breathtaking» speed and frenzied activity of American civilization. With genuine regret, Crane strikes the note of *ubi sunt,* calling out for the redeemers of the country, the old «patriarch race» for whom America was holy land.[93] These kinsmen and patriarchs refer both to the poet's pioneer ancestors and to the noble Indians. As in «The Dance,» the Indians are invoked as the poet's true guides to the land. The old battles between white rangers and Indian braves are recalled, and the «Iroquois» are extolled as true ancestors and spiritual teachers: «But I must ask slain Iroquois to guide/ Me farther than scalped Yankees knew to go:/ Shoulder the curse of sundered parentage.» The last line has a double meaning and refers both to the cleavage between white and Indian culture and the alienation between the poet and his parents. The waiting for mail that is alluded to concerns, according to Philip Horton, a quarrel between Hart Crane and his mother over his grandmother's inheritance, which he for a while suspected his mother of withholding from him.[94]

In the final two stanzas of «Quaker Hill,» Crane fully regains his usual lyric power and presents a dazzling, complex texture. The tone gains authority and the imagery becomes both subtle and impressive. The conclusion of the poem raises hopes that were denied by the foregoing paragraphs, and we are presented with another vision of beauty, unity in love and spiritual rebirth:

> So, must we from the hawk's far stemming view,
> Must we descend as worm's eye to construe
> Our love of all we touch, and take it to the Gate
> As humbly as a guest who knows himself too late,
> His news already told? Yes, while the heart is wrung,
> Arise — yes, take this sheaf of dust upon your tongue!
> In one last angelus lift throbbing throat —
> Listen, transmuting silence with that stilly note
>
> Of pain that Emily, that Isadora knew!
> While high from dim elm-chancels hung with dew
> That triple-noted clause of moonlight —
> Yes, whip-poor-will, unhusks the heart of fright,
> Breaks us and saves, yes, breaks the heart, yet yields
> That patience that is armour and that shields
> Love from despair — when love foresees the end —
> Leaf after autumnal leaf,
> > > break off,
> > > > descend —
> > > > > — descend

Freedom, the vision of the spiritual unity of being are symbolized in *The Bridge* by winged flight, whether it be that of a seagull, a moth, an eagle or an airplane. Here it is represented by «the hawk's far stemming view,» and the position of the bird equals the high vantage point of «the central cupola.» The meaning of the fall and the vow to love «all we touch» is a confirmation of the Whitmanian doctrine of total identity and love, and Crane sees himself in what may be regarded as his favorite role or mask, that of the guest who brings a message that was brought earlier but has been forgotten. The message is the dream of a mystic America; its carrier knows that he is too late, and yet he feels compelled to take his «news» to the «Gate,» a word which may refer both to the door of the Avalon Hotel and to the symbolic «Gates of Wrath» of the Blakeian epigraph to «The Tunnel.» These gates symbolize the final ordeal which must be endured before the complete vision can be released. «Quaker Hill» brings us up to them, but «The Tunnel» takes us through them.

Again it is emphasized that poetic creation is linked with suffering; «the heart is wrung» as the imagination reshapes reality. The poet realizes that he must somehow embrace and accept even the lowest and most meaningless aspects of modern reality as parts of the mystic whole, and this is the symbolic meaning of the poet-worm that eats dust like the Biblical serpent. The passage calls to mind the conclusion of *The Re-Discovery of America,* in which Frank also uses the image of dust to denote the raw material out of which America's artists must fashion the ideal: «Although they know the dust that may lie in their hands, making America, they will pursue their way, because all other ways to them are void. Having found wholeness in themselves, what else could they choose? They will act each hour to make themselves more true and to bring truth to bear upon the unborn world: not for any issue in time or person, but for the joy of the eternity of the moment lived in the image of God. The life of such men will be the fulfillment of America's oldest tradition. And it may be that in their fulfillment a world called America will be discovered.»[95]

At his lowest point, as worm, another ascent is indicated as the reinspired protagonist of «Quaker Hill» fixes his gaze upward in worship. After the perils of their voyage the crew of Columbus said their «angelus,» and the repetition of this word in «Quaker Hill» suggests that the poet reaffirms the dream of Cathay in the modern world. A manuscript fragment of this stanza shows that Whitman's doctrine of total love was part of the motivation behind the renewed commitment. The following two lines seem particularly relevant: «O secret throb, O vow to know, to love/ Henceforth not one — but all —.»

Isadora Duncan, one of the guiding spirits of «Quaker Hill,» identified love, beauty and art in a manner which must have struck Crane as an attitude close to the one expressed in this poem: «I have sometimes been asked whether I consider love higher than art, and I have replied that I cannot separate them, for the artist is the only lover, he alone has the pure vision of beauty, and love is the vision of the soul when it is permitted to gaze upon immortal beauty.»[96]

The upturned gaze and «last angelus» is finally answered by the song of another bird, a whippoorwill in a tree-top, and the «triple-noted clause» of this bird is a voice of affirmation for the poet. The word «clause» is linked with the linguistic vocabulary employed throughout *The Bridge* when the reference is to the integrated consciousness of America. The song of the bird symbolizes the returning faith in the validity of the poetic image, and it relieves the poet of the «fright» of complete dejection and pessimism in the face of modern reality. However, the connection between poetry and suffering is again emphasized; in order to preserve the vision one has to pay the heavy price of laying oneself open to the injuries inflicted by a world which seems to be devoid of any spiritual dimension whatever. At the time when he wrote «Quaker Hill» Crane felt particularly keenly the discrepancy between the noble dimension of *The Bridge* and the spiritual wreckage of the land and people that the poem set out to celebrate. However, the saving vision is upheld, though the seer's personal happiness is sacrificed and his heart broken.[97] And yet he gets his reward, a «patience» or deep inner confidence in the essential truth of his poetic message, and this is the «armour» that protects him from despair. The same kind of patience is referred to at the end of «The River:» «Patience! and you shall reach the biding place!» Apart from the frequent pessimistic outbursts, Crane's letters also contain certain utterances, serene and religious in tone, that testify to his abiding faith in his work. In 1923, after a year of hardships as an incipient poet in New York, he wrote Charlotte Rychtarik on September 23: «I have been through the hardest summer in my life — the hardest year, perhaps, when you consider the developments I have been through and the material difficulties that I have encountered. I want to keep saying 'YES' to everything and never be beaten a moment, and I shall, of course, never be really beaten.» In spite of what he uttered to the contrary, this sentiment never left Crane completely, and even the darkest sections of *The Bridge* contain some positive or affirmative note, though it may sound desperate at times.

The essence of the renewed faith at the end of «Quaker Hill» is the vision of love, first presented fully in «Cape Hatteras.» The phrase «love foresees the end» seems to have two levels of meaning. Related to the «Atlantis» section, it refers to the artistic fulfillment of the vision of universal love, and as a variation on the poetry of Emily Dickinson it refers to spiritual rebirth into eternity. Dickinson's poem «The

Gentian Weaves her Fringes,» from which Crane took the epigraph, is
a parable of the death and rebirth of man in terms of the seasonal cycle
of flowers:

> The Gentian weaves her fringes
> The maple's loom is red.
> My departing blossoms
> Obviate parade . . .
>
> A brief, but patient illness,
> An hour to prepare;
> And one, below this morning,
> Is where the angels are.
>
> It was a short procession, —
> the bobolink was there,
> An aged bee addressed us,
> And then we knelt in prayer.
>
> We trust that she was willing, —
> We ask that we may be.
> Summer, sister, seraph.
> Let us go with thee![98]

Identifying with the dying blossom in the fall, the poet prays for rebirth into the summer of eternity. This poem, like «Quaker Hill,»
deals with autumn and uses imagery of flowers and leaves. The rebirth
pattern of «The Gentian Weaves» occurs in the larger context of the
poems of the second half of *The Bridge*, the autumn of «Quaker Hill»
corresponds to the sterility depicted in «Southern Cross» and «National Winter Garden,» and the rejuvenating spring of «Virginia» is cli-
maxed in «Atlantis.» That Crane regarded the faith in rebirth as
Dickinson's principal poetic concern or theme is evident in his poem
«To Emily Dickinson:»

> — Truly no flower yet withers in your hand,
> The harvest you descried and understand
> Needs more than wit to gather, love to bind.
> Some reconcilement of remotest mind —

Leaves Ormus rubyless, and Ophir chill.
Else tears heap all within one clay-cold hill.

Dickinson has the ability, which Crane admired and found in Whitman, to perceive the eternal in the temporal and believe that man's soul is part of eternity. The metaphor of vegetative rebirth is again employed: the flowers that the poet plucks are her premonitions of immortality, and the harvest that she is looking forward to is not of this world. Immortality is her hope, here represented by rubies and gold, and without that hope she will have to despair and confront the grave as the end of all.

The curvature of the final passages of «Quaker Hill» runs from the high point of the hawk to the realm of the worm; from there it turns upward again in the gaze toward the whippoorwill and the moonlight, and finally it descends again in the concluding image of falling leaves. In *The Bridge* such a fall is always followed by a later resurrection, as, for example, the rainbow is sunk at the end of «Cutty Sark» and rises again at the end of «Cape Hatteras.» In a similar way the leaves of «Quaker Hill» are resurrected in the emblem of the serpent and the eagle in the leaves in «Atlantis.»

8. *The Tunnel*

The autumnal descent of falling leaves, which is only mildly and lyrically depicted in «Quaker Hill,» is in a sense continued and completed in the night journey through the nether realm of demons and burlesque which the poet undertakes in «The Tunnel.» Like «National Winter Garden» this section is wholly derived from the lowest regions of Crane's poetic world, but it goes far beyond the former in the range and scope of its assemblage of figures and themes that constitute a total inversion of the positive meaning of the bridge symbol.

«The Tunnel» is also the particular section which is most markedly influenced by Eliot's early poetry; its rendering of the sterility and seediness of modern big cities and portrayal of the emptiness and lack of meaning of the people who inhabit them are strongly reminiscent of the poems of *Prufrock and Other Observations, The Waste Land* and *The Hollow Men.* In his repeated comparisons of *The Bridge* and *The Waste Land* Crane emphasized that his poem had a more positive direction than that of Eliot, for example, in his letter of reply, of May

22, 1930, to Seldon Rodman's review of *The Bridge*: «Your criticism of *The Bridge* was very much to the point, and I am grateful for your enthusiasm. I also share your admiration for the poetry of Archibald MacLeish, though I feel that at times he betrays too evidently a bias toward the fashionable pessimism of the hour so well established by T. S. Eliot. I tried to break loose from that particular strait-jacket, without however committing myself to any oppositional form of didactism . . . The poem, as a whole, is, I think, an affirmation of experience, and to that extent is 'positive' rather than 'negative' in the sense that *The Waste Land* is negative.»

Long before this letter was written, Crane had maintained that Eliot's poetry was dead and pessimistic, though at the same time honoring him as the greatest poetic craftsman and the most authentic literary voice of the time. This comes out most clearly in a letter to Gorham Munson of January 5, 1923: «You already know, I think, that my work for the past two years (those meagre drops) has been more influenced by Eliot than any other modern . . . There is no one writing in English who can command so much respect, to my mind, as Eliot. However, I take Eliot as a point of departure toward an almost complete reverse of direction. His pessimism is amply justified, in his own case. But I would apply as much of his erudition and technique as I can absorb and assemble toward a more positive, or . . . ecstatic goal . . . After this perfection of death — nothing is possible in motion but a resurrection of some kind.»

It is worth noticing that despite his ardent vows to combat what he regarded as the destructive pessimism of Eliot and his followers, Crane involved himself in the style and outlook of the older poet to a considerable extent, and nowhere is this influence more keenly felt than in «The Tunnel.» Taken in isolation, the poem serves as an affirmation of Eliot's pessimism, but *The Bridge* as a whole is an affirmation of experience that differs from the outlook of Eliot. As for «The Tunnel» itself, it is the intimate personal background of the poem (Crane lived in Brooklyn and rode home on the subway from Manhattan) and the poet's own powerful and sweeping vision that makes this poem something more than an Eliotic *pastiche*. Crane's own comment on the poem is very illuminating: «It's rather ghastly, almost surgery — and, oddly almost all from the notes and and stitches I have written while swinging on the strap at late midnights going home.» (Letter to Frank, August 23, 1926.)

Crane's awareness of the evils of modern civilization and of the chaotic life of its people quite matches that of Eliot, but unlike the latter, he incorporated this awareness into the total meaning of *The Bridge,* making it part of the consciousness of the «mystic Whole.» In this larger design even chaos and darkness has a place; and in «Cape Hatteras» the consciousness was symbolized by the «undenying eyes» of Whitman and reaffirmed in the vow to love «all we touch» given in «Quaker Hill.» Following this attitude to its logical conclusion, Crane also confronted the ghastly world of «The Tunnel» and incorporated it in the «Whole.»

This visionary redemption, or resolution of conflict, is the final outcome of a process of total identification with and acceptance of all of reality, a process that involves suffering and a surrender of the ego to forces larger than oneself. Only thus can the divine harmony be perceived. Speaking of suffering, Crane wrote: «I have had enough, anyway, to realize that it is all very beautiful in the end if you will pierce through to the center of it and see it in relation to the real emotions and values of Life. Do not think I am entirely happy here, — or ever will be, for that matter, except for a few moments at a time when I am perhaps writing or receiving a return of love. The true idea of God is the only thing that can give happiness, — and that is the identification of yourself with *all of life.*» (Letter to Charlotte Rychtarik, July 21, 1923.) This penetrating vision includes darkness as well as light and leads to resolution of conflict. The idea is expressed in Waldo Frank's work, for example, in his novel *The Death and Birth of David Markand* (1935). Helen Markand, the wife of the main character, experiences just such an illumination after having been involved in the death of a child in an accident. She is on her way home to look after her own child, who has fallen off a swing, and she also feels obliged to help her driver, who may be brought before the magistrate for having knocked down the child. Helen Markand is torn between irreconcilable demands and feels the agony of an impossible situation, but at the height of her suffering, she experiences a sudden insight: «Helen's agony suffused into a light. The three impossible conjunctions were all true; all of them true together! The light flooded the dark room. Helen saw there was no separateness in the world.»[99] Helen Markand becomes a Catholic, and her vision is identified with the experience of Christ. Nevertheless, it is Frank's philosophy of the «Whole» that is implied in Helen Markand's thoughts: «The world and self, and all their agonies of burden, could be burned away by the fire of the impact of their contradictions . . . of their false separateness. And then, illumination! And then, peace.»[100]

Against this background, the epigraph from William Blake's «Morning» assumes its natural function as an introduction to «The Tunnel.» It is a poem which portrays a perilous pilgrimage toward a holy land:

> To find the Western path
> Right thro' the Gates of Wrath
> I urge my way;
> Sweet Mercy leads me on:
> With soft repentant moan
> I see the break of day.
>
> The war of swords & spears
> Melted by dewing tears
> Exhales on high;
> The Sun is freed from fears
> And with soft grateful tears
> Ascends the sky.[101]

This poem characterizes not only «The Tunnel,» but the whole of *The Bridge,* which also follows a «Western path,» sometimes through dark labyrinths, and its theme of the new world that will arise is symbolized by dawn, just as the «break of day» suggests the release from the gates of wrath in «Morning.»

The opening passage of «The Tunnel» returns to the downtown Manhattan that serves as the background of the proem, «The Harbor Dawn» and «Virginia.» It is evening and the poet wanders the streets, confronting the masses of the city in a direct and searching way:

> Performances, assortments, résumés —
> Up Times Square to Columbus Circle lights
> Channel the congresses, nightly sessions,
> Refractions of the thousand theatres, faces —
> Mysterious kitchens . . . You shall search them all.
> Some day by heart you'll learn each famous sight
> And watch the curtain lift in hell's despite;

145

You'll find the garden in the third act dead,
Finger your knees — and wish yourself in bed
With tabloid crime-sheets perched in easy sight.

The confusion of this paragraph is intentional. It presents a welter of impressions and images as registered by a passing glance. One is reminded of the opening of «The River,» which presents a series of scattered objects and impressions, or of «Faustus and Helen,» in which the mind has become reduced to the «labelled dough/ Divided by accepted multitudes.» The leading idea is that man is separated from reality; the throng either comes from or is being «channelled» into theatres to witness performances which are imitations of real life. This resembles the situation of the «multitudes» in the cinemas of the proem; the difference is in the poet, who now identifies more strongly with the passive spectators. These people invite comparison with the masses flowing over London Bridge in Eliot's *The Waste Land.* This concept of modern man as a creature of complete passivity and emptiness became tremendously popular and influential in the poetry of the 1920s, and Crane's subway passengers have a great deal in common with Eliot's Londoners.

The poet finds himself in one of the theatres, and what he sees becomes symbolic of the total urban reality, the modern hell. His own time is the third act of the historic drama of America, originally the garden of a new Eden which he now believes is dead, suppressed by the total encroachment of a mechanical civilization. The poet wants to leave the scene and go to his home in Brooklyn and read newspapers, but that he should wish to concentrate on the cheap and repulsive sensationalism of these «crime-sheets» is another indication of his surrender to the pressure of the environment.

Before he finally descends into the subway, he wavers and hesitates, and a vague atmosphere of dread is created. Walking down under the street he exclaims to those who are coming up and out his «subscription praise» of the America that has failed to materialize in the course of the historical development and that he as poet has subscribed to in the sense of pledging himself to it and being its prophetic spokesman. The walk down to the platform is imaginary, in reality he has difficulties making up his mind about the method of getting to his home and finally decides in favor of the subway because of the cold weather, «preparing penguin flexions of the arms.» The entrance «yawns the quickest promise home,» and the word «yawn» is used later in the poem when the subway is seen as a demonic personification: «Daemon, demurring and evenful yawn!» A final moment of fear precedes the actual descent:

Be minimum, then, to swim the hiving swarms
Out of the Square, the Circle burning bright —
Avoid the glass doors gyring at your right,
Where boxed alone a second, eyes take fright
— Quite unprepared rush naked back to light;
And down beside the turnstile press the coin
Into the slot. The gongs already rattle.

Merging with the mass of people around him, reducing himself to the nothingness that they represent, the protagonist heads for the subway entrance, the lights of Columbus Circle forming a sinister and lurid version of the «crescent ring» of «modulated fire» that revealed itself to Columbus in «Ave Maria.» The figure of rotation appears in the image of the gyrating glass doors that suggest a maelstrom pulling the poet down and in which he sees his eyes as in a mirror. The eyes register terror of the hellish depths and at the aspect of going down into them alone, and he rushes back to the other passengers. In «Van Winkle» he had started his journey across America with a sense of elation and promise as he boarded the subway train, but now he presses the nickel into the slot with dark premonitions. The subway is seen as a kind of underground river, an image which vaguely suggests the river Styx which separates Hades from the world of the living:

And so
of cities you bespeak
subways, rivered under streets
and rivers . . . In the car
the overtone of motion
underground, the monotone
of motion is the sound
of other faces, also underground —

In the subway car daylight has been shut out and everything is reduced to a monotone of motion and sound, including the lives of the passengers, whose faces express the staleness and emptiness of their existence. Here one has lost sight of the harmonious, integrating curve of the bridge and the flight of seagulls. As in *The Waste Land,* the keynote is sterility and fragmentation, whether spiritual or sexual. This state of affairs is objectified in the snatches of conversation overheard and recorded impressionistically:

«Let's have a pencil Jimmy — living now
at Floral Park
Flatbush — on the Fourth of July —
like a pigeon's muddy dream — potatoes
to dig in the field — travlin the town — too —
night after night — the Culver line — the
girls all shaping up — it used to be —»

Our tongues recant like beaten weather vanes.
This answer lives like verdigris, like hair
Beyond extinction, surcease of the bone;
And repetition freezes —

Even in these highly mundane remarks there are echoes of another America; Independence Day is referred to, and Pocahontas, here reduced to a «pigeon's muddy dream» among the tenements of Brooklyn and other urban areas. The whole conversation renders the empty chat of beings who are as passively moved around as weather vanes blown by the wind. Like Eliot's people in *The Waste Land* they are already dead, their speech a mechanical activity which paradoxically continues after physical death, like hair that grows «beyond extinction» or a parasitical element that nourishes itself on the destruction of something else, like verdigris on copper. Here we are in a realm similar to Eliot's «rat's alley/Where the dead men lost their bones.»

The poet feels that the remarks that he overhears in the train are like «phonographs of hades» that constantly «rewind themselves» in his brain; dominated by the darkness of his soul, he is the victim of an evil vision which he cannot escape from and which he has to face. The degradation of love, initiated as a theme in «National Winter Garden,» reaches an ultimate level in the image of «A burnt match skating in a urinal.» The image has multiple levels of meaning within the context of *The Bridge.* In «Ave Maria» fire is the emblem of God's essence, which is love; in «The Dance» the sacrificial burning of Maquokeeta/

Quetzalcoatl suggests the total love and devotion associated with the apotheosis of a god. The black ashes of the burnt-out match symbolize the ruin and waste of the power of love, whether religious or sexual, in modern society, and the urinal, emphasizing the body as a seat of excrement rather than a temple of love, reinforces the general symbolic impression of sterility and dissolution. The image also reminds one of the way in which Eliot uses the cigarette butt as a metaphor of an existence without vitality or promise, for example, in Prufrock's question: «How would I begin/ To spit out all the butt-ends of my days and ways?» and the «burnt-out ends of smoky days» in «Preludes I.»[102]

Maquokeeta was united with the earth, Pocahontas, in a ritual fire, and the god was described in terms of flames and lightning. This rise is followed by a vision of the reborn, fertile and beautiful earth-mother in spring. Though it goes underground in the city, the subway journey does take place within Pocahontas' body, which now assumes a sinister and ravaged shape:

Whose head is swinging from the swollen strap?
Whose body smokes along the bitten rails,
Bursts from a smoldering bundle far behind
In back forks of the chasms of the brain, —
Puffs from a riven stump far out behind
In interborough fissures of the mind . . .?

The questions remind one of Crane's gloss in the margin of «The Harbor Dawn:» «Who is the woman with us in the dawn? . . . Whose is the flesh our feet have moved upon?» In «The River» and «The Dance,» this question was answered, but in «The Tunnel» the poet has lost his knowledge of the spirit of the continent and repeats his question in despair.

Degraded by the encroachment of a mechanical civilization, the image of Pocahontas has been reduced to the smoking remnants of a cremated body, vaguely conceived in the deep recesses or «chasms» of the poet's mind. The ritual fire of «The Dance» is now recalled only as a «smoldering bundle far behind,» an image of ashes and waste which is linked with that of the burnt match. This passage thus also refers back, to the decay of love suggested by sexual exploitation: «after/ the show she cried a little afterwards but —.» Love, whether it is directed toward an ordinary woman or the body of Pocahontas, has become replaced by violation and ravage, sexual or technological. In this world, Poe is invoked as a guide, but his «visage» does not emerge until the next stanza.[103]

The words «swollen» and «bitten» suggest a diseased condition, and the «chasms» and «riven stump» connote cleavage and disruption, the qualities that are opposed to the meaning of the bridge symbol. What we have is a mental picture of the subway; the mind is conceived of as completely dominated by and organized on the pattern of the city and the subway system, it is construed of «interborough fissures.»

Like Whitman in «Cape Hatteras,» Poe is Crane's guide in the world of «The Tunnel.» Looking into the window of the car, he sees an appararition of Poe's face staring at him and invokes some of the circumstances of the older poet's death:

And why do I often meet your visage here,
Your eyes like agate lanterns — on and on
Below the toothpaste and the dandruff ads?
— And did their eyes like unwashed platters ride?
And Death, aloft, — gigantically down
Probing through you — toward me, O evermore!
And when they dragged your retching flesh,
Your trembling hands that night through Baltimore —
That last night on the ballot rounds, did you
Shaking, did you deny the ticket, Poe?

Crane read and admired Poe, who is listed first, followed by Whitman, among a number of favorite poets mentioned in a letter to William Wright, October 17, 1921. The above passage has one clear reference to «The City in the Sea,» and the image of «agate lanterns» suggests the poem «To Helen,» in which a poetic vision of the beautiful queen is addressed in lines like these: «Lo! in yon brilliant window-niche/ How statue-like I see thee stand,/ The agate lamp within thy hand!»[104]

As a symbol of beauty Helen held similar meanings for both Poe and Crane, who in «The Tunnel» seems to be drawing attention to two aspects of Poe's work: the worship of beauty as it appears in poems like «To Helen» and the fascination with gothic horrors that appears in other poems and in the short stories. Poe was the literary spokesman of sorrow and death, but he was also the uncompromising craftsman and artist, totally devoted to poetry and the world of letters in spite of all the misery of his life. He is the archetype of the crucified poet, and the idea of crucifixion is implied in the image of the eyes of Poe's unreceptive contemporaries, whose condemning stares pierce his side like the spear that the Roman soldier ran through the body of Christ. In contrast to the «agate» eyes of Poe their eyes are like «unwashed platters,» coarse, dirty and unable to appreciate either beauty or the idea of sacrifice for its sake.

However, it is Poe's obsession with death and corruption which presents itself most insistently to Crane and reinforces his own concept of the underworld. The image of death looking down at the subway passengers is taken from these lines in «The City in the Sea:» «While from a proud tower in the town/ Death looks gigantically down.» The sunken city described is a perennially lost Atlantis, a ghostly place illumined not by the sun, but by its own infernal light:

No rays from the holy heaven come down
On the night-time of that town;
But light from out the lurid sea
Streams up the turrets silently —
Gleams up the pinnacles far and free —
Up domes — up spires — up kingly halls —
Up fanes — up Babylon — like walls —[105]

This poem can hardly have failed to strike Crane as a demonic counterpart to his own vision of the beautiful city of white buildings and towers that appears in «The Harbor Dawn» and «Atlantis.» In fact, Poe's picture of the light of the sea streaming upward along the turrets and spires is very closely related to the repetitive imagery of upward moving rays that occurs in the opening stanzas of «Atlantis.»

Recalling the tragic last phase of Poe's life, Crane turns him into the figure of a derelict poet who has something in common with the sailor of «Cutty Sark,» but who is actually Crane's *alter ego,* the condemned seer who upholds the sanctity of his art in the face of the most devasting external and personal circumstances. According to one unverified account of what happened to Poe in Baltimore, he was made drunk on an election night and more or less forced to represent a certain «ticket» or list of candidates.[106] The challenge thus put to him was whether he was able to withstand the pressure of society, at least mentally, and thus deny the ticket. As Dembo says, «Crane seems to be asking here whether or not Poe was able to maintain his moral strength, even at the time of his most obvious humiliation.»[107]

In the letter to Frank of November 21, 1926, in which he comments on Williams' *In the American Grain,* Crane noticed the similarity between Williams' and his own evaluation of Poe: «I was so interested to note that he puts Poe and his 'character' in the same position as I had *symbolized* for him in 'The Tunnel' section.» Williams devoted a chapter of his book to Poe and praises him as the first great American poetic genius who fought an unceasing battle for order and beauty to «clear the ground» for serious artistic expression in the midst of a cultural and geographical wilderness. He was «a light in the morass — which *must* appear eerie, even to himself, by force of terrific contrast, an isolation that would naturally lead to drunkenness and death.»[108] Williams goes on to state that one cause of the atmosphere of dread which prevails in much of Poe's poetry is the horror of trying to create order in such a formless environment: «It is especially in the poetry where 'death looked gigantically down' that the horror of the formless resistance which opposed, maddened, destroyed him has forced its character into the air, the wind, the blessed galleries of paradise, above a morose, dead world, peopled by shadows and silence, and despair.»[109]

The «morose, dead world» refers to the sunken city of despair that Crane compares the subway realm with; Williams makes the observation that even when Poe wrote of an ideal existence, the dread and the melancholy followed suit. He is thinking of poems like «The Haunted Palace» and «To One in Paradise.»

Before going into the actual tunnel under the river, the train stops and unloads a number of passengers who rise in elevators toward the street. They are conceived of as a «serenade» of «shoes, umbrellas, each eye attending its shoe;» they exist in complete individual isolation, contemplating their separate selves, and their melancholy serenade contrasts with the triumphant «One Song» of love and unity in «Atlantis.» These people again call to mind Eliot's crowds on London Bridge where «each man fixed his eyes before his feet.» The departure of some passengers emphasizes the perilous nature of the still deeper descent which lies ahead. Carrying fewer passengers, the interior of the car is the quintessence of resignation and hopelessness, with its rumpled newspapers littering the floors and the old «washerwoman» riding home after work. This woman is addressed as «Genoese;» as «wop» she may be regarded as a descendant of Columbus and his followers. The «Daemon» of the subway is taking her home, and the poet asks this rhetorical question: «O Genoese, do you bring mother eyes and hands/ Back home to children and to golden hair?» This is a direct and striking contrast to the lines in «Passage to India» in which Whitman triumphantly exclaims: «(Ah genoese thy dream! thy dream!/ Centuries after thou art laid in thy grave,/ The shore thou foundest verifies thy dream.)»[110] Crane replaces Whitman's assurance with a low burlesque on the Mary-Pocahontas image, his «washerwoman» is obviously poorly equipped to be a representative of the maternal principle that is sought after, and the «gaunt sky-barracks» with their «cuspidors» where she does her work are a sardonic mockery of Whitman's idea that «the shore» of America has verified Columbus' dream.

All the dark and negating qualities that the subway stands for are gathered up in its personification, the «daemon» who «yawns» ominously and whose laughter is a «bellows mirth.» The bellows suggest the inflating of infernal fire, and the whole figure of the daemon has vague associations with traditional mythic figures of hell, Satan, Hades and even Cerberus, the monstrous dog at the gates of the underworld.

This daemon defeats, quenches the very dawn of a new day, the symbol of the ever returning hope for a new America. Against the «brinking dawn» with all its promise, the daemon presents «worlds that glow and sink,» a derelict Atlantis of the kind that Poe envisioned and that occurred in the «Cutty Sark» refrain about «remnants of the skeletons of cities.» The daemon guards an Atlantis which is sunken and darkened. The obscure imagery of «liquid» and «star» is apparently linked with the metaphor of moving among people like a swimmer in the sea suggested earlier: «swim the hiving swarms.» The daemon reduces people in his world to mere nonentities, mere «locutions» that are swept along in the dark underground flow of the subway. The «conscience» may refer to the poet's awareness of another tradition; his vision is born, «navelled,» in the wind, a symbol of inspiration, but the daemon destroys the possibility of survival for the vision and it dies. In «The Tunnel» darkness is the victor, but even the daemon cannot completely extinguish the «word» of the poet, the possibility of renewed faith:

O caught like pennies beneath soot and steam,
Kiss of our agony thou gatherest;
Condensed, thou takest all — shrill ganglia
Impassioned with some song we fail to keep.
And yet, like Lazarus, to feel the slope,
The sod and billow breaking, — lifting ground,
— A sound of waters bending astride the sky
Unceasing with some Word that will not die . . .!

Again, the predicament of the «multitudes,» the masses who are mere victims of a historical process, is emphasized. Like the hoboes caught in the flow of the river of time, the people in the subway are mere pennies, tossed, as it were, underground. And yet, unlike the inhabitants of a traditional hell, these passengers are engaged in a journey which leads upward and out of the infernal regions. Though they are agonized and without hope, their suffering is gathered up and assimilated by the divine being above, who in this context is hard to distinguish from the actual bridge itself which spans the river over their heads. The second line of this passage was originally part of a version of «Atlantis» sent to Waldo Frank on January 18, 1926: «O Bridge! Kiss of our agony thou gatherest.»[111]

The bridge is the symbol of total integration and fusion, of a spiritual reality that includes even agony and darkness, as stated at the beginning of this analysis of «The Tunnel.» Thus it is «condensed» and «takest all;» it is the «Word» that unites everything, both that which is under it and that which is above it. In the story «Hope,» which is part of *City Block* (1922), Waldo Frank attributes the same symbolic significance to the structure of the elevated railroad in New York. The protagonist, a young man walking in the city, experiences the railroad like this: «Above his hat, the Elevated Road . . . a balance in sonorous black where all that was over it and under was contained. The structure so immediate above him, so infinite beyond him, was a Word.»[112]

Toward the end of «The Tunnel» the poet returns from the world of the dead in order to sustain his message, the «Word» that is greater than himself and that will not die. However, in this poem the word is only pointed to, not fleshed in any such glorious imagery as that found in Columbus' vision after his struggle with *his* darkness, the storm, in «Ave Maria.»

The final part of the poem finds the familiar figure of the solitary poet at the riverside. The time is midnight and the situation is similar to that of the proem, in which he stands under the shadow of the bridge. Having traversed vast geographical and historical expanses, he has gone through the great cycle or totality of experience which the bridge as symbol represents; like Satan in the Book of Job he has spanned the earth and can report on what he has seen. The epigraph of *The Bridge* as a whole is Satan's words to the Lord: «From going to and fro in the earth, and from walking up and down in it.» Listening to the sounds from the river traffic, he counts the «echoes» that reach the pier where he walks, observing the «coasting» lights of the passing tugboat. The «echoes» may be taken to refer not only to the sounds from the river, but to the vestiges of glorious hopes and images that remain in his mind after the journey through the American experience.

«The Tunnel» ends on a note of resignation rather than one of despair:

> And this thy harbor, O my City, I have driven under,
> Tossed from the coil of ticking towers . . . Tomorrow,
> And to be . . . Here by the River that is East —
> Here at the water's edge the hands drop memory;
> Shadowless in that abyss they unaccounting lie.
> How far away the star has pooled the sea —
> Or shall the hands be drawn away, to die?
>
> Kiss of our agony Thou gatherest,
>   O Hand of Fire
>   gatherest

The poet sees himself as one who is «tossed» from the towers and into the underground world. In the proem the elevator dropped him down to the street; this fall was less deep than that experienced in «The Tunnel,» and it left the poet with faith in and ability to pray to the bridge to provide him with a sustained vision. There the revelation and the promise were imminent and vivid, but for the prophet who has just emerged from the subway passage the bridge, symbol of wholeness, is felt as something distant and remote. In the proem the stars, manifestations of the divine, had descended and merged with the traffic lights across the bridge; Eden was near, but now the poet feels expelled from it. God has withdrawn, and the star, like «Hesperus» in «Cape

Hatteras,» is far away and mirrored in the sea. Standing on the East River, the poet is facing west, like the homeward bound Columbus who looks toward the «Indian emperies» that lie beckoning on the other side of the sea. Columbus sees himself embarking anew on a voyage toward Cathay, and the memory of his discovery and the revelations that accompanied it is still vivid in his mind. Confronting the harbor and city of New York more than four hundred years later, the poet has created his own version of the dream of a new world and found his «usable past.» Now the time has come to «drop memory» of the past in the sense of not looking back toward it any more and, having faced the present in its total aspect, to sum up all the elements of both past and present and give his own personal, highly emblematic, vision of the mystic America in «Atlantis.»

9. Atlantis

The finale of *The Bridge* was the first section to be composed, and it seems appropriate to consider the remarks made by Crane on the project of *The Bridge* in the letters of 1923 in order to throw light on the initial enthusiasm or ecstasy with which the poet was outlining his worksheets of «Atlantis». Although he was referring to *The Bridge* as a planned whole in these observations, the poem nearest at hand, the finale, was uppermost in his mind.

Though it was first thought of as a major symbol of American mysticism in «Atlantis,» the bridge as a significant object had occurred to Crane as early as 1921. In April of that year he had written a poem called «The Bridge of Estador;» it was not included in *White Buildings* and is reprinted in Brom Weber's book on Crane. The poem is important because it demonstrates the earliest evidence of the meaning consistently attributed to the bridge symbol later on:

Walk high on the bridge of Estador
No one has ever walked there before.
There is a lake, perhaps with the sun
Lapped under it, — or the dun
Bellies and estuaries of warehouses,
Tied bundle-wise with cords of smoke.

Do not think too deeply, and you'll find
A soul, an element in it all.[113]

The bridge symbol has a meaning which is close to the one it has in «Atlantis.» By ascending the bridge of Estador one obtains a view of a beautiful lake as well as ugly warehouses; and from this vantage point a poetic vision emerges which harmonizes the conflicting elements of the scenery. A deeper harmony and beauty, a «soul,» is perceived in it all. However, the reader is asked to refrain from thinking «too deeply» if he wants to discover the «soul» of the scenery. Even at this early stage in his career, Crane revealed his doubts about that vision. But «Atlantis» remains his grandest expression of it.

The main theme of «Atlantis» is the voyage toward a Belle Isle of the imagination that presents an experience of ultimate integration, or «mystical synthesis of America,» as Crane put it in a letter to Gorham Munson of February 18, 1923, in which he vowed that if *The Bridge* became a success, «such a waving of banners, such ascent of towers, such dancing, etc., will never before have been put down on paper!» At this time, Crane had just finished «Faustus and Helen» and had started to gain real confidence in his powers. He wrote to Munson again on March 2: «Potentially I feel myself quite fit to become a suitable *Pindar* for the dawn of the machine age, so called. I have lost the last shreds of philosophical pessimism during the last few months.»

The poet's exaltation is evident in the first sketches of «Atlantis,» for example, in the lines sent to William Underwood in February 1923:

And midway on that structure I would stand
One moment, not as a diver, but with arms
That open to project a disk's resilience
Winding the sun and planets in its face.
Water should not stem that disk, nor weigh
What holds its speed in vantage of all things
That tarnish, creep or wane; and in like laughter,
Mobile yet posited beyond even that time
The Pyramids shall falter, slough into sand, —
And smooth and fierce above the claim of wings,
And figured in that radiant field that rings
The Universe: — I'd have us hold one consonance
Kinetic to its poised and deathless dance.

The situation of «The Bridge of Estador» is maintained: the poet standing high on the bridge envisages a totality of experience. But the style has become more condensed and emblematical, and the dominant image of the disk evolves from the concrete observation of the bridge and its cables. The glorious disk floats above water, like the «Anemone» in later versions, and it is superposed on everything imperfect, «things that tarnish,» enveloping them in a larger, harmonious design. It represents a state of consciousness or vision in which ugliness and darkness have been totally assimilated and have no power to disturb, but this supreme insight resides above ordinary human experience and is accessible only to the elect imagination.

A worksheet from the spring of 1923 shows a slightly different approach to the formulation of the vision of totality and centrality, focusing on the gothic arches of the bridge towers. This fragment was incorporated into a six-paragraph version sent to Alfred Stieglitz on July 4, 1923:

And, steady as the gaze incorporate
Of flesh affords, we turn, surmounting all
With keenest transience to that sear arch-head,
Expansive center, purest moment and electron . . .

Feeling himself and the bridge turning, rising over the city, the poet has a sense of surmounting all obstacles and following a symbolic path toward the top of the gothic arches which constitutes the «expansive center» of a widening circle or wheel. This spiral narrows upward toward its apex, and a motion of ascent is suggested. From the upper vantage point of the spiral-image, eyes look down on the totality of time and existence, possessing a coordinated vision denied to ordinary cognizance.[114] From the cablework of the bridge springs the natural metaphor of a great «loom» upon which everything is woven into a beautiful fabric of sight and sound.

Early in 1923 Crane read P. D. Ouspensky and found that his own poetic experiences were related to the theories advocated by the Russian philosopher. The poet wrote to Allen Tate on February 15: «I have also enjoyed reading Ouspensky's *Tertium Organum* lately. Its corroboration of several experiences in consciousness that I have had gave it particular interest.» The experience of totality that is so important in «Atlantis,» depends on a particular concept of time that Crane may have derived from Ouspensky. According to the latter, the development of a «higher consciousness» involves the power to transcend ordinary time limits and apprehend all of time as an eternal present, and he describes the evolution of such an awareness in these terms: «Let us imagine a consciousness that is not bound by the conditions of sensuous receptivity. Such a consciousness can rise above the plane upon which we are moving; it can see far beyond the limits of the circle enlightened by our usual consciousness . . . it can see the past and the future, lying together and existing simultaneously.»[115] This experience of the simultaneity of all time became a major theme in «Atlantis.»

In the draft of July 4, 1923, the drama of ascent from the deep is also rendered, and though Crane did not decide to call the finale «Atlantis» until the summer of 1926, the image of Atlantis, the lost continent, is beginning to emerge here; it is a «baited rock» sounding through water, a vast «porch» that rises through «brimming clay.» The position of the poet midway on the bridge creates the illusion that he, the bridge and a whole world are moving up into sight. The bridge as a «nave of time» corresponds to the «purest moment;» these are the beginnings of what in «Atlantis» became an attempt at a synthesis of time and history. The second stanza introduces more themes and figures that have become familiar to readers of Crane:

O whitest instruments, in pain addressed
And so applied in beams of driven fire,
In ordered sheaves remission gathered up
And multiplied with steps to such a sum, —
That, scathless, we assume and guide
The tempered axis of the world . . .

The color white symbolizes the purifying power of the poetic consciousness, and the familiar association of suffering and artistic creation is implicated. Integration of a chaotic experience into an ordered whole is suggested by the «sheaves» or cables forming themselves into a design whose beauty has redemptive power. In the final version the image of the bridge as a white flower which is a «pardon for this history» forms a related redemptive climax.

The experience of turning around as in a dance and simultaneously being lifted upwards is based on the poet's actual sensations when walking across his Brooklyn Bridge. In a beautiful and moving letter to

Frank of April 21, 1924, he tells of the bliss granted him by a new and intense friendship and records his ecstasy when mounting the footwalk of the bridge with his friend: «I have been able to give freedom and life which was acknowledged in the ecstasy of walking hand in hand across the most beautiful bridge of the world, the cables enclosing us and pulling us upward in such a dance as I have never walked and never can walk with another.» The personal fulfillment experienced in love goes beyond itself and becomes linked with the spiritual-poetic vision obtained on the bridge. Crane used to tell his companion that «all of life is a bridge,» or «the whole world is a bridge.»[116]

The 1923 drafts of «Atlantis» were either abandoned, carried over into other poems, or changed radically, and the themes they presented were later developed in an increasingly complex and sophisticated manner. During the period between 1923 and 1926 Crane seems to have laid aside work on *The Bridge* and wrote short poems as well as «Voyages.» In 1926 work on «Atlantis» was resumed, and a number of worksheets and drafts were written before the poem got its final form sometime during the fall. On January 18 of that year Crane sent the first full-length version, a ten-stanza manuscript, to Frank, and he commented that in his poem «the bridge in becoming a ship, a world, a tremendous harp (as it does finally) seems to really have a career.» The rock or porch rising from the deep in the Stieglitz version of 1923 was now, three years later, developing into a more complete presentation of the birth of a new world:

> we feel
> Beneath us lift a world, a new concourse
> Outspanned of silver parallels that strike
> Upward, till razor paces tilt the slow
> Pale rings of rebirth, aureate horns of snow.

The image of a continent ascending into sight is here so clearly formulated that the idea of drawing on the Atlantis legend may already have occurred to Crane at this point. The idea of rebirth connects both with Frank's notion of America as the grave of Europe and cradle of an entirely new cultural order and with Spengler's cyclical theory of history. Crane vacillated between agreement with Spengler's conviction that the West was caught in an irreversible decline and a belief in the validity of his own vision.

The Columbus section was in embryo as Frank got the «Atlantis» version, and Crane wrote to him: «I'm now busy on the Nina, Santa Maria, Pinta episode — Cathay being an attitude of spirit, rather than material conquest throughout, of course.» Crane saw himself as a modern Columbus, a discoverer of a new religious dimension whose birth he describes in Christian terms in the seventh stanza of the Frank version, where the bridge becomes a Mary-figure: «From thy glittering thighs this white nativity!»

After the completion of his first full-length manuscript, Crane continued to ruminate on *The Bridge* throughout the spring of 1926. He was beginning to feel doubts about the validity of the project, but he always regarded it as an affirmation that was needed to counteract the influence of Eliot and Spengler. Crane felt particularly challenged by Spengler's contention that great and original art and literature is no longer possible in the present phase of world history: «We are civilized, not Gothic or Rococco, people; we have to reckon with the hard cold facts of a *late* life, to which the parallel is to be found not in Pericles's Athens but in Caesar's Rome. Of great painting or great music there can no longer be, for Western people, any question. Only architectural possibilities are left to them.»[117]

Crane refused to accept this thesis, but his remarks in the letters show that he felt threatened by it and had doubts about his own chosen position. Referring to Spengler in a letter to Frank of June 20, 1926, he wrote: «This man is certainly fallible in plenty of ways but much of his evidence is convincing — and is there any good evidence forthcoming from the world in general that the artist isn't completely out of a job?» That the poet was beginning to have reservations is also evident in the textual development of «Atlantis.» The first version of what became the final stanza was included in the manuscript of January 18, 1926, and its last four and half lines, from «Is it Cathay . . .» to the end, remained unchanged. A question is put here which remained unanswered, and a tone of doubt emerges which was not present in the fragments of 1923.[118] On August 3, 1926, Crane sent an eleven-stanza manuscript of the finale to Frank. Some time later what is now the eleventh stanza of the final version, which has twelve stanzas, was added. The August 3 draft was only very slightly altered before it became the last version.

While on the Isle of Pines in May of 1926, Crane read Lewis Spence's book *Atlantis in America* and was fascinated by its theory about a continent that had once existed between the landmasses of America and Europe. It seems likely to assume that this book prompted the poet to give the title «Atlantis» to the finale of *The Bridge,* a decision which was mentioned in his letter to Frank of July 26, 1926: «You have the last section ('Atlantis,' as I have decided to call it) haven't you? I have discovered that it IS the real Atlantis, even of geology!»

Spence furnished Crane with a legend which was singularly fitted to act as a visionary image of America in *The Bridge.* According to the theory, there once was a vast continental island stretching from the Azores to the West Indies, and Plato's account of its civilization in *Critias* is a fragment of a world-memory of Atlantis. Plato describes the downfall of the people in this ideal society, in which the inhabitants lived in close communion with their gods: «When that portion of divinity, or divine destiny, which they enjoyed, vanished from among them, in consequence being frequently mingled with much of a mortal nature, and human manner prevailed, — then, being no longer able to bear the events of the present life, they acted in a disgraceful manner.»[119]

Spence maintains that as Atlantis disintegrated, some of its inhabitants migrated both eastward and westward, and he presents as evidence the existence of the relatively well-developed culture of the Cro-Magnon cave-dwellers of the regions of the Bay of Biscay and the highly civilized societies of the Mayas, Toltecs and Aztecs in Central America and Mexico. Thus the myth of Quetzalcoatl, the culture-bringer from the land beyond the western ocean, is based on historical fact. What later became a god was originally the leader of the first Maya colonists to land in America. Spence regards Mayas and Toltecs as parts of one cultural entity and sees Quetzalcoatl as the central deity of the old Indian civilizations of Central America and Mexico.[120]

Debatable as it is, this hypothesis about Atlantis provided very significant background material for Crane's project. If the Indian cultures came from Atlantis, it means that Europe and America once were a primordial unity, and such a union is eminently symbolized by the bridge. Moreover, the theory puts back further than Columbus the tradition of America as a new world colonized by refugees from an older society. With the discovery of America by the white man history repeated itself, and the possibility arose of establishing a counterpart to the old Atlantis, a new synthesis of European and Indian elements. Within this context Crane's New York became another Tollan or Tenochtitlan, the fabulous and glorious cities of Toltecs and Aztecs, as well as a modern Troy or Tyre.

In its final form «Atlantis» is the most complex and elaborate of all of Crane's poems, and it presents one of the most intricate, condensed and dazzling poetic textures that exists in English. It seems to defy interpretation; each new critical attack is repelled by the hard diamond light of its lines, and yet the reader is always attracted anew by the promise of marvelous revelations that this poem extends.

«Atlantis» has no thread of narration or development of action like «Ave Maria,» «The Dance,» «The River,» and «The Tunnel;» nor does it present historical and geographical vistas in the way these and other sections do, apart from focussing on the object of the bridge itself. It is both severely restrictive and infinitely expansive, and its texture is emblematical to a degree unsurpassed in Crane's work. It is an ambitious attempt to gather up all the significant ideas and images of *The Bridge* into one coherent poetic unity. In his letter to Frank of January 18, 1926, Crane presented this gloss of «Atlantis:» «It is symphonic in including the convergence of all the strands separately detailed in antecedent sections of the poem — Columbus, conquest of water, land, etc., Pokahantus, subways, offices, et., etc . . .» The term «symphonic» is very close to and perhaps directly derived from Frank's *The Re-Discovery of America*, where the author calls for the development of America into a «symphonic nation» in which the various forces and institutions of the country might work in consort and harmony.

«Atlantis» has no progression of any definite nature, for example, of philosophic argument. Nor is it purely presentational and imagistic, but consists of blocks of interconnected figures and symbols which revolve around the basic theme of Atlantis, which is less a vision of a society than a symbol of the poet's representation of the essence of America, and the recurring motif of voyage. In «Ave Maria» the expedition of Columbus provides the total structural framework of the poem, but in «Atlantis» the voyage is thematic rather than specific, a recurring figure rather than a plot-like structure with a beginning, middle and end.

The opening stanza is an arresting example of Crane's luminous texture:

Through the bound cable strands, the arching path
Upward, veering with light, the flight of strings, —
Taut miles of shuttling moonlight syncopate
The whispered rush, telepathy of wires.
Up the index of night, granite and steel —
Transparent meshes — fleckless the gleaming staves —
Sibylline voices flicker, waveringly stream
As though a god were issue of the strings . . .

If the imagery of «The Tunnel» was predominantly suggestive of cleavage and disruption, that of «Atlantis» connotes fusion and integration in multiple ways. Images of winged flight and references to harps and music abound, and the connections with the proem are particularly striking. Both poems are primarily hymns to the bridge itself, though in «Atlantis» it has become even more transsubstantiated.

Different images constantly fuse and blend into each other, «the flight of strings,» for example, repeats the recurring figure of flight and the idea of music. Besides repeating the images of the poems preceding it, «Atlantis» employs repetition with variation as its main structural device. The «arching path» refers to the towers as well as the cables curving up toward them and points back to the «path» of the bridge in the proem. It is also linked with the «aisle» that is envisaged in the third stanza.

Light and sound are synesthetically fused; the moonlight that filters down through the cablework «syncopates,» gives rhythmic accent to the music of the wind rushing through the cables.[121] The idea of «telepathy of wires» suggests a communication between the poet and the divine spirit that reveals itself in the bridge. Telepathy, pure and cerebral rapport, aptly characterizes the expansion of consciousness that makes audible the flickering voices that emanate from the bridge. The granite of the towers and the steel of the span blend in a new harmony which resolves the conflict, the «iron-dealt cleavage» between rock and soil and technological inventions that is emphasized in «Powhatan's Daughter.» In this vision everything partakes of the same essence, no dualities remain. On another level such fusion occurs in the multiple puns of the poem. The word «staves,» for example, may refer to the planks of a ship, the rungs of a rack or ladder (perhaps a Jacob's ladder), or the stanzas of a poem, the bridge being a symbol of poetic organization.

The voices are «sibylline;» they prophesy the imminent incarnation of a god. The word «issue» means both offspring in a literal sense and the music that flows from the harp-bridge, and the incarnation theme was present in the version of January 18, 1926, with its reference to the «white nativity» of the bridge. In the proem the protagonist stands under the bridge and prays for divine revelation; now he has entered the sanctuary and listens to the holy music. But he never faces his deity or explains its nature, and its presence is only hypothetical, an «as though.» Like the proem, «Atlantis» describes both faith and doubt.

The second stanza pauses from the concentrated upward thrust of the imagination, which subsides as the larger meaning of the bridge is defined:

And through that cordage, threading with its call
One arc synoptic of all tides below —
Their labyrinthine mouths of history
Pouring reply as though all ships at sea
Complighted in one vibrant breath made cry, —
«Make thy love sure — to weave whose song we ply!»
— From black embankments, moveless soundings hailed,
So seven oceans answer from their dream.

Now the bridge emerges as the «one arc,» the perfect emblem, not of the *details* of a Utopia, but of a new consciousness which fuses and interlinks all the traditions of the past into a new whole within which they are fulfilled. The sea represents the vast, unordered reservoir of the world's different races, creeds, ideas etc., as they are gathered throughout history, and above this conglomerate soars the triumphant span of the bridge, symbol of the new totality, of the resolution of historical conflict and the ultimate end of all history. This poetic version of the idea of America as a new cultural whole must have appealed strongly to Waldo Frank, who must have seen in Crane's work evidence that his own concept of «the Whole» was gaining ground in the minds of some. The following statement by Frank can be employed as a paraphrase of the second stanza: «America, from its historic outset, has had the *mystic tradition:* a tradition, that is, which rose from consciousness of the whole of man and of God; which linked the land with all lands and all men; which identified the self of our land with the destiny of human kind.»[122] The experience which the bridge stands for is

165

present and accessible, but not yet attained by all; the span runs far above ordinary reality, it is present yet apart, like Whitman's eyes in «Cape Hatteras,» which shine in the labyrinth of the city which is «not our empire yet.» The «labyrinthine mouths» are not only those of history, but those of the people of the subway, who pray for a redemptive vision.

The voyage across the ocean in quest of the ideal land is a favorite theme in myth and literature, and America, the great bridge, sums up all the aspirations of all voyagers: Jason, Aeneas, Columbus, transforming their dreams into one «breath» or song, the essence of which is love, the great unifying power. All the voices of history and tradition, speaking in an eternal presence, combine into the supreme song of the bridge of America, the bridge of pure and universal love and harmony. Its span embodies the dreams of all the earth, of the «seven oceans» of the whole world.

The image of America as the common goal of the historical development of mankind was celebrated by Whitman, for example, in «Pioneers! O Pioneers!:» «All the pulses of the world,/ Falling in they beat for us, with the Western movements beat,/ Holding single or together, steady moving to the front, all for us.»[123] History and its cultures move continually westward, flourishing here and there, but always starting anew in search of a higher fulfillment, which becomes possible in America.

Stanzas three through five return to the pattern of ascension in a series of flights reaching ever higher and higher:

And on, obliquely up bright carrier bars
New octaves threstle the twin monoliths
Beyond whose frosted capes the moon bequeaths
Two worlds of sleep (O arching strands of song!) —
Onward and up the crystal-flooded aisle
White tempest nets file upward, upward ring
With silver terraces the humming spars
The loft of vision, palladium helm of stars.

The association of bridge and music is further developed, and so is the wordplay. The «carrier bars» refer to the vertical suspenders that extend from the main cables and to the diagonal stays that intersect them. As the bridge becomes a harp, the bars assume a musicological meaning, the measures of a stave. «Carrier» means not only a suppor-

166

ting device, but a messenger bringing spiritual communications. The music of the bridge climbs the octaves, ever soaring upward, but the word «octave» may also refer to an eight-line stanza, which, incidentally, is the verse form chosen in «Atlantis.» The braced framework or «threstle» of the suspenders and the stays suggest the image of a sheet of music. The «two worlds of sleep» are obscure references. The word «cape» suggests the sea, and it may be that the Atlantic and the Pacific oceans are alluded to here. The sea can be a symbol of rest and oblivion in Crane's work, for example, in «At Melville's Tomb,» where the sea keeps the «fabulous shadow» of the «mariner.» However, «Atlantis» presents a struggle to overcome the everpresent lure of the sea and does it by repeated emphasis on the upward drive of the imagery.

The «crystal-flooded aisle» leads up to some high altar, and the imagery of gems, precious metals, stars and whiteness becomes more concentrated than ever as the poet probes the essence of his revelation. Different emblems relieve each other throughout the poem, each containing the supreme insight which is the end of the poetic quest. The «silver terraces» recall the aerial flight of the «silvery biplane» of «Cape Hatteras» and the «nimble blue plateaus» of the air described in «Faustus and Helen.»

The «spars» refer to parts of an airplane wing, but the word can also mean the mast of a ship. In this pun is foreshadowed the figure of a two-dimensional voyage through sea and air that is developed in stanza five. An image of a ship running across the sky and leaving a wake is related to the «orbic wake» of Elohim in «Ave Maria» and is suggested by the word «helm,» meaning a rudder. It also refers to a helmet, in particular the one belonging to Pallas Athena, the goddess from whose name «palladium» is derived. Athena supervised the construction of «Argo,» the ship of Jason, whose voyage is invoked further on in the poem.

The first part of stanza four contains a vision of eyes that fly or swim upward like frosty seagulls or fish propelled by «fins of light.» The dual nature of this flight reinforces the projected air-and-sea voyage.[124] The «looms» of the bridge «press» or condense

— Tomorrows into yesteryear — and link
What cipher-script of time no traveller reads
But who, through smoking pyres of love and death,
Searches the timeless laugh of mythic spears.

The Ouspenskian idea of the eternal present may have influenced these lines. The poet sees past and future lying together, co-existing in the consciousness of that «traveller» or voyager who can read the signs that are present in ordinary human time, the structure of the bridge, for example. In the high vision all time is fused, and he who achieves it knows the future as well as the past and pronounces everything good. The poet or «traveller» identifies himself with Quetzalcoatl, like him he sacrifices himself on «smoking pyres,» but he is also the returning god, a modern counterpart to the conquistadores whom the Aztecs hailed as the founders of a new order.

As the past merges with the present, Crane creates a synopsis of voyages in search of fabulous realms or cities, going back to the story of Jason and the Argonauts. Jason's «Argo» was, according to legend, the first ship ever to be built, and his is the archetype of all voyages. The bridge resurrects the glory of legendary ancient cities, other instances of the Belle Isle or Atlantis vision. «Tyre,» the great and wealthy city of the seafaring Phoenicians, was situated on an island near the mainland. The poem suggests an image of an island-city floating in the air, and the image of the disk that we recall from the 1923 drafts is alluded to in the vision of «planet-sequined heights,» «sequin» meaning gold coin or metal disk. Imagery of steelwork construction, of hammers and anvils, suggests that a new «Troy,» the heroic city whose fate was linked with that of Helen, is being «riveted» or constructed. Such a fusion of present and past, of New York and ancient capitals of culture and religion, is described in a lyrical letter to Frank of April 21, 1924. Referring to the view from his window in Columbia Heights, the poet wrote: «That window is where I would be most remembered of all: the ships, the harbor, and the skyline of Manhattan, midnight, morning or evening, — rain, snow or sun, it is everything from mountains to the walls of Jerusalem and Nineveh, and all related and in actual contact with the changelessness of the many waters that surround it. I think the sea has thrown itself upon me and been answered, at least in part, and I believe I am a little changed — not essentially, but changed and transubstantiated as anyone who has asked a question and been answered.»

The sea-and-sky voyage bodies forth in the vision of Jason, who «hests» or commands the air as if he were harnessing a horse. Here is an echo of the «harnessed jelly of the stars» of «Cape Hatteras;» and perhaps also of «the saddled sky» of the warring planes of «Faustus and Helen.» In these instances the poet seems to want to conceive of air as some sort of liquid or concrete substance, thus in a sense fusing the elements of sea and air. Another example is the plane that cuts across the «foaming anthracite» of the sky in «Cape Hatteras.»

The expedition of the Argonauts is connected with that of Columbus in that is was undertaken to recover the golden fleece; gold, as we know, being associated with the Cathay image. The silvery wake of the «Argo» links with the wake of Elohim, and the «yelling beams» are an oblique allusion to the oracular beam put into the prow of the ship by Athena. Aeolus ruled the winds and the floating island Aeolia, which invokes the Belle Isle emblem. The «straits» are presumably the Symplegades, the rocks guarding the Bosporus that crushed all ships that attempted to pass between them. The «Argo» avoided this fate, but its stern ornament was caught, «splintered» between the rocks.

Stanza six brings the upward movement to a climax. From the great «gulf» of human history and experience rises the bridge, the goal of all voyages, real as well as spiritual:

> From gulfs unfolding, terrible of drums,
> Tall Vision-of-the-Voyage, tensely spare —
> Bridge, lifting night to cycloramic crest
> Of deepest day — O Choir, translating time
> Into what multitudinous Verb the suns
> And synergy of waters ever fuse, recast
> In myriad syllables, — Psalm of Cathay!
> O Love, thy white, pervasive Paradigm . . .

In «The Dance» the sound of drums signals the apotheosis of Maquokeeta; in «Atlantis» the drums accompany the vision of the bridge as movement or voyage and as source of light, defying night and «lifting» it into all-encompassing or «cycloramic» day. Atlantis itself is a kind of voyage, something sallying forth, emerging. Drums accompany the sunken Atlantis rose in «Cutty Sark:» «drums wreathe the rose.» The bridge as woman is subtly suggested in the metaphor of «lifting night,» which harks back to the proem, in which we saw night «lifted in thine arms.» The recurring metaphors of the bridge as a great poem or word find their climax in this stanza. A massive choir issues from the bridge-harp, it is the «Verb» or poem which expresses the consciousness of spiritual unity which Crane defined as the meaning of

Cathay. The linguistic metaphor is sustained here: love, the unifying power, is a «Paradigm.» The same linguistic analogy is used by Frank, who stated that it is necessary to look upon the state, the church or the person as «Verbs» instead of «Nouns.» In conceiving of the idea of America, we must regard both people and institutions as verbs, elements that act dynamically together to form a whole.[125] The Platonic epigraph to «Atlantis» defines love as a state of harmony analogous to that of music: «Music is then the knowledge of that which relates to love in harmony and system.» The sentence is taken from *The Symposium,* in which the concept of harmony is further elaborated upon: «harmony is composed of differing notes of higher or lower pitch which disagreed once, but are now reconciled by the art of music; for if the higher and lower notes still disagreed, there could be no harmony . . . For harmony is a symphony, and symphony is an agreement . . .»[126]

The poet goes on to rehearse again the theme of the voyage of discovery, now with clear overtones of «Ave Maria:»

We left the haven hanging in the night —
Sheened harbor lanterns backward fled the keel.
Pacific here at time's end, bearing corn, —
Eyes stammer through the pangs of dust and steel.

The harbor may be both Palos and New York; the poet in his imagination spans both the sea and the American continent in his sea-and-air voyage, reaching the Pacific. The end of his journey is the end of time, the experience of the eternal presence of all time that was expressed by the «arc synoptic» and «multitudinous Verb». Eternity for Crane is conceived of less as the timeless, the non-existence of time, than as the coexistence of all time fused in one, mystic moment.

Pocahontas, the American corn goddess, is subtly invoked here; the eyes of the seer wrestle with the «iron-dealt cleavage» of the conflicting elements of nature and civilization, earth and steel, until harmony is restored. The «one song» of the poem binds everything together in a perfect wholeness, and its «vernal strophe chimes from deathless strings!» The promise of a new world, emerging in the poem or «strophe,» is a «vernal» theme that ever returns, like spring itself. The seasonal rebirth pattern is active throughout *The Bridge*; in «Van Winkle» the poet receives a lilac twig from his father in spring, and we have the springtime flowering of Pocahontas in «The Dance.» Another spring-time is associated with Whitman's poetry in «Cape Hatteras,» and, again, in the light and sprightly rhythms of «Virginia.»

In moments of faith Crane felt his vision as something complete and perfect and presented it in the belief that a cultural springtime would occur. In such moments the «steeled Cognizance» of the bridge, the vernal vision, is consummate:

O thou steeled Cognizance whose leap commits
The agile precincts of the lark's return;
Within whose lariat sweep encinctured sing
In single chrysalis the many twain, —
Of stars Thou art the stitch and stallion glow
And like an organ, Thou, with sound of doom —
Sight, sound and flesh Thou leadest from time's realm
As love strikes clear direction for the helm

Like the seagull that takes wing each dawn, the flight of the lark, re-turning in spring, suggests the renewal of vision, the very meaning of which is manifest in the steely «leap» of the bridge. The word «com-mit» must here be taken to mean consign or preserve. More metaphors of encirclement, totality, are introduced: «lariat sweep» and «encinc-tured,» and the theme of the Many in One, the unified cognizance, is concretized in the image of a chrysalis out of which a wonderful future is born like a beautiful butterfly.

The traffic lights that became starlike beads in the proem reappear as a «stitch» of stars in the fabric of the sky, and the stars are also like the white teeth of stallions, a curious image which Crane referred to as «the motif of the holy tooth» in the letter of January 18, 1926, to Frank. The image occurs in «The Dance:» «stag teeth foam about the raven throat,» and in the description of flowers in «Cape Hatteras» as «bared teeth of stallions.» The poet may have had in mind some use of teeth as talismans or sacred objects. In «Van Winkle» the sound of a hand organ evokes the spanning of the whole American continent. In «Atlantis» the bridge is both harp and organ, the music of which re-veals the unifying principle of love beyond the dimensions of material reality: «sight, sound and flesh.» The bridge-ship voyages toward love, and the word «helm» now refers to rudder rather than helmet.

The power of revelation is anchored in man's consciousness, his «veins:»

Swift peal of secular light, intrinsic Myth
Whose fell unshadow is death's utter wound, —
O River-throated — iridescently upborne
Through the bright drench and fabric of our veins;
With white escarpments swinging into light,
Sustained in tears the cities are endowed
And justified conclamant with ripe fields
Revolving through their harvests in sweet torment.

Apart from the first two lines, this stanza was preserved unchanged through all the versions of «Atlantis,» from its initial appearance in the draft of July 4, 1923, to the final version. In the first draft the first two lines went like this: «To be, Great Bridge, in vision bound of thee,/ So widely straight and turning, ribbon-wound,» and they were not significantly altered until 1926. The change seems to imply that the poet to begin with believed in the power of the bridge vision to sustain him permanently; the harmony it yielded was felt to be present in a reality outside of the poet and his words. The earliest drafts have almost none of the repeated later references to the poetic medium itself as the primary instrument of revelation. The «Great Bridge» became the «*intrinsic* Myth,» the capacity of our own faculties to achieve spiritual insight. The sound of bells and light itself are fused, synesthetically, in a «peal of secular light;» the word «secular» reinforcing the awareness that the light resides in man's poetic consciousness. The word «fell» must be taken to mean «fierce» in this context. The supreme poetic insight was never easily achieved by Crane.

The «myth» or light is always with us, perhaps buried in the «throat» of the river of time (in «The River» the Mississippi «drinks the farthest dale»). The rainbow, representing the same quality as the bridge, inheres in our very flesh and bones, as in the «rainbows currying each pulsant bone» in «The Dance.» The vein image occurs in the «sanskrit charge» of the «wrist» of the pilot of «Cape Hatteras,» and also in the phrase «It is blood to remember,» that is, remember revelation, in «Southern Cross.»[127] In «The Broken Tower» Crane questioned seriously this very ability to create and sustain the tower of poetic vision: «The steep encroachments of my blood left me/ no answer (could blood hold such a lofty tower . . .?)»

Echoes of «Faustus and Helen» occur in the ninth stanza of «Atlantis,» for example, the beautiful «white cities passed on to assume/

That world which comes to each of us alone.» Also, Waldo Frank describes the ideal New York of his dreams as a «scintillant city rising like an army of arrows toward the Sun, its Father.»[128] These cities are «justified» or redeemed by the poet's vision, symbolized by the eye image which is implied in the reference to tears, which also suggest the association of poetry and suffering.[129]

The tenth stanza concludes what in terms of imagery constitutes the first part of «Atlantis.» The final two paragraphs are the second part. Part one mainly revolves around the physical and spiritual phenomenon of the bridge, whereas part two leaves the bridge and its construction largely behind and develops fully the image of the «Atlantis rose.» Stanza ten presents us with more idioms denoting the music of the bridge; it is a «canticle,» meaning religious hymn, which links with «Deity's glittering Pledge,» the divine covenant or promise that America shall be holy land. Being new, the sacred song produces «fresh» spiritual bliss in the modern worshipper.

The final mystic emblems of «Atlantis» are determined by circular imagery. The curve of the bridge has become a circle:

Migrations that must needs void memory,
Inventions that cobblestone the heart, —
Unspeakable Thou Bridge to Thee, O Love.
Thy pardon for this history, whitest Flower,
O Answerer of all, — Anemone, —
Now while thy petals spend the suns about us, hold —
(O Thou whose radiance doth inherit me)
Atlantis, — hold thy floating singer late!

So to thine Everpresence, beyond time,
Like spears ensanguined of one tolling star
That bleeds infinity — the orphic strings,
Sidereal phalanxes, leap and converge:
— One Song, one Bridge of Fire! Is it Cathay,
Now pity steeps the grass and rainbows ring
The serpent with the eagle in the leaves . . .?
Whispers antiphonal in azure swing.

Love is the essence of the monistic reality revealed by the symbol of the anemone. The «Atlantis rose» has developed into a great seaflower, a Belle Isle afloat in the ocean. The emblem represents the ultimate integration, the harmony of a total design which alone can redeem the imperfections of history as it is. The white flower of Atlantis lies on the sea, as it were, and its radiance sustains the poet in a moment's consummation. He asks his symbol to «hold» him, to keep him from sinking, or drowning, in the sea of life.

Whitman's cosmic self and Frank's «mystic sense of the Whole» are intimately related to Crane's idea of the bridge as a symbol of «consciousness spanning time and space.» These thought-complexes find poetic form in the figure of a circular, wheel-like emblem of ultimate synthesis in the last stanza of «Atlantis.» The emblem seems to have been inspired by an illustration in *Scientific American,* which he told Frank in the letter of August 3, 1926, that he wanted to reprint in *The Bridge.* The illustration is an angle chart, and Crane wrote that it «embodies a complete symbolism of both Bridge and Star.»[130] The chart shows a large circle, within which is another figure consisting of a smaller circle from whose center spokes radiate as in a wheel. This hub is the focus of the upper, converging lines of a third, heart-shaped figure larger than the small circle. The spokes of the small circle continue beyond its circumference into the heart-shaped figure.

The «one tolling star» corresponds to the focus of the small circle, toward which all the spokes aspire and converge. Similarly, the «spears» of the poem «leap and converge» like «sidereal,» starlike, columns or «phalanxes» toward the star. The overall effect is one of lines that veer toward a focal point, suggesting the figure of a cone. That the apex of this cone is pointing upward cannot be determined from the angle chart itself, but we may assume that we are confronted with the figure of the ascending spiral that we know from the 1923 versions of «Atlantis» and other contexts. The «One Song» of the final experience of the mystical unity of being issues from «orphic strings,» a fitting epithet. Crane conceived of himself as an orphic poet, one whose words had magic powers of transformation and revelation.[131]

The apotheosized bridge, transformed into this circular emblem, culminates in the ultimate, unitive conditions of music and fire, and the Whitmanian vision of an immutable essence of All of «Cape Hatteras» is reaffirmed. In «Passage to India» this center of all being is celebrated in light imagery: «O Thou transcendent/ Nameless, the fibre and the breath,/ Light of the light, shedding forth universes, thou centre of them.»[132] Frank, in his discursion on «Mystic America,» distinguishes between modes or foci of the vision of wholeness: «The experience of true wholeness is a light that can be centered sharp and wide; illuming by its focus what is called self, what is called the nation, what is called the cosmos.»[133] The wholeness of the nation was what Crane wanted to realize in *The Bridge*, and the radiance of «Atlantis» is the most forceful expression of his longings.

«Atlantis» has a cosmic significance, but when the poet returns to the Cathay-image in the concluding lines and repeats the symbolism of the serpent and the eagle, he returns to the main theme, the search for a new world, the Cathay-consciousness. In «The Dance,» the serpent and the eagle represent Pocahontas; in «Atlantis» one should consider a supplementary meaning of this symbolism. According to their myths, the Aztecs founded their great city of Tenochtitlan at the place where they saw the following omen: «they beheld a high rock with a cactus growing on it. Upon the cactus was an eagle. Up he rose; he flew towards the rising sun, and in his talons he held a serpent.»[134] The return of the white gods heralded the founding of a new society, a new world. The moment of radiance and harmony which is Atlantis is the message that the poet wants to bring, but the question mark in the second last line records his continued doubt concerning the truth of his revelation. The doubt is as real as the faith, the renewed possibility of which is suggested in the last line of *The Bridge,* with its «Whispers antiphonal» that promise a new dawn.[135]

Crane felt himself isolated in his vision, and yet he felt compelled to present it in his poem. He struggled between a private and esthetic contemplation of the vision and the urge to make it public, to spread it as a national mystique. We may take the very fact that *The Bridge* was published as evidence that Crane felt that his poem might have some public significance and be related to a living tradition in America. Moreover, he commented to Frank in a letter of February 19, 1931, that «Present day America seems a long way off from the destiny I fancied when I wrote that poem.»

In spite of all his doubts and reservations, then, Crane did pursue a mystic-Utopian vision of America, but his presentation of it was modified by the less than glorious realities of his life and times, and «progress» as he conceived of it, was only something that could come from within the consciousness of man, if at all. *The Bridge,* with its alternating moods of faith and despair, is an eloquent testimony of the gap that separates the visionary poet from his audience in the twentieth century, and the question mark at the end is parallelled by the hesitant, doubtful tone of the concluding, prophetic pages of Frank's *The Re-Discovery of America*: «We are dealing with a world that never yet has been; a world which may come true if it is true (as I believe) that man is still an infant and all his history a cradle story. But it may never be. The dangers besetting this recreated man are subtle and vast. I am sure he can exist. I am sure, if he comes together with his kind, that there will be strength to transform the pliant American world. The doubtful test is that which will decide whether such men, each overwhelmed by the mechanical and inner Jungle of our life whose every power is a scattering and a marshalling against them, can join; or whether they must live alone, each one; and die alone.»[136]

Both Frank and Crane were aware of the great difficulties that lay ahead for anyone who devoted himself to the propagation of their vision of the new America, but the strength of Crane's visionary conviction is evident in the powerful symbols of «Atlantis.» Here emerges, more clearly than anywhere else, the notion or image of America as holy land, divinely infused whole. However, it does not refer back to an ideal that was real somewhere in the past and that must be revived, but it does reaffirm various *promises* of the past and presents a synthesis that is paradoxical in the sense that it is timeless yet points to the future. Thus the image finally relates itself to American history as the possible growth of an awareness in the minds of men. Within *The Bridge* itself, the «myth of America» emerges as a mystical, supralogical synthesis of several historical and modern episodes, images and scenes that combine into the grand unity of the finale of the poem.

IV. Concluding note

In writing a poem such as *The Bridge,* Hart Crane set himself a task
of such magnitude that he had to confront challenges and problems of
enormous proportions. He accepted the challenge and produced a
large-scale poem on a theme which could hardly have been greater or
more significant — the destiny of America itself. The national idealism
which *The Bridge* expresses represents a central factor of the American
psyche which is a continual challenge both for the artist and the public.
Ezra Pound demanded of American poets that they must «make it
new,» start from the beginning, and Crane answered this call in the
most literal sense. In *The Bridge* he created a mystic, national symbolism, constituting a new set of heraldic images that were to represent a
new religion, a truly American *mystique.* He wanted to believe in this
mystique, though he was never wholly convinced by it or comfortable
within it. However, since the publication of *The Bridge* in 1930, there
has been no comparable effort in American poetry, with the possible
exception of the work of William Carlos Williams and Allen Ginsberg,
to create such a *mystique.* Crane may have been the last poet to reaffirm the grand attempt of American romanticism, to transmute the divine in uniquely American terms. The accelerating secularization of
the twentieth century certainly has made this effort increasingly difficult. In Crane's own era, which now lies more than fifty years back,
the traces of the utopian hopes were still relatively fresh. These religious and social hopes and aspirations were expressed in some of the
architecture of the times and the period immediately preceding it. The
neo-Gothic construction of The Brooklyn Bridge itself was completed
in 1883, sixteen years before Crane's birth, and a similar architecture
can be seen in some of the buildings of lower Manhattan, notably the
Woolworth tower, the «temple of commerce» which was erected in
1912.[1] For a man of Crane's generation it was still possible to entertain
hopes of the emergence of a religious Utopia where the forces of

technology, religious faith and even capitalism would combine into a new synthesis. But the spiritual aspirations of *The Bridge* serve only too well to illuminate the gap between them and the American reality, even as it was in Crane's own time: the virtual absence of any communal sharing or even knowledge of the poem's vision, an obsession with power and material gain, the dominance of superficial and conventional forms of religious life.

And yet, in a very fundamental sense, Crane's poem expresses a principle which traditionally, at least, has been perceived as a fundamental part of the American experience. This principle, which has both banal and lofty aspects, is that of synthesis, of unification and bridging of the diversities, disparities and conflicts of all sorts that have beset human history in general and European in particular. The American imagination has been a synthesizing one, giving the artist the freedom to use any available material, creed or influence to create new harmonies. Crane's bridge of love and divine power is one such attempted leap into an affirmation of a harmony hitherto largely unknown and unrecognized.

The Bridge has been regarded as a failure by more than one critic, and it is certainly not flawless. However, when we think back on it as a visionary poem about America, published in 1930, we might ask ourselves if it may not be possible to apply the work «failure» in a wider sense. Crane's dream of a land filled with spiritual love and beauty was always precariously upheld in a modern, industrialized and commercialized world, but it was brutally smashed by the central world event that occurred during Crane's last years, the financial crash of 1929 and the ensuing great economic depression. The America that Crane was praising in *The Bridge* failed utterly to live up to his expectations. Thus, the questions posed in *The Bridge* go beyond the personal life of the poet and beyond the difficulties and shortcomings of the poem as a work of art. Because of its utopian theme, *The Bridge* is related to the social and political sphere, and when regarded from this perspective, its dilemma is the same that confronts any liberal utopian literature or ideology within the context of a capitalist society. The poem expresses a desire to transcend the conditions of its own time and place, to envisage a better and more glorious future for America, but during the period when the work was written, conditions in the country changed from boom to economic collapse. The hopeful vision of *The Bridge* came to seem unreal and abstract in the face of grim reality, although the poem retained, and retains, the power to illuminate the still existing gap between the ideal and the real.

The enduring importance of *The Bridge* is perhaps due to its serving as a reminder to the country to try and fulfill its historical promise. The poem refuses to stop within the realm of the purely esthetic, and herein lies its persistent, if perhaps unfashionable, challenge. Crane's poem is evidence of a desire to accept the facts of twentieth-century experience, including works of technology, and even regard them as evidence of a divine design, in an age which seems to have abandoned all religious certainties.

However, when one speaks of Crane's religiosity, it is important to recall that it was not a Puritan faith at all. Like Frank and Whitman, Crane sought the spiritual element by getting closely involved with a wide range of experience, including the act of physical love-making, the cultivation of the senses so as to be able to respond strongly and sharply to the environment, the readiness to appreciate the dynamism and beauty of machinery. By thus identifying with «all of life,» as Crane put it, it would be possible to discern, gradually but ever more clearly, the wholeness of it all, which alone could redeem and justify modern America.

In their insistence on the importance of wholeness and spiritual unity, the hopeful and visionary parts of *The Bridge* still stand as denials of and counterweights against the modern trend towards social atomization and the withdrawal into the privatistic life and sphere. A bridge is something we create in order to span and connect the gaps that tend to develop between people themselves and people and their world. All too often, societies seek to unite on a negative basis, against common enemies or scapegoats, or against a background of broad social and ideological divisions. Crane's poem about the bridge of love is different in that its premise is a positive, affirmative one that, ideally speaking, everyone should be able to accept. The bridge of love that is Crane's mystic America is all-embracing and tolerant rather than discriminating and evaluating; it represents an abundant, spontaneous generosity that is more in keeping with America's historical view of itself than the sophistication and reserve of older and different cultures. The poet's pursuit of his vision is a process of continual struggle, even suffering. In *The Bridge*, he confronts experience headlong, as it were, and opens himself up to its hopeful as well as destructive aspects. Then, occasionally, the vision is released, revealing the hidden structures of beauty and harmony that exist in the reality around him. The emotional poles of the poet's experience were great despair and ecstatic joy, and *The Bridge* reflects these extremes throughout all of its sections without really committing itself to either one of these positions. In «The Tunnel,» the darkest section, the poet is said to rise like Lazarus from the dead, and in the grand finale, «Atlantis,» the last lines question the very existence of the vision.

This position is unusual, but it is in keeping with the whole structure of *The Bridge* and with the split or division within Crane himself. His letters contain ample evidence of the fact that he was capable both of a naive, religious enthusiasm and of skeptical rationalism, and the two attitudes are present in his poetry as well. *The Bridge* reflects a thoroughly divided attitude toward the synthesis of America, a visionary conviction that coexists, as it were, with disbelief and disillusionment.

This dualistic attitude is in fact quite simple. It consists of a wholly affirmative, loving attitude to everything, whether it be people, the city, nature or machinery, and a black pessimism, in which everything that looked so promising suddenly becomes transformed, so to speak, before the poet's eyes, and assumes all sorts of sinister and threatening forms and shapes. Both responses are equally real for the poet; both are experienced with the same degree of intensity. As we have seen, this division is reflected in the poem in several ways. There is the separation between the hopeful or ecstatic sections, like «The Harbor Dawn,» «The Dance,» «To Brooklyn Bridge» and «Atlantis,» and the disillusioned or tragic poems like «Southern Cross,» «Quaker Hill» and «The Tunnel.» Within the context of individual poems there are also shifts of emphasis and dramatic changes of action and atmosphere, as in the suggested fall of the bedlamite in the proem, the tempest in «Ave Maria,» the satirical view of technology in the power house scene of «Cape Hatteras,» and the question mark in the last stanza of «Atlantis.» Finally, there is the consistently dual pattern of imagery, whereby the figures of hope and visionary unity, such as curves and circles, flight, birds, women images, dance, fire and spiralling movements, occur in sinister and ironic versions in certain passages and sections.

The Bridge reveals the drama of the poet's faith and doubt in relation to his mystic America. The faith assimilated by Crane via Walt Whitman and Waldo Frank envisages a unification of the American experience in which evil and darkness are included and transcended. The doubt concerns the validity or possibility of this vision itself, a suspicion that reality is intractable, disordered, flawed beyond repair, that the divine whole, in fact, does not exist.[2]

In terms of its ideas about America, *The Bridge* expresses both absolute faith and absolute doubt. Thereby it presents a pattern that is repetitive rather than evolving, changing, maturing. The spiritual never finds any secure foothold in the real, because of the poem's violent vacillations between despair and hope. However, the poem also derives a certain strength from this, a quality of infinite longing that is typical of «To Brooklyn Bridge,» «Ave Maria,» «The Harbor Dawn,» «The Dance» and «Atlantis».

The Bridge, as a whole, is an impressive poetic performance, but all of its sections and passages are not equally successful. At its best, Crane's poetry is intense, visionary, complex without being too complicated. At its worst, it is strained, obscure and overwrought. The beginning and the end of «The Dance» contain poignant and enchanting poetry, but the middle, the ritual dance and sacrifice, is artificial and melodramatic. The reader has the feeling that the poet is protesting too much. Even «Atlantis,» for all its undeniable splendor, is occasionally marred by abstract, overblown rhetoric, as in stanzas six and ten. In those parts of «Cape Hatteras» where Crane announces his faith in Whitman's vision or celebrates the beauty of the airplanes, genuine conviction seems to have been replaced by loud proclamations and a form of adolescent worship of technology.

A weakness of another kind is demonstrated in poems like «Indiana» and «Quaker Hill.» Large parts of these poems are prosaic and pedestrian and lack the richness and tension of the texture that more successful sections present. Both poems, however, are necessary parts within the larger plan of *The Bridge*. «Indiana» is a link between the mythic past of «The Dance» and the poet's own twentieth-century experience in «Cutty Sark,» and «Quaker Hill» forms a natural transition from the light lyricism of «Virginia» to the bleak despair of «The Tunnel.» Also, the story of the pioneer woman and the decay of the New England countryside are interesting and worthwhile subjects both as elements of *The Bridge* and as subjects in themselves. But the straightforward emotionalism of «Indiana» and the directness of the attack on materialism in «Quaker Hill» are incongruous in relation to the sophisticated technique and complex emotional appeal of the poem

as a whole. A similar objection can be raised with regard to
«Virginia,» although the graceful rhythms of this poem do much to
make up for the relatively insubstantial impression that it creates.[3]

However, the best poems of *The Bridge* are superb examples of Romantic American poetry of the modern age, and that in itself is a rare achievement. Sections like «To Brooklyn Bridge,» «Ave Maria,» «The Harbor Dawn,» «Van Winkle,» «The River,» «Cutty Sark,» «The Tunnel,» as well as much of «The Dance,» «Cape Hatteras» and «Atlantis» contain poetry of the highest order and convey a sense of pure, magic beauty that transforms the American realities and makes the reader believe in the poet's vision. In the history of American poetry, Hart Crane was one of those who devoted themselves to the task of «making America» so that its civilization could be affirmed and embraced. His poem therefore still stands at the centre of an unresolved dilemma of the technological society we have created. The mystic vision of *The Bridge* attempts a reconciliation of the spirit and the machine which we can ill afford to abandon because of man's continued need to feel that some vital relation beyond the utilitarian one exists between himself and the technological works he produces. This vital relation does not stop at the level of our sense of artistic form and of the power represented by technology and architecture; an awareness of these aspects is more or less inevitable. The unique contribution of *The Bridge* is its insistence on the religious function of the manifestations of American life, the millenial hopes that it sees in bridges, skyscrapers, trains and airplanes. Such a hopeful vision may yet prove to be an important element for the continued progress and development of the technological civilization that America still is.

Bibliography

The following bibliography is limited to works quoted in this study.

The American Long Poem: An Annotated Selection, ed. Stephen Fender. London, 1977.

Andreach, Robert. *Studies in Structure: The Stages of the Spiritual Life in Four Modern Authors.* Fordham University Press, 1964.

Arpad, Joseph. «Hart Crane's Platonic Myth: The Brooklyn Bridge,» *American Literature,* 34 (1967).

Blackmur, R. P. *The Double Agent: Essays in Craft and Elucidation.* Gloucester, Mass., 1962.

Blake, William. *The Complete Writings of William Blake,* ed. Geoffrey Keynes. New York, 1957.

Brinton, Daniel. *American Hero-Myths: A Study in the Native Religions of the Western Continent.* Philadelphia, 1882.

Butterfield, R. W. *The Broken Arc: A Study of Hart Crane.* Edinburgh, 1969.

Cambon, Glauco. *The Inclusive Flame: Studies in Modern American Poetry.* Bloomington, 1965.

Chase, Richard. *Quest for Myth.* Baton Rouge, 1949.

Coffman, Stanley. «Symbolism in *The Bridge,*» *PMLA,* 66 (1951).

Colum, Padraic. *Orpheus: Myths of the World.* New York, 1930.

Columbus, Christopher. *The Journal of Christopher Columbus (During his First Voyage, 1492—1493),* trans. Clements R. Markham. London, 1893.

Cowley, Malcolm. «A Preface to Hart Crane,» *The New Republic,* 62 (1930).

Dembo, Lawrence. *Hart Crane's Sanskrit Charge: A Study of The Bridge.* Ithaca, 1960.

Deutsch, Babette. *Poetry in Our Time.* New York, 1952.

Dickinson, Emily. *The Complete Poems of Emily Dickinson with an Introduction by her Niece Martha Dickinson Bianchi.* Boston, 1926.

Drew, Elizabeth. «The Trouble with Modern Poetry,» *Saturday Review of Literature,* 14 (1936)

Duncan, Isadora. *My Life.* New York, 1927.

Eliot, T. S. *The Complete Poems and Plays.* New York, 1952.

Frank, Waldo. *In the American Jungle: 1925—1936.* New York 1937.

—«—. *Our America.* New York, 1919.

—«—. *Salvos.* New York, 1924.

—«—. *The Re-Discovery of America.* New York, 1929.

—«—. *Virgin Spain.* New York, 1926.

—«—. *Rahab.* New York, 1922.

—«—. *City Block.* New York, 1922.

—«—. *The Death and Birth of David Markand.* New York, 1934.

—«—. *Memoirs of Waldo Frank,* ed. Alan Trachtenberg. The University of Massachussetts Press, 1973.

Frye, Northrop. *Anatomy of Criticism.* Princeton, 1957.

Grigsby, Gordon K. «Hart Crane's Doubtful Vision: A Note on the 'Intention' of *The Bridge,*» *College English,* 24 (April 1963).

Hazo, Samuel. *Hart Crane: An Introduction and Interpretation.* New York, 1963.

Hoffman, Frederick. *The Twenties: American Writing in the Postwar Decade,* New York, 1949.

Horton, Philip. *Hart Crane: The Life of an American Poet.* New York, 1937.

Jennings, Elizabeth. *Every Changing Shape.* London, 1961.

Lawrence, D. H. *The Plumed Serpent.* London, 1926.

—«—. *Studies in Classic American Literature.* New York, 1964.

Lewis, R. W. B. *The Poetry of Hart Crane: A Critical Study.* Princeton, 1967.

Marlowe, Christopher. *Marlowe's Plays and Poems,* ed. M. R. Ridley. London, 1961.

Matthiessen, F. O. «American Poetry 1920—40,» *Sewanee Review,* 55 (1947).

Melville, Herman. *The Selected Poems of Herman Melville,* ed. Hennig Cohen. Carbondale, 1964.

Metzger, Deena Posy. «Hart Crane's Bridge: The Myth Active,» *Arizona Quarterly,* 20 (1964).

Modern Poetry: American and British, eds. Malcolm Friar and John Brinnin. New York, 1951.

Moss, Howard. «Disorder as Myth: Hart Crane's *The Bridge,*» *Poetry,* 57 (1943).

Munson, Gorham. *Waldo Frank: A Study.* New York, 1923.

Nassar, Eugene Paul. *The Rape of Cinderella: Essays in Literary Continuity.* Bloomington, 1970.

Ouspensky, P. D. *Tertium Organum: The Third Canon of Thought. A Key to the Enigmas of the World.* New York, 1922.

Paul, Sherman. *Hart's Bridge.* Urbana, 1972.

Perry, Robert. *The Shared Vision of Waldo Frank and Hart Crane.* Lincoln, 1966.

Plato. *The Dialogues of Plato,* trans. B. Jowett. New York, 1937.

—«—. *The Timaeus and the Critias or Atlanticus,* trans. Thomas Taylor. Washington, D. C., 1944.

Poe, Edgar Allan. *Selected Writings of Edgar Allan Poe.* Boston, 1956.

Prescott, William. *The History of The Reign of Ferdinand and Isabella.* Boston, 1859.

Quinn, Vincent. *Hart Crane.* New York, 1963.

Quinn, Sister M. Bernetta. *The Metamorphic Tradition in Modern Poetry.* New Brunswick, 1955.

Rosenfeld, Paul. *Port of New York.* 1924; rpt. Urbana, 1961.

Sandburg, Carl. *Cornhuskers.* New York, 1918.

—«—. *Smoke and Steel.* New York, 1921.

Schlauch, Margaret. *Modern English and American Poetry: Techniques and Ideologies.* London, 1956.

Shakespeare, William. *Antony and Cleopatra.* The Arden Edition of the Works of William Shakespeare. London, 1954.

Spence, Lewis. *Atlantis in America.* New York, 1926.

—«—. *The Myths of the North American Indians.* London, 1914.

Spengler. Oswald. *The Decline of the West: Complete in One Volume,* trans. Charles F. Atkinson. New York, 1937.

Sugg, Richard. *Hart Crane's The Bridge: A Study of its Life,* The University of Alabama Press, 1976.

Tate, Allen. «A Distinguished Poet,» *The Hound and Horn,* 3 (1930).

Trachtenberg, Alan. *Brooklyn Bridge: Fact and Symbol.* New York, 1956.

Unterecker, John. *Voyager: A Life of Hart Crane.* New York, 1969.

Untermeyer, Louis. «Prophetic Rapsody,» *Saturday Review of Literature,* 6 (1930).

Waggoner, Hyatt Howe. *The Heel of Elohim: Science and Values in Modern American Poetry*. Norman, 1950.

Weber, Brom. *Hart Crane*. New York, 1948.

Whitman, Walt. *Complete Poetry and Selected Prose and Letters,* ed. E. Holloway. London, 1938.

Wilder, Amos. *The Spiritual Aspects of the New Poetry*. New York and London, 1940.

Williams, William Carlos. *I Wanted to Write a Poem: The Autobiography of the Works of a Poet*. London, 1967.

—«—. *In the American Grain*. Norfolk, Conn., 1925.

Winters, Yvor. «The Progress of Hart Crane,» *Poetry,* 36 (1930).

Young, Philip. «The Mother of Us All: Pocahontas Reconsidered,» *The Kenyon Review,* 24 (1962).

Notes

CHAPTER 1

1 Chase, *Quest for Myth* (Baton Rouge, 1949), p. 73.
2 Tate, «A Distinguished Poet,» *The Hound and Horn,* 3 (1930), 582.
3 *Ibid.,* p. 583.
4 Winters, «The Progress of Hart Crane,» *Poetry,* 36 (1930), 153.
5 The other first reviews of *The Bridge* are interesting items of literary history and were written by, among others, such critics as Malcolm Cowley, Granville Hicks and Louis Untermeyer. In his «A Preface to Hart Crane,» *The New Republic,* 62 (1930), 276, Cowley wrote that «although this book of poems . . . begins with a modest apostrophe to a bridge over the East River, it ends bravely as an attempt to create the myth of America.» The rest of Cowley's review was dedicated to an analysis of «The River.» Hick's review in *Nation,* 130 (1930), did not attempt to define the myth. In his review «Prophetic Rhapsody,» *Saturday Review of Literature,* 6 (1930), 1125, Untermeyer praised *The Bridge* as «A set of disparate poems» that were «integrated by vital figures, the figures having been lifted into the realm of national myth.» He went on to state that the poem «approaches . . . a highly sophisticated, highly syncopated local epic.»
6 Drew, «The Trouble with Modern Poetry,» *Saturday Review of Literature,* 14 (1936), 14.
7 Wilder, *The Spiritual Aspects of the New Poetry* (New York and London, 1940), p. 124.
8 Matthiesen, «American Poetry 1920—40,» *Sewanee Review,* 55 (1947), 38.
9 Weber, *Hart Crane* (New York, 1948), p. 323.
10 *Modern Poetry: American and British,* eds. Malcolm Friar and John Brinnin (New York, 1951), p. 427.
11 *Ibid.,*p. 428.
12 Deutsch, *Poetry in Our Time* (New York, 1952), p. 325.
13 Quinn, *Hart Crane* (New York, 1963), p. 73.
14 See Young, «The Mother of Us All: Pocahontas Reconsidered,» *The Kenyon Review,* 24 (1962), 391—415.
15 Waggoner, *The Heel of Elohim: Science and Values in Modern American Poetry* (Norman, 1950), p. 159.
16 Quinn, «Eliot and Crane: Protean Techniques,» *The Metamorphic Tradition in Modern Poetry* (New Brunswick, 1955), p. 148.
17 See Cambon, «Hart Crane's *The Bridge,*» *The Inclusive Flame: Studies in Modern American Poetry* (Bloomington, 1965), p. 160.
18 Dembo, *Hart Crane's Sanskrit Charge: A Study of The Bridge* (Ithaca, 1960), p. 17. Samuel Hazo, in his *Hart Crane: An Introduction and Interpretation* (New York, 1963), is influenced mainly by Dembo's Platonic definition of the myth.
19 Andreach, «Hart Crane,» *Studies in Structure: The Stages of the Spiritual Life in Four Modern Authors* (Fordham University Press, 1964), pp. 126—127.

20 See Trachtenberg, *Brooklyn Bridge: Fact and Symbol* (New York, 1965). See also Chapter 3, note 3.

21 R. W. B. Lewis, *The Poetry of Hart Crane: A Critical Study* (Princeton, 1967), p. 231.

22 See R. W. Butterfield, *The Broken Arc: A Study of Hart Crane* (Edinburgh, 1969), p. 189.

23 Paul, *Hart's Bridge* (Urbana, 1972), p. 192.

24 For an example of Paul's psychoanalytic readings, see his comments on the poet's dream of Pocahontas, in «The Harbor Dawn,» in *Hart's Bridge,* p. 200. One argument against the psychoanalytic interpretation of Crane's poem would be that it tends to reduce the general significance of *The Bridge* to a special case, or case history.

25 Cf. the statement of Elizabeth Jennings: «Crane employed many Christian words, signs and symbols. But, as with Rilke, he removed these things from the realm of strict orthodoxy and gave them a free life of their own. His imagination unyoked them from the bondage of dogma in order to liberate them for a visionary but less easily defined activity.» *Every Changing Shape* (London, 1961), p. 232.

26 *Ibid.,* p. 187. On page 303, Paul concludes that Crane's imagination is neither «religious» nor «visionary,» but «cubist.» A purely esthetic, almost formalist, approach is used in the latest full-length analysis of *The Bridge,* that of Richard P. Sugg, whose thesis is that «*The Bridge* is a poem about the creation of a poem.» *Hart Crane's The Bridge: A Description of its Life* (The University of Alabama Press, 1976), p. 4.

CHAPTER 2

1 Whitman, *Complete Poetry and Selected Prose and Letters,* ed. E. Holloway (London, 1938), p. 585. For further comments on Whitman's influence on Crane, see the analysis of «Cape Hatteras» in Chapter 3.

2 *Ibid.,* p. 721. For another account of Crane's indebtedness to Whitman, see Bernice Slote, *Start with the Sun: Studies in the Whitman Tradition* (University of Nebraska Press, 1960). For Slote, «Passage to India» is the poem that is most closely related to *The Bridge.*

3 Frank, *Our America* (New York, 1919), p. 8.

4 *Ibid., p. 10.*

5 *Ibid.,* pp. 81—82.

6 *Ibid.,* pp. 123—135.

7 *Ibid.,* p. 141.

8 *Ibid.,* pp. 231—232.

9 Frank, *The Re-Discovery of America* (New York, 1929), p. 24.

10 *Ibid.,* p. 245.

11 *Ibid.,* p. 31.

12 *Ibid.,* p. 42.

13 *Ibid.,* p. 140.

14 *Ibid.,* p. 177. In an essay on Stieglitz' art, Paul Rosenfeld wrote that «it stood, perpetual affirmation of a faith that there existed, somewhere, here in very New York, a spiritual America.» *Port of New York* (1924; rpt. Urbana, 1961), p. 260.

15 *Ibid.,* p. 306.

16 Robert L. Perry has written a short study on Frank's influence on Crane; *The Shared Vision of Waldo Frank and Hart Crane,* University of Nebraska Studies: New Series, 33 (Lincoln, 1966), 73 pp. Perry calls his study an essay in «biographical criticism» which intends to show the parallels between Frank's ideas and those expressed in *The Bridge.* The author interprets the bridge as a mystic symbol in the general sense, whereas the present writer emphasizes the utopian, national meaning of the mysticism. In many respects, however, this study is in agreement with Perry, and the main objection to his essay is that it does not carry out the implications of its own premises. The author's analysis of *The Bridge* is incomplete, amounting to no more than twelve pages.

17 Frank, *Salvos* (New York, 1924), p. 276.

18 Waldo Frank's final assessment of Hart Crane and his own influence upon the poet is found in his *Memoirs,* in which he lists such works of his as *Rahab, City Block, Holiday, Virgin Spain* and *America Hispana* and maintains that «Crane took them to be within his own apocalyptic vision.» *Memoirs of Waldo Frank,* ed. Alan Trachtenberg (The University of Massachussetts Press, 1973), p. 242.

19 According to John Unterecker, Crane intended the poems of «Powhatan's Daughter» to represent «the spiritual core of the entire American people.» *Voyager: A Life of Hart Crane* (New York, 1969), p. 652.

20 Munson, *Waldo Frank:* A Study (New York, 1923), p. 25.

NOTES TO CHAPTER 3

1   Speaking of the «sails,» Alan Trachtenberg states that «in a further transmutation, they become a 'page of figures'.» *Brooklyn Bridge: Fact and Symbol,* p. 154. This reading is difficult to reconcile with the grammar of this stanza. The first three lines constitute one coherent statement, and the third line does not express the same idea as the second. A comma, or full stop, would be required after «cross» in order for lines two and three to be regarded as parallel statments. Samuel Hazo interprets the lines in the same way as the present writer. Commenting on the «inviolate curve» of the seagull, he states that «it suggests freedom to all those who turn momentarily away from a 'page of figures' to observe it.» *Hart Crane,* p. 73.

2   Cf. Dembo: «Crane is implying that only the poet has the 'Visionary Eye' that sees beyond the gull and into the Bridge.» *Hart Crane's Sanskrit Charge,* p. 46. Some readers think that the «other eyes» are those of the audience, or the «multitudes.» See Hazo, *Hart Crane,* p, 73, and R. W. B. Lewis, *The Poetry of Hart Crane,* p. 247.

3   Joseph Arpad regards the belamite as a symbol of a man trying to escape from the shadowy cave that most men inhabit, according to Plato's well-known metaphor of man's condition on this earth. On the bridge, the bedlamite confronts the blinding light of reality, which in Plato's context means the world of ideas, and being «unwilling to consummate his escape by jumping . . . he is suspended there . . . as though vacillating between two worlds.» «Hart Crane's Platonic Myth: The Brooklyn Bridge,» *American Literature,* 34 (1967), 83. Frederick Hoffman, on the other hand, interprets the action of the bedlamite as «the suicide of one of the crowd.» *The Twenties: American Writing in the Postwar Decade* (New York, 1965), p. 264. See also R. W. Butterfield, *The Broken Arc,* p. 152.

4   See «The Dynamo and the Virgin,» *The Education of Henry Adams* (Boston, 1918), pp. 379—390.

5 For a psychoanalytic study of the bridge as a symbol of sexual union in mythology and in Crane's *The Bridge,* see Paul Friedman, «The Bridge: A Study in Symbolism,» *Psychoanalytic Quarterly,* 21 (1952), 49—79.

6 Schlauch, *Modern English and American Poetry: Techniques and Ideologies* (London, 1956), p. 36.

7 Referring to the discovery of Cathay as the great cause to which Columbus had devoted his life, Prescott writes: «the glorious enterprise which he had achieved almost justified the conviction of his acting under the influence of some higher inspiration than mere human reason, and led his devout mind to discern intimations re-
   specting himself in the dark and mysterious annunciation of sacred prophecy.» *The
   History of the Reign of Ferdinand and Isabella* (Boston, 1859), III, 243.

8 Frank, *The Re-Discovery of America,* p. 214.

9 This translation is taken from Dembo's *Hart Crane's Sanskrit Charge,* p. 54.

10 «Far from being displeased, Isabella was moved by his honest eloquence. She con-
   templated the proposals of Columbus in their true light; and refusing to hearken
   any longer to the suggestions of cold and timid counsellors, she gave way to the natural impulses of her own noble and generous heart.» Prescott, *The History,* II,
   128.

11 *The Journal of Christopher Columbus (During his First Voyage, 1492—1493),*
   transl. Clements R. Markham (London, 1893), p. 35. (Printed for the Hakluyt Society.)

12 Dembo writes that «Columbus is a Great White Bird in that he has completed the
   sea gull's arc and has reached the world of his dream.» *Hart Crane's Sanskrit
   Charge,* p. 55. The seagull and the white birds are structural symbols in *The Bridge,*
   suggesting visionary discovery, but Columbus belongs to another category, that of
   the various protagonists and *personae* that occur in the poem. R. W. B. Lewis also
   relates the «White Birds,» not Columbus, to the seagull of the proem and maintains
   that Crane thus connects the symbol of the gull to «the historic vision of the New
   World.» *The Poetry of Hart Crane,* p. 259. A similar reading is found in Sherman
   Paul, *Hart's Bridge,* p. 192.

13 Whitman, *Complete Poetry and Selected Prose,* p. 375.

14 Stanley K. Coffman argues in a similar vein, stating that the recurring curve and
   circle imagery of *The Bridge* represents a universal law, or principle, of union and
   reconciliation of opposites. «Symbolism in *The Bridge,*» *PMLA,* 66 (1951), 65—77.
   See also Robert L. Perry, *The Shared Vision of Waldo Frank and Hart Crane,* pp.
   43—60, and Bernice Slote, *Start with the Sun,* p. 147.

15 Vincent Quinn, *Hart Crane,* p. 83. R. W. B. Lewis describes Columbus' prayer as
   «a single cry of appeal and of praise to a cruel, an omnipotent, a loving, and an un-
   fathomable God.» *The Poetry of Hart Crane,* p. 264. Similar views are found in
   Dembo, *Hart Crane's Sanskrit Charge,* p. 59, and in Robert J. Andreach, «Hart
   Crane», *Studies in Structure,* p. 105.

16 «and they saw the God of Israel, and there was under his feet as it were a pavement
   of sapphire stone.» Exodus 24:10.

17 «the king and queen, together with all those present, prostrated themselves on their
   knees in grateful thanksgivings, while the solemn strains of the Te Deum were
   poured forth by the choir of the royal chapel . . .» Prescott, *The History,* II, 166.

18 Frank, *Virgin Spain* (New York, 1926), p. 298.

19 *Ibid.,* p. 297.

20 Lawrence, *Studies in Classic American Literature* (New York, 1964), pp. 35—36.

21 William Strachey's *History of Travaile into Virginia Britannica* (1615). According
   to R. W. B. Lewis, Crane took this passage from a review of William Carlos Williams' *In the American Grain* in *transition,* by Kay Boyle. Williams quotes from

Strachey in his book, and some of his citations were reprinted in the review. See *The Poetry of Hart Crane*, p. 289.

22 According to Philip Young, «Crane, in *The Bridge* (1930), raised Pocahontas to full mythic stature . . . Thus we have a sort of American Ceres, or Demeter, or Gaea, developed from Pocahontas, a fertility Goddess, the mother of us all.» «The Mother of Us All: Pocahontas Reconsidered,» p. 408.

23 See Hazo, *Hart Crane*, p. 83.

24 R. W. B. Lewis thinks that the word «blond,» used to describe the light in the window, is a pun on «blind,» thus indicating «the spiritual blindness of the awakened poet.» For Lewis, the transition from the dream-vision of Pocahontas to awakening and daylight represents the loss of the «vision of beauty.» Consequently, the «bright window-eyes» of the skyscrapers across the river are, in Lewis' words, «glittering and sightless.» *The Poetry of Hart Crane,* pp. 290, 292. This reading seems to me to go against the generally accepted meaning of the symbolic images of sun, whiteness and seagulls as ciphers of visionary hope in *The Bridge.* See R. W. Butterfield, *The Broken Arc,* p. 159, for a reading similar to the one presented in this study.

25 *The Broken Arc,* p. 161. See also Vincent Quinn, *Hart Crane,* p. 85.

26 Greeley's advice to the American youth of the nineteenth-century was: «Go west, young man.» The reference to Greeley is made by R. W. B. Lewis. See *The Poetry of Hart Crane,* p. 297.

27 The author is indebted to Sherman Paul for the explanation of «Thomas a Ediford» and for the reference to Byrd's expedition. See *Hart's Bridge,* pp. 208—209. Crane's use of words and phrases from *As You Like It* are pointed out by R. W. B. Lewis, and also by Paul. See *The Poetry of Hart Crane,* pp. 297—298, and *Hart's Bridge,* p. 209. This source was originally identified by John Unterecker, in his «The Architecture of *The Bridge,*» *Wisconsin Studies in Contemporary Literature,* 3 (1962), 16. «Tintex» and «Japalac» are brand names for, respectively, a dye and a lacquer. See *The American Long Poem: An Annotated Selection,* ed. Stephen Fender (London, 1977), p. 52.

28 From «Cool Tombs» in Sandburg's *Cornhuskers* (New York, 1918), p. 120.

29 This information derives from Unterecker, «The Architecture of *The Bridge,*» p. 15.

30 This postcard, now in the Butler Library collection, shows a woman lying on her side, enveloped by a serpent. Her head rests against a large birdwing, and below Crane's mark in the margin one can discern the head and wings of an eagle.

31 Eliot, *The Complete Poems and Plays* (New York, 1952), p. 133.

32 Lewis, *The Poetry of Hart Crane,* p. 304. See also Dembo, *Hart Crane's Sanskrit Charge,* p. 71. Other critics interpret the ending of «The River» more negatively, as Crane's expression of his sense of the meaninglessness of human life. See Vincent Quinn, *Hart Crane,* pp. 87—88, and Sherman Paul, *Hart's Bridge,* pp. 214—215.

33 Frank, *Our America,* p. 109.

34 According to Daniel G. Brinton, «Ataensic threw herself through a rift in the sky and fell toward the earth . . . Her body was buried, and from it sprang the various vegetable productions which the new earth required to fit it for the habitation of man. From her head grew the pumpkin vine; from her breast, the maize; from her limbs, the bean . . .» *American Hero-Myths: A Study in the Native Religions of the Western Continent* (Philadelphia, 1882), p. 54. It has not been established that Crane read this book.

35 The author is indebted to R. W. B. Lewis for this detail of the interpretation. See *The Poetry of Hart Crane,* p. 308.

36 Paul, *Hart's Bridge,* p. 217.

37 According to Brinton, pp. 48—49: «In the calendar of the Aztecs the day and god Tecpatl, the Flint-Stone, held a prominent position. According to their myths such a stone fell from heaven at the beginning of things and broke into sixteen hundred pieces, each of which became a god.» In his *Atlantis in America* (New York, 1926), which Crane read, Lewis Spence speaks of the Maya thundergod whose image was a stone: «The flint of thunder-stone was the chisel of the Maya masons and sculptors, the magical implement that shaped the idol and the pyramid.» (p. 199).

38 William Carlos Williams' *In the American Grain* (1925) also contains a female personage who symbolizes the virgin land. Williams has since confirmed that Crane was influenced by his book: «The chapter on De Soto was used by Hart Crane in 'The Bridge' — he took what he wanted, why shouldn't he — that's what writing is for.» *I Wanted to Write a Poem* (London, 1967), p. 54.

39 Lewis Spence informs that Haokah, a Sioux thundergod, «beat the tattoo of the thunder on his great drum, using the wind as a drumstick.» *The Myths of the North American Indians* (London, 1914), p. 125. One does not know if Crane knew this work.

40 Frederick J. Hoffman, *The Twenties,* p. 268. The same view is held by several other critics. See Quinn, *Hart Crane,* p. 89, Hazo, *Hart Crane,* p. 93, and Butterfield, *The Broken Arc,* p. 168. R. W. B. Lewis, on the other hand, writes that Crane employed the «sacred lie» of the «modern romantic tradition.» See *The Poetry of Hart Crane,* p. 311. See also Sherman Paul, *Hart's Bridge,* p. 219.

41 Crane's interest in Aztec mythology and history is well known. In 1931 he went to Mexico to write an epic poem on the downfall of Montezuma, «a blank verse tragedy of Aztec mythology — for which I shall have to study the obscure calendar of dead kings.» Apart from these myths, «The Dance» seems to contain allusions to the legends of North American Indians as well, though no particular tribe is referred to.

42 Metzger, «Hart Crane's Bridge: the Myth Active,» *Arizona Quarterly,* XX (1964), 37. Crane knew Padraic Colum, and Metzger holds that the poet may have obtained the details of the Quetzalcoatl myth from him through conversation, although Colum's *Orpheus* was published in 1930, the same year as *The Bridge.* In his biography, Philip Horton mentions that Crane knew Prescott's *History.* See *Hart Crane: The Life of an American Poet* (New York, 1957), p. 291.

43 Lawrence, *The Plumed Serpent* (London, 1926), p. 220.

44 Frank, *In the American Jungle: 1925—1936* (New York, 1937), pp. 125—126.

45 Richard P. Sugg, *Hart Crane's The Bridge: A Description of Its Life,* p. 61.

46 *The Broken Arc,* p. 173. See also Dembo, *Hart Crane's Sanskrit Charge,* p. 83.

47 The word «grass» in the third line has been corrected to «glass» in *The American Long Poem,* ed. Stephen Fender, p. 62.

48 For a discussion of «Cutty Sark» in relation to Baudelaire's «Le Voyage,» see Sherman Paul, *Hart's Bridge,* pp. 225—226.

49 Vincent Quinn maintains that the sailor has had a real experience of eternity, and that this knowledge has overwhelmed him. See *Hart Crane,* p. 91.

50 *Selected Writings of Edgar Allan Poe* (Boston, 1956), p. 26.

51 See note 129.

52 *The Rainbow* has been considered the first real American clipper and was designed by the famous naval architect John W. Griffeths. Three years after it was launched it was lost with all hands. The *Flying Cloud* was generally regarded as the finest of all clippers. The *Taeping* and the *Ariel* were British and competed in several races. The *Thermopylae* and the *Cutty Sark* were also British clippers. See Hawthorne Daniel, *The Clipper Ship* (New York, 1928), *passim.*

53 R. W. Butterfield argues that this synthesis, which is glimpsed in «the inebriated mind of the protagonist,» has no relation to the realities of America. See *The Broken Arc*, p. 178.

54 According to Hoffman, the last word of the poem, «Ariel,» expresses the poet's «appeal to Ariel of *The Tempest* to help him find his way back.» *The Twenties*, p. 269. See also Dembo, *Hart Crane's Sanskrit Charge*, p. 89.

55 Frank, *Our America*, p. 204.

56 Whitman, *Complete Poetry*, p. 380.

57 Hazo believes that the reptilian imagery refers to the shape of Cape Hatteras itself as it disappears out of sight. *Hart Crane*, p. 100. See also Sugg, *Hart Crane's The Bridge*, p. 71. Because the poet uses the words «slow» and «slowly» and employs geological terms, this interpretation seems unlikely. Sherman Paul, on the other hand, says that «the cape sinks while the mountain range rises» and speaks of an «evolutionary naturalistic vista» in connection with these lines. *Hart's Bridge*, pp. 233—234. Interestingly, R. W. Butterfield suggests that the sinking cape refers to Atlantis. See *The Broken Arc*, p. 182.

58 See Sugg, *Hart Crane's The Bridge*, p. 75, and Butterfield, *The Broken Arc*, p. 183. An interesting discussion of the symbolic meaning of the word «pool» in *The Bridge* is found in Jean Guiguet, *L'universe poétique de Hart Crane* (Paris, 1965), p. 37.

59 Whitman, *Complete Poetry*, p. 231.

60 *Ibid.,* p. 210.

61 *Ibid.*

62 R. W. B. Lewis thinks that the «power house» refers to the whole world of machinery. See *The Poetry of Hart Crane*, p. 330. Some critics believe that this passage describes an airplane. See, for example, Hazo, *Hart Crane*, p. 101, Quinn, *Hart Crane*, p. 93, and Dembo, *Hart Crane's Sanskrit Charge*, p. 98. Sherman Paul and R. W. Butterfield suggest that the first part of the passage refers to the dynamos of electric machinery, whereas the second part, beginning with «The forked crash of split thunder,» refers to an airplane engine. See *Hart's Bridge*, p. 238, and *The Broken Arc*, p. 183. Against this one could point out that the word «armature» refers to a part of a dynamo and thus links with the dynamos described in the previous lines.

63 Frank, *The Re-Discovery*, p. 93.

64 Whitman, p. 380.

65 One of the many worksheets of «Cape Hatteras» contains some leftout lines which emphasize the poet's awareness of a distinct poetic tradition springing from Whitman: «For who was he, but thou, who undertook the plunge/ O Carrier-creator of song's breakless chain.»

66 Whitman, p. 57.

67 *Ibid.,* p. 103.

68 *Ibid.,* p. 677.

69 *Ibid.,* p. 209.

70 *Ibid.,* pp. 109—110.

71 Frank, *Salvos* (New York, 1924), p. 278.

72 *Marlowe's Plays and Poems,* ed. M. R. Ridley (London, 1961), p. 375.

73 Crane's image of the sky as a woman in the process of denudation is formally related to the opening lines of Eliot's «The Love Song of J. Alfred Prufrock.» Crane was very interested in Eliot's early poetry and its novel techniques of imagery, and on the back page of an unpublished letter to Otto Kahn, dated April 10, 1926 (in the Butler Library), he discussed what he saw as two types of sky metaphors, the conventional «sky is a dome» and the radical metaphor of the sky as «a patient ether-

ized upon a table.» According to Crane's note, the former is «logical-objective. Here is aroused recognition by relationships between objects in simple statement — outside of self.» The latter, on the other hand, is «extra-logical-subjective. Sensibility is here *acted upon*.» Moreover, in the case of Eliot's image, we have «the ego's participation in an event of consciousness signalled by the image.» Another clue to the obscure opening of «Southern Cross» may be found in an «Atlantis» fragment in the Butler Library where the poet writes about «the girdles of thy thighs, O bridge.» The bridge may be seen as a goddess of night and stars whose form or outline is dissolved in «Southern Cross.»

74 See Dembo, *Hart Crane's Sanskrit Charge*, pp. 110—111.

75 See Frye, *Anatomy of Criticism* (Princeton, 1957), pp. 147—150. Frye's terminology is also used by Sherman Paul. See *Hart's Bridge*, pp. 237—238.

76 See R. W. Butterfield, *The Broken Arc*, pp. 191—192. Similar readings of this line are found in Dembo, *Hart Crane's Sanskrit Charge*, pp. 111—112, and R. W. B. Lewis, *The Poetry of Hart Crane*, p. 343.

77 The last lines of Crane's poem may have been influenced by Melville's *Clarel*, which laments the loss of the Christian faith:

> Emblazoned bleak in Austral skies —
> A heaven remote, whose starry swarm
> Like Science lights but cannot warm —
> Translated Cross, hast thou withdrawn,
> Dim paling too at every dawn.

The Selected Poems of Herman Melville, ed. Hennig Cohen (Carbondale, 1964), p. 74. See also Hazo, *Hart Crane*, p. 106.

78 According to Norttrop Frye, «the demonic erotic relation becomes a fierce destructive passion that works against loyalty or frustrates the one who possesses it. It is generally symbolized by a harlot, witch, siren, or other tantalizing female, a physical object of desire which is sought as a possession and therefore can never be possessed.» *Anatomy*, p. 149.

79 *Antony and Cleopatra*, The Arden Edition of the Works of William Shakespeare (London, 1954), p. 41.

80 The burlesque dancer is modelled not only on Pocahontas and Cleopatra, but also on Astarte, the Phoenician goddess of love and fertility. In a manuscript version of the last stanza of «National Winter Garden,» Astarte is substituted for Magdalene. Astarte was associated with Aphrodite in the Greco-Roman tradition. This version of the last stanza is rather different and is given here in its entirety:

> Yet, in the empty trapeze of your flesh,
> Astarte, each comes back to die alone . . .
> Death is a ululation at so many wrists,
> — So much per death, so much per bone.

81 Willingham, «'Three Songs' of Hart Crane's *The Bridge*,» *American Literature*, 27 (1955/57), 66.

82 Printed in Weber, *Hart Crane*, pp. 396—397.

83 Hoffman, *The Twenties*, p. 271. R. W. Butterfield thinks that «Virginia» expresses the poet's «sentimental dream.» See *The Broken Arc*, pp. 195—196.

84 Horton, *Hart Crane: The Life of an American Poet*, p. 261.

85 Sherman Paul thinks very highly of the poem because it presents «a moment of tragic realization» of the problems of modern America. See *Hart's Bridge*, p. 254.

86   Frank, *The Re-Discovery*, p. 136.
87   See Dembo, *Hart Crane's Sanskrit Charge*, p. 116, Hazo, *Hart Crane*, p. 108, and Lewis, *The Poetry of Hart Crane*, p. 348. Richard P. Sugg believes that the cows refer to the Quakers. *Hart Crane's The Bridge*, p. 93, and Robert L. Perry asserts that the first stanza refers to «the asceticism of the New England Brahmins.» *The Shared Vision of Waldo Frank and Hart Crane*, p. 65. Among those who think that the cows are simply cows are R. W. Butterfield, *The Broken Arc*, p. 197, Vincent Quinn, *Hart Crane*, p. 97, and Sherman Paul, *Hart's Bridge*, p. 255.
88   See Horton, *Hart Crane*, pp. 199—200.
89   Frank, *The Re-Discovery*, p. 96.
90   *Ibid.*, pp. 214—215.
91   See John Unterecker, *Voyager: A Life of Hart Crane*, pp. 4—5.
92   Butterfield, *The Broken Arc*, p. 200.
93   On a manuscript fragment of the sixth stanza Crane wrote:
       «The Promised Land, the mandate, the legacy,»
     and underlined the words with red ink. The manuscripts also contain a left-out stanza which mentions the degradation of America: «that playful, generous heart gone filched.»
94   See Horton, pp. 246—251.
95   Frank, *The Re-Discovery*, p. 310.
96   Duncan, *My Life* (New York, 1927), p. 5.
97   Waldo Frank's novel *Rahab* (1922) is the story of a woman, Fanny Luve, who becomes a martyr in the cause of spiritual love. In a letter to Gorham Munson, August 1922, Crane called *Rahab* «a beautiful book.»
98   *The Complete Poems of Emily Dickinson with an Introduction by her Niece Martha Dickinson Bianchi* (Boston, 1926), p. 104. A copy of this edition is in the Crane Collection of the Butler Library, and the poet has marked the two opening lines with red ink.
99   Frank, *The Death and Birth of David Markand* (New York, 1934), p. 63.
100 *Ibid.* Frank has also explained the doctrine in philosophic terms: «Adversity by imposing limits upon self enables the self to transcend these limits by spiritual assimilation of what opposes it.» *The Re-Discovery of America*, p. 263 n.
101 *The Complete Writings of William Blake* (New York, 1957), p. 421.
102 Eliot, *The Complete Poems and Plays*, p. 5, 12. For further comparisons between «The Tunnel» and *The Waste Land,* see George S. Lensing, «Hart Crane's Tunnel from *The Waste Land*,» *Ariel: A Review of International English Literature*, 6 (1975), 20—35.
103 Several critics interpret this passage differently, regarding the «head» and the «body» as references to Poe. See R. W. Lewis, *the Poetry of Hart Crane*, p. 359, R. W. Butterfield, *The Broken Arc*, p. 203, Richard P. Sugg, *Hart Crane's The Bridge*, p. 101, and Robert J. Andreach, *Studies in Structure*, p. 121. Others suggest that it is the poet himself who is referred to. See Vincent Quinn, *Hart Crane*, p. 99, Dembo, *Hart Crane's Sanskrit Charge*, p. 122, and Sherman Paul, *Hart's Bridge*, p. 268—269.
104 *Selected Writings of Edgar Allan Poe*, p. 23.
105 *Ibid.*, p. 26.
106 See James A. Harrison, *The Life of Edgar Allan Poe,* The Complete Works of Edgar Allan Poe, ed. James A. Harrison, I, Biography (New York, 1965), pp. 330—331.
107 Dembo, *Hart Crane's Sanskrit Charge*, p. 123. See also R. W. B. Lewis, *The Poetry of Hart Crane*, p. 361. R. W. Butterfield thinks that Crane is referring to «the ticket to Atlantis,» and that Poe would have denied it, thus cancelling Crane's vision. See

The Broken Arc, p. 203. Robert J. Andreach believes that the «ticket» is a reference to the dark night of the soul that is part of the mystical experience.

108 Williams, *In the American Grain* (Norfolk, Conn., 1925), p. 222.

109 *Ibid.,* p. 231.

110 Whitman, *Complete Poetry,* p. 374.

111 Printed in Weber, *Hart Crane,* p. 431.

112 Frank, *City Block* (New York, 1922), pp. 170—171. Crane was very enthusiastic about «Hope,» and pointed out «the beautiful manipulation of symbolism» in the story. (Letter to Frank, November 30, 1922.) See also Robert L. Perry, *The Shared Vision of Waldo Frank and Hart Crane,* p. 35.

113 Quotations from «The Bridge of Estador» and from the «Atlantis» manuscripts are from the «Appendix» of Weber, *Hart Crane,* pp. 425—440.

114 M. D. Uroff has a similar interpretation of this early stanza, speaking of its «vision of totality.» *Hart Crane: The Patterns of his Poetry* (Urbana, 1974), p. 148. In his comment on «Atlantis,» R. W. B. Lewis uses the same phrases as Uroff. See *The Poetry of Hart Crane,* p. 373. However, neither Uroff nor Lewis thinks of this «totality» as being first and foremost a divine revelation.

115 Ouspensky, *Tertium Organum: The Third Canon of Thought. A Key to the Enigmas of the World* (New York, 1922), p. 42.

116 The author of this study obtained this information from Crane's friend himself, Emil Opffer, in Denmark in 1977. Opffer, a retired Danish-American sailor, was then 81 years old. See the essay-interview «Memories of Hart Crane: A Talk with Emil Opffer,» *Hart Crane Newsletter,* I, no. 2 (1978).

117 Spengler, *The Decline of the West: Complete in One Volume,* transl. Charles F. Atkinson (New York, 1937), p. 40.

118 For an account of Spengler's influence on Crane, see Philip Horton, *Hart Crane,* pp. 204—206. See also John Unterecker, *Voyager,* pp. 446—448.

119 Plato, *The Timaeus and the Critias or Atlanticus,* trans. Thomas Taylor (Washington D. C., 1944), p. 248.

120 See Spence, *Atlantis in America,* pp. 30—64.

121 For further comment on the «synesthetic images» of the first three stanzas of «Atlantis,» see Herbert A. Leibowitz, *Hart Crane: An Introduction to the Poetry* (New York, 1968), pp. 137—143.

122 Frank, *The Re-Discovery,* pp. 212—213. R. W. B. Lewis has a similar interpretation of the «One arc synoptic,» stating that it «unites all the tides beneath it; while those tides, in turn, represent all the phases of history bound together by vision.» *The Poetry of Hart Crane,* p. 367. See also Vincent Quinn, *Hart Crane,* p. 101.

123 Whitman, *Complete Poetry,* p. 213.

124 «Crane's implied fusion of the images of bird and fish (gull and fin) reflects the correspondence of sky and sea that the was making throughout the sequence.» Dembo, *Hart Crane's Sanskrit Charge,* pp. 128—129.

125 See Frank, *The Re-Discovery,* pp. 243—245.

126 *The Dialogues of Plato,* trans. B. Jowett (New York, 1937), I, 314.

127 R. W. Butterfield thinks that the «bright drench and fabric of our veins» refers to the people of the nation that are being transformed by the bridge. See *The Broken Arc,* p. 208.

128 Frank, *In the American Jungle,* p. 17.

129 R. P. Blackmur has analysed Crane's use of the tear-eye image in poems like «The Wine Menagerie» and «Lachrymae Christi.» From the latter Blackmur comments on the line: «Thy Nazarene and tinder eyes:» «Note, from the title, that we are here again concerned with tears as the vehicle-image of insight.» *The Double Agent: Essays in Craft and Elucidation* (Gloucester, Mass., 1962), p. 135.

195

130 The chart is from an article on «Counterbalancing the Unbalance» in shafts and other rotating objects of machinery. See *Scientific American,* 135 (1926), 43. A copy of the chart is in the «Appendix» of this study. The Black Sun Press edition of *The Bridge* contained three photographs of the Brooklyn Bridge by Walker Evans. A study of their function in relation to *The Bridge* has been made by Gordon K. Grigsby in his «The Photographs in the First Editon of *The Bridge,*» *Texas Studies in Language and Literature,* 4 (1962/63), 5—11. At one time, Crane wanted to use Joseph Stella's painting of the Brooklyn Bridge as frontispiece for the poem. For a discussion of the «apocalyptic visions» inherent in Stella's painting of the bridge, see Alan Trachtenberg, *Brooklyn Bridge: Fact and Symbol,* pp. 133—136. See the «Appendix» for a copy of the painting.

131 According to Dembo, «it is only the poet who endures the 'spears ensanguined of one tolling star/That bleeds infinity' and can express his knowledge.» *Hart Crane's Sanskrit Charge,* p. 129. See also Robert J. Andreach, *Studies in Structure,* p. 124. R. W. Butterfield believes that the «ensanguined spears» are those that were used to massacre the Indians. See *The Broken Arc,* p. 209.

132 Whitman, p. 379.

133 Frank, *The Re-Discovery,* p. 309. In *Rahab,* Frank endows his heroine, Fanny Luve, with a vision similar to that of the last stanza of «Atlantis:» «She saw the world all One: and of it, like a throbbing heart, like a high radiant head, she saw that there was God.» *Rahab* (New York, 1922), p. 120.

134 Colum, *Orpheus: Myths of the World* (New York, 130), p. 306.

135 Frederick J. Hoffman emphasizes only the doubt that is implied in the poet's question: «the poem concludes with questioning and doubt. *Is* this Cathay? *Does* 'this history' lead without doubt and fear to this worship?» *The Twenties,* p. 273. Samuel Hazo maintains that the last lines of «Atlantis» indicate that the poem's meaning lies in the search rather than the answer: «It could well be that Crane is insisting that the true meaning of the search is not in the thing sought, but in the seeking.» *Hart Crane,* p. 118. See also R. W. Butterfield, *The Broken Arc,* pp. 209—210, M. D. Uroff, *Hart Crane: The Patterns of his Poetry,* p. 150, and R. W. B. Lewis, *The Poetry of Hart Crane,* pp. 369—371. According to Sherman Paul, the question indicates the uncertainty that is part of the experience of the vision, «affirmation enclosing skepticism.» *Hart's Bridge,* p. 282. Richard P. Sugg regards the question as a rhetorical one, the answer to which is clearly affirmative and given in the last line. See *Hart Crane's The Bridge,* pp. 117—118.

136 Frank, *The Re-Discovery,* p. 309.

CHAPTER 4

1 At the opening ceremonies of the Brooklyn Bridge in May 1883, the Reverend Richard S. Storrs expressed the utopian hopes that the bridge symbolized for him. See Trachtenberg, *Brooklyn Bridge: Fact and Symbol,* pp. 124—127.

2 Philip Horton arrives at the same conclusion: «That these two attitudes — a buoyant idealism and an almost macabre pessimism — exist side by side in his work in irreconcilable opposition is a further token that he was completely a man of his time. *Hart Crane: The Life of an American Poet,* pp. 312—313. Naturally enough, Horton's main emphasis lies on the poet's life, not the poetry. Gordon K. Grigsby expresses a similar view, although he states that it is a mistake to read the poem as «some kind of nationalistic paean to America.» «Hart Crane's Doubtful Vision: A Note on the 'Intention' of *The Bridge,*» *College English,* 24

(April 1963), 522. A poem which deals with the «myth of America» can be said to be nationalistic, although *The Bridge,* as Grigsby himself shows, demonstrates the complexity of Crane's approach. Eugene P. Nassar also emphasizes the dualistic nature of *The Bridge,* but maintains that the poem is about the phenomenon of myth as such instead of an expression of true faith: «The poem *The Bridge* is not Crane's myth of America or God, but *about* myth.» «Hart Crane's *The Bridge* and its Critics,» *The Rape of Cinderella: Essays in Literary Continuity* (Bloomington, 1970), p. 188.

3 The weaknesses of Crane's poetry have been pointed out by many critics. In his comment on «Atlantis,» Yvor Winters attacks Crane in a negative way and says that the poem consists of «aspects which cannot possibly be imbued with any definite significance.» «The Progress of Hart Crane,» p. 157. In a letter to this author, dated June 14, 1966, Winters wrote about Crane that «I lost all serious interest in him a good many years ago.» See also Brom Weber, *Hart Crane,* p. 375, and Odell Shepard's review of *The Bridge* in *Bookman,* 72 (1930). In his comment on «Cape Hatteras,» Howard Moss objects to Crane's use of the airplane because it expresses «a phony optimism which is belied by the material.» «Disorder as Myth: Hart Crane's *The Bridge,*» *Poetry,* 62 (1943), 38. See also R. W. Butterfield, *The Broken Arc,* p. 180, Vincent Quinn, Hart Crane, pp. 93—94, and Karl Shapiro, «Study of *Cape Hatteras* by Hart Crane,» *The Merrill Studies in the Bridge,* compiled by David R. Clark (Columbus, 1970). pp. 37—43. For critical comments on «Indiana» and «Quaker Hill,» see R. W. B. Lewis, *The Poetry of Hart Crane,* pp. 316—317 and p. 350.

The Bridge. Oil. One of five panels by Joseph Stella entitled. New York Interpreted, 1922
(Courtesy of the Newark Museum)

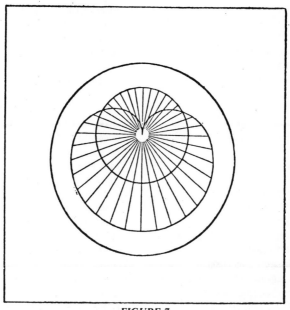

FIGURE 7
Based on this Chart of Angles, Newkirk's Law is developed and applied

199

INDEX